Pittsburgh Series in Bibliography

# JOHN O'HARA

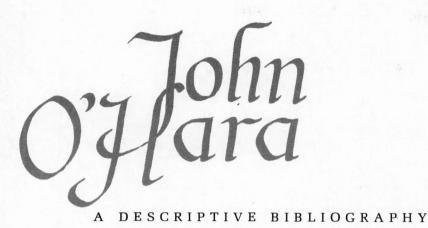

# John O'Hara

A DESCRIPTIVE BIBLIOGRAPHY

Matthew J. Bruccoli

UNIVERSITY OF
PITTSBURGH PRESS
1978

Published by the University of Pittsburgh Press, Pittsburgh, Pa. 15260
Copyright © 1978, University of Pittsburgh Press
Feffer and Simons, Inc., London
Manufactured in the United States of America

Library of Congress Cataloging in Publication Data

Bruccoli, Matthew Joseph, 1931–
   John O'Hara: a descriptive bibliography.

   (Pittsburgh series in bibliography)
   Includes index.
   1.  O'Hara, John, 1905–1970—Bibliography.  I.  Series.
Z8642.32.B72   [PS3529.H29]     016.813′5′2     77-15737
ISBN 0-8229-3349-7

In Memory of Maxine Dickey

# Contents

# Acknowledgments

BIBLIOGRAPHERS incur great debts because they have to rely on so many people for verification of information. My greatest debt for this volume is to my old friend Charles Mann, keeper of the John O'Hara Collection at the Pennsylvania State University Library. I am also obligated to his able staff. The help of Albert Erskine of Random House has been crucial to my work on O'Hara. The late Katharine Barnes O'Hara, the widow of John O'Hara, offered me every encouragement with my work.

I am obligated to Patrick O'Connor and Diane Vespi of Popular Library, Roger Palmer of Hodder & Stoughton, Muriel Hamilton of Hampton Books, Joseph I. O'Hara, Jerry Talmer of the *New York Post,* Robert Nance, Richard Taylor, Graham Watson, Frank Darchinger, Philip B. Eppard, Glenda Fedricci, and C. E. Frazer Clark, Jr. I could not have assembled the books from which to compile this bibliography without the assistance of many bookdealers, and Anthony Rota was particularly helpful in providing English editions of O'Hara.

The staffs of the Library of Congress, the British Library, the Bodleian Library, and the Historical Society of Schuylkill County, Pa., were generously helpful. Ian Willison of the British Library made crucial assistance available. Claudia Drum and her colleagues at the Interlibrary Loan Department of the University of South Carolina Library are always marvels.

Vice-President H. Willard Davis and Professor William Nolte of the University of South Carolina arranged travel grants for this project; and I received a research grant from the National Endowment for the Humanities.

Secretarial labors were performed by Frances Ponick, Cara White, and Diane Dalton. The index was prepared by Linda Berry. Proofing was done by Karen Rood. Mary F. Bruccoli made the color identifications for her color-blind father.

My manuscript was vetted by William Cagle of the Lilly Library and by Charles Mann. I am grateful to Beth E. Luey and Louise Craft of the University of Pittsburgh Press for giving the manuscript its final editing. Frederick A. Hetzel, Director of the Press, has made the Pittsburgh Series in Bibliography possible.

# Introduction

PUBLICATION is the essential act of scholarship; but all bibliographies are works in progress.

This bibliography builds on my *John O'Hara: A Checklist* (New York: Random House, 1972), but it is still incomplete. Besides the things I do not know about, there is a serious gap for O'Hara's work on the *Pottsville Journal:* for which there is no file for the period of his employment in 1924–1926.

FORMAT

Section A lists chronologically all books and pamphlets by John O'Hara—including all printings of all editions in English. The form of entry for the first English printings is less full than for the first American printings. The numbering system for Section A designates the edition and printing for each entry. Thus for the first English edition of *Appointment in Samarra, A2.2.a* indicates that the volume described is the second book by O'Hara *(A2)* and that it is the second edition, first printing *(2.a)*. Issues are designated by asterisks: *A2.1.a\** indicates the presentation issues of the first printing of the first edition of *Appointment in Samarra*. States are designated by inferior numbers: *A6.1.a₁*. At the end of this section there is an AA supplemental list of collections of O'Hara's work, arranged chronologically.

Section B lists chronologically all titles in which material by O'Hara appears for the first time in a book or pamphlet. Previously unpublished items are so stipulated. The first printings only of these items are described, but republication in England is noted.

Section C lists chronologically the first appearances of all O'Hara short stories in periodicals or books.

Section D lists chronologically magazine and newspaper appearances of O'Hara's writings other than stories: articles, letters, reviews, verse, statements, and interviews.

Section E lists chronologically O'Hara's newspaper and magazine columns.

Section F lists chronologically blurbs by O'Hara that appeared on books by other authors. Quotes from his reviews are not included.

Appendix 1 lists journalism jobs held by O'Hara.

Appendix 2 summarizes O'Hara's employment as a movie writer.

Appendix 3 contains the compiler's notes on the known lacunae in this bibliography.

Appendix 4 lists all books or pamphlets and the most useful articles about O'Hara.

TERMS AND METHODS

*Edition.* All the copies of a book printed from a single setting of type—including all reprintings from standing type, from plates, or by photo-offset processes.

*Printing.* All the copies of a book printed at one time (without removing the type or plates from the press).

*States.* States occur only within single printings and are created by an alteration not affecting the conditions of issue to *some* copies of a given printing (by stop-press correction or cancellation of leaves). There are two states of the first printing of *Files on Parade* (A 6).

*Issues.* Issues occur only within single printings and are created by an alteration affecting the conditions of publication or sale to *some* copies of a given printing (usually a title-page alteration). Issues occur in *Appointment in Samarra* (A 2) and *Sermons and Soda-Water* (A 18).

*Edition, printing, state,* and *issue* have been restricted to the sheets of the book. Binding or dust-jacket variants have no bearing on these terms.[1] Binding or jacket variants in this bibliography are treated simply as binding or jacket variants.

*State* and *issue* are the most abused terms in the vocabulary of bibliographical description. Many cataloguers use them interchangeably as well as ignorantly. Much would be gained for the profession of bibliography by the consistent and precise usage of these terms. *State* is easy to use correctly, but *issue* is more troublesome. Some able bibliographers prefer to define *issue* in terms of publication or distribution, rather than in terms of type pedigree. They argue that a new issue results whenever a complete printing is released by a new publisher. Under this usage the reprinting of the Harcourt, Brace plates for *Appointment in Samarra* by the Modern Library (A 2.1.j) would constitute the "Modern Library issue." Nonetheless, because the damage to bibliographical accuracy resulting from the idiosyncratic usage of *issue* has been so great, I have elected to treat the term conservatively. It may well be that a new term is needed to cover cases when plates are leased to a new publisher—that is, when a complete printing is published by a different publisher from the one who first made the plates.

Dust jackets for Section A entries have been described in detail because they are part of the original publication effort and sometimes provide information about how the book was marketed. There is, of course, no certainty that a jacket now on a copy of a book was always on it.

For binding-cloth descriptions I have used the method proposed by G. Thomas Tanselle;[2] most of these cloth grains are illustrated in Jacob Blanck,

---

1. This statement holds for twentieth-century publishing. It is not possible to be so dogmatic for nineteenth-century publishing, when parts of a printing were marketed in different formats—for example, cloth, paper, and two-in-one bindings. In such cases it is difficult to avoid regarding the different bindings as *issues* because they do represent a deliberate attempt to alter the conditions of publication.

2. G. Thomas Tanselle, "The Specifications of Binding Cloth," *The Library,* 21 (September 1966), 246–247.

ed., *The Bibliography of American Literature* (New Haven: Yale University Press, 1955– ).

Color specifications are taken from the *ISCC-NBS Color Name Charts Illustrated with Centroid Colors* (National Bureau of Standards).[3] A color holds for subsequent lines until a color change is stipulated.

In the descriptions of title pages, bindings, and dust jackets, the color of the lettering is always black, unless otherwise stipulated. The style of type is roman, unless otherwise stipulated.

The spines of bindings and dust jackets are printed horizontally unless otherwise stipulated. The reader is to assume that vertically printed spines read from top to bottom, unless otherwise stipulated.

The term *perfect binding* refers to books in which the pages are held together with adhesive along the back edge after the folds have been trimmed off—for example, most paperbacks.

Dates provided within brackets do not appear on the title pages. Usually—but not invariably—they are taken from the copyright pages.

Locations are provided by the following symbols:

BL: British Library, London
Bod: Bodleian Library, Oxford University
LC: Library of Congress
Lilly: Lilly Library, Indiana University
MJB: Collection of Matthew J. Bruccoli
PSt: Pennsylvania State University Library

For paperbacks, the serial number provided is that of the first printing. Paperback publishers normally change the serial number for later printings, but this information has not been noted.

It is desirable in bibliographical descriptions to avoid end-of-line hyphens in transcriptions. Because of word lengths and a measured line, however, it is impossible to satisfy this requirement in every case. End-of-line hyphens have been avoided wherever possible, and always where a hyphen would create ambiguity.

A bibliography is outdated the day it goes to the printer. Addenda and corrigenda are earnestly solicited.

The University of South Carolina
21 August 1976

---

3. G. Thomas Tanselle, "A System of Color Identification for Bibliographical Description," *Studies in Bibliography,* 20 (1967), 203–204.

# A. Separate Publications

Books and pamphlets by O'Hara, including all printings of all editions in English, arranged chronologically. At the end of Section A there is an AA supplemental list of collections of O'Hara's work.

A 1 REMINISCENCES FROM "KUNGSHOLM"
*Only printing (1934)*

$\mathcal{R}$EMINISCENCES FROM
"KUNGSHOLM"
WEST INDIES CRUISE
MARCH 9—MARCH 28, 1934

SWEDISH AMERICAN LINE

A 1: 6" × 9"

[1–42]

Stapled through side: probably [1]¹ [2]⁴ [3–10]²

*Contents:*   1: title; p. 2: 'Extract from the Log of the "Kungsholm" '; pp. 3–10: 'POST CRUISE EDITION'; pp. 11–14: 'NUMBER 1' (10 March 1934); pp. 15–18: 'NUMBER 2' (13 March); pp. 19–22: 'NUMBER 3' (14 March); pp. 23–26: 'NUMBER 4' (15 March); pp. 27–30: 'NUMBER 5' (18 March); pp. 31–34: 'NUMBER 6' (21 March); pp. 35–38: 'NUMBER 7' (22 March); pp. 39–42: 'NUMBER 8' (27 March).

*Typography and paper:*   8″ × 4⁷/₈″. Double-columned. Pp. 1–10 on slick wove paper; rest on plain wove paper. Each page of *The Kungsholm Cruise News* has logo at head.

*Binding:*   Stiff strong red (#12) paper covers, goldstamped: '[script] Cruising the Caribbean | and the | Spanish Main | [illustration of pirates] | [roman] ON BOARD | M. S. "KUNGSHOLM" '. Back has circular seal of Swedish American Line.

*Publication and printing:*   The 8 numbers of the *Cruise News* were printed aboard the *Kungsholm.* After the voyage, 10 pages of front matter were added to these numbers and bound as a souvenir by the Swedish American Line. Unknown number of copies. Not for sale.

*Location:*   MJB.

*Note:*   Each number of *The Kungsholm Cruise News* consists of 4 pages—of which p. 3 is canned tourist information. For the final number O'Hara wrote a parody guide to Manhattan. Each number lists O'Hara as the editor. The extra number with the front matter, called the 'POST CRUISE EDITION', includes " 'TILL WE MEET AGAIN!" on p. 8, signed 'JOHN O'HARA, EDITOR.' No separate copies of the *Cruise News* have been located.

A 2 APPOINTMENT IN SAMARRA

A 2.1.a
*First edition, first printing (1934)*

# APPOINTMENT IN SAMARRA

## A NOVEL BY JOHN O'HARA

DEATH SPEAKS: There was a merchant in Bagdad who sent his servant to market to buy provisions and in a little while the servant came back, white and trembling, and said, Master, just now when I was in the market-place I was jostled by a woman in the crowd and when I turned I saw it was Death that jostled me. She looked at me and made a threatening gesture; now, lend me your horse, and I will ride away from this city and avoid my fate. I will go to Samarra and there Death will not find me. The merchant lent him his horse, and the servant mounted it, and he dug his spurs in its flanks and as fast as the horse could gallop he went. Then the merchant went down to the market-place and he saw me standing in the crowd and he came to me and said, Why did you make a threatening gesture to my servant when you saw him this morning? That was not a threatening gesture, I said, it was only a start of surprise. I was astonished to see him in Bagdad, for I had an appointment with him tonight in Samarra.                    —W. SOMERSET MAUGHAM

## HARCOURT, BRACE AND COMPANY
### NEW YORK

A 2.1.a: 5⁵/₁₆″ × 8″

[i–viii] [1–2] 3–301 [302–304]

[1–19]⁸ [20]⁴; erratum slip tipped on 1$_{4r}$

*Contents:* pp. i–ii: blank; p. iii: half title; p. iv: blank; p. v: title; p. vi: copyright; p. vii: 'to | F. P. A.'; erratum slip (1³/₄″ × 5¹/₄″) tipped on dedication page: '*The quotation on the title page appears in* | *"Sheppey," a play by W. Somerset Maugham,* | *which will be published in the fall of 1934* | *by Doubleday, Doran and Company.*'; p. viii: blank; p. 1: half title; p. 2: blank; pp. 3–301: text, headed '1'; pp. 302–304: blank.

*Typography and paper:* Caslon, 12 point on 15. 6″ (6¹/₄″) × 3¹¹/₁₆″; 28 or 29 lines per page. No running heads. Wove paper.

*Binding:* Black varnished V cloth (smooth). Spine goldstamped: 'APPOINT- | MENT IN | SAMARRA | *John O'Hara* | *Harcourt, Brace* | *and Company*'. All edges trimmed. Top edge stained yellow. White wove calendered endpapers.

*Dust jacket:* Front and spine have continuous illustration of car rounding curve in green, yellow, black, white, and gray. Front: '[in black on 2 white curved panels] APPOINTMENT | IN SAMARRA | [against dark green] [yellow] by | JOHN | O'HARA | [black] *MAURER*'. Spine: '[black on white] APPOINTMENT | IN | SAMARRA | [yellow against dark green] O'HARA | [black on white] HARCOURT, BRACE | AND COMPANY'. Back: 'RECENT FICTION'. Front flap has a blurb for *AIS*. Back flap has ad for *The Last Adam*.

*Publication:* Unknown number of copies of the first printing. Published 16 August 1934. $2.50. Copyright #A74572.

*Printing:* Set, printed, and bound by Quinn & Boden, Rahway, N.J.

*Locations:* Lilly (dj), MJB (dj), PSt (dj).

*Note:* Galley proofs are at MJB and Yale.

A 2.1.a*
*Presentation issues*

An unknown number of copies of the first-printing sheets were bound in cloth or wrappers for advance distribution. These were almost certainly used as review copies.

*Clothbound*

First-printing sheets with special first gathering. On p. i: 'PRESENTATION EDITION | NOT TO BE SOLD'. p. ii: blank.

Dust jacket for A2.1.a

Bound in light gray yellowish brown (#79) V cloth (smooth). Spine goldstamped: 'APPOINTMENT | IN | SAMARRA | [wavy rule] | O'HARA'. Light yellowish brown (#76) wove endpapers.

*Location:* MJB.

*Wrappers*

First-printing sheets with special first gathering. On p. i: 'PRESENTATION EDITION | NOT TO BE SOLD'; p. ii: blank. Noted with or without rubber-stamped notice on front endpaper: 'TO BE PUBLISHED [holograph] August 16 | PRICE [holograph] Probably $2.50'.

Bound in the dust jacket for the book.

*Location:* MJB (2 copies, with and without rubber-stamping).

A 2.1.b
*Second printing:* New York: Harcourt, Brace, 1934.

Not seen.

A 2.1.c
*Third printing:* New York: Harcourt, Brace, [1934].

On copyright page: 'Third printing, September, 1934'. Acknowledgment for "Sheppey" printed on p. viii.

A 2.1.d
*Fourth printing:* New York: Harcourt, Brace, 1934.

Not seen.

A 2.1.e
*Fifth printing:* New York: Harcourt, Brace, [1935].

On copyright page: 'Fifth printing, February, 1935'.

A 2.1.f
*Sixth printing:* New York: Grosset & Dunlap, [1936].

Reprinted 1940.

A 2.1.g
*Seventh printing:* New York: Duell, Sloan & Pearce, [1941?].

A 2.1.h
*Eighth printing:* New York: Dover, 1946.

A 2.1.i
*Ninth printing:* Cleveland and New York: World, [1947].

A 2.1.j
*Tenth printing:* New York: Modern Library, [1953].

With a previously unpublished "Foreword" by O'Hara.

On copyright page: 'First Modern Library Edition, 1953'. 9 printings: April 1953, April 1954, August 1956, April 1957, January 1958, January 1960, February 1961, March 1962, April 1964.

A 2.1.k
*Eleventh printing:* New York: Literary Guild, 1963.

Not seen.

A 2.1.l
*Twelfth printing:* New York: Dollar Book Club, 1964.

Not seen.

A 2.2.a
*First English edition, first printing (1935)*

# APPOINTMENT IN SAMARRA

## BY JOHN O'HARA

DEATH SPEAKS: There was a merchant in Baghdad who sent his servant to market to buy provisions and in a little while the servant came back, white and trembling, and said, Master, just now when I was in the market-place I was jostled by a woman in the crowd and when I turned I saw it was Death that jostled me. She looked at me and made a threatening gesture; now, lend me your horse, and I will ride away from this city and avoid my fate. I will go to Samarra and there Death will not find me. The merchant lent him his horse, and the servant mounted it, and he dug his spurs in its flanks and as fast as the horse could gallop he went. Then the merchant went down to the market-place and he saw me standing in the crowd and he came to me and said, Why did you make a threatening gesture to my servant when you saw him this morning? That was not a threatening gesture, I said, it was only a start of surprise. I was astonished to see him in Baghdad, for I had an appointment with him tonight in Samarra.

—W. SOMERSET MAUGHAM

## FABER & FABER LIMITED
## LONDON

A 2.2.a: 4⁷/₈″ × 7¹/₄″

*Copyright page:* 'FIRST PUBLISHED IN JANUARY MCMXXXV | BY FABER AND FABER LIMITED | 24 RUSSELL SQUARE LONDON W.C.1 | PRINTED IN GREAT BRITAIN BY | LATIMER TREND AND CO PLYMOUTH | ALL RIGHTS RESERVED'.

[1–6] 7–300

[A] B–I K–S⁸ T⁶

*Contents:*  p. 1: half title; p. 2: blank; p. 3: title; p. 4: copyright; p. 5: dedication; p. 6: blank; pp. 7–300: text, headed 'I'.

*Typography and paper:*  31 lines per page. Wove paper.

*Binding:*  Medium red (#15) V cloth (smooth). Spine goldstamped: '[on blue panel within gold single-rule frame] *Appointment | in | Samarra* | [circle] | *John O'Hara* | [below panel] *Faber and | Faber'*. All edges trimmed. White wove endpapers.

*Dust jacket:*  Same illustration as American dust jacket. Front: same lettering as American dust jacket, but artist's name omitted. Spine: '[black on white] APPOINT-MENT | IN | SAMARRA | [yellow on dark green] O'HARA | [black on white] FABER & | FABER'. Back: 'THE FABER LIBRARY'. Front flap has blurb for *AIS*. Back flap has Faber & Faber ad.

*Publication:*  No fewer than 6,000 copies of the first printing. Published 14 February 1935. 7s. 6d.

*Locations:*  BL (6 FEB 35), MJB (dj).

*Note:*  Substantive variants between American and English editions

| HARCOURT, BRACE (1934) [ | | FABER & FABER (1935) | |
|---|---|---|---|
| 23.10 | county | 27.6 | country |
| 41.28 | a [twice] | 45.20 | an [twice] |
| 42.6 | a | 45.30 | an |
| 42.8 | a | 46.1 | an |
| 57.3 | table | 60.18 | tables |
| 64.15 | day | 67.16 | days |
| 65.1 | October 29, | 68.1 | 29 October |
| 65.22 | as nearly anyone | 68.22 | as nearly as anyone |
| 80.29 | January 6, | 83.19 | 6 January |
| 105.26 | went | 108.18 | gone |
| 115.4 | ass | 117.21 | arse |
| 118.6 | ass | 120.23 | arse |
| 118.20 | ass | 121.7 | arse |
| 119.17 | ass | 122.3 | arse |
| 121.27 | ass | 124.9 | arse |
| 122.2 | ass | 124.12 | arse |
| 126.25 | hid | 128.26 | hidden |
| 152.13 | clubs, in | 153.25 | clubs, and in |
| 158.5 | ass | 159.5 | arse |
| 160.7 | ass | 161.7 | arse |
| 203.26 | the | 204.6 | that |
| 204.28 | such merger | 205.7 | such a merger |
| 245.13 | forgot | 244.31 | forgotten |
| 278.4 | suspenders | 276.31 | braces |
| 279.23 | suspenders | 278.20 | braces |

O'Hara to Bruccoli, 12 February 1966: "I think you may find some tinkering with APPOINTMENT IN SAMARRA and maybe some others in the Faber & Faber trade editions. I seem to recall their fucking around with the dialog, trying to make my characters talk like Fellows of All Souls, which Geoffrey Faber was. But once I have read proof on the U.S. trade editions I have to trust to luck."

A 2.2.b
*Second printing:* London: Faber & Faber, [1935].

On copyright page: 'SECOND IMPRESSION MARCH MCMXXXV'.

A 2.2.c
*Third printing:* London: Faber & Faber, [1936].

On copyright page: 'THIRD IMPRESSION JANUARY MCMXXXVI'.

There were at least 6 more printings through 1951, none of which has been seen.

A 2.2.d
*Faber Paperback printings:* London: Faber & Faber, [1961].

"Faber Paper Covered Editions." 6s. Unknown number of printings 1961–1975.

A 2.3
*Third edition:* Hamburg, Paris & Bologna: Albatross, [1935].

#291. Location: MJB.

A 2.4
*Fourth edition:* New York: Pocket Books, [1939].

#27. 25¢. 2 printings: November, December 1939.

A 2.5
*Fifth edition:* Harmondsworth & New York: Penguin, [1944].

#472. 9p. Reprinted 1945.

A 2.6
*Sixth edition:* New York: Penguin, [1945].

#563. 2 printings: August, October 1945.

A 2.7
*Seventh edition:* Stockholm & London: Continental Book Co., [1948].

Zephyr #199. Location: PSt.

A 2.8
*Eighth edition:* New York: Signet, [1945].

25¢. 5 printings: August 1945, September 1945, January 1950, November 1953, September 1957.

A 2.9
*Ninth edition:* London: Pan, [1958].

#G107. 2s. 6d.

A 2.10
*Tenth edition:* New York: Signet, [1961].

#D1895. 50¢. 3 printings in 1961.

A 2.11
*Eleventh edition:* New York: Signet, [1963].

#CP177. 60¢.

A 2.12
*Twelfth edition:* [London]: Corgi, [1965].

#FN7203. 5s. 3 printings: 1965, 1966, and 1967.

A 2.13.a
*Thirteenth edition, Bantam printing:* New York: Bantam, [1966].

#S3094. 75¢.

A 2.13.b
*Thirteenth edition, Popular printing:* New York: Popular Library, [1976].

#445-08441-195. $1.95.

A 2.14
*Fourteenth edition: Appointment in Samarra—Butterfield 8—Hope of Heaven.* New York: Random House, [1968].

See AA 6.

*Note*

Abridged in *New York Post,* 30 January 1950, 35; 31 January, 35; 1 February, 65; 2 February, 37; 3 February, 59; 5 February, 1S–8S.

A 3 THE DOCTOR'S SON AND OTHER STORIES

A 3.1.a
*First edition, first printing (1935)*

# THE
# DOCTOR'S SON

## AND OTHER STORIES

## BY JOHN O'HARA

HARCOURT, BRACE AND COMPANY

NEW YORK

A 3.1.a: 5³/₈″ × 8″

[i–viii] [1–2] 3–294 [295–296]

[1–19]⁸

*Contents:*  p. i: half title; p. ii: *'Also by John O'Hara'*; p. iii: title; p. iv: copyright; p. v: acknowledgments; p. vi: blank; pp. vii–viii: 'Contents'; p. 1: half title; p. 2: blank; pp. 3–294: text, headed 'The Doctor's Son'; pp. 295–296: blank.

*37 stories:* "The Doctor's Son," "Early Afternoon," "Pleasure," "New Day," "The Man Who Had to Talk to Somebody," "Mary," "Ella and the Chinee," "Ten Eyck or Pershing? Pershing or Ten Eyck?" "Alone," "Coffee Pot," "The Girl Who Had Been Presented," "Mort and Mary," "On His Hands," "It Wouldn't Break Your Arm," "I Never Seen Anything Like It," "Lombard's Kick," "Frankie," "Mr. Cass and the Ten Thousand Dollars," "Of Thee I Sing, Baby," "Screen Test," "Mr. Sidney Gainsborough: Quality Pictures," "Mr Cowley and the Young," "Never a Dull Moment," "Master of Ceremonies," "Mrs. Galt and Edwin," "Hotel Kid," "Dr. Wyeth's Son," "Except in My Memory," "The Public Career of Mr. Seymour Harrisburg," "Straight Pool," "Back in New Haven," "Salute a Thoroughbred," "All the Girls He Wanted," "Sportsmanship," "In the Morning Sun," "It Must Have Been Spring," "Over the River and Through the Wood." "The Doctor's Son" had not been previously published.

*Typography and paper:*  Caslon, 12 point on 15. 5¹/₂″ (5¹³/₁₆″) × 3¹¹/₁₆″; 25 lines per page. Running heads: rectos and versos, story titles. Wove paper.

*Binding:*  Black varnished V cloth (smooth). Spine goldstamped: 'THE | DOCTOR'S | SON | & | OTHER STORIES | John O'Hara | Harcourt, Brace | and Company'. All edges trimmed. White wove sized endpapers of heavier stock than text.

*Dust jacket:*  Front lettered on green, gold, and black: '[black] *by* JOHN O'HARA | [script] author of [roman] APPOINTMENT IN SAMARRA | [sketch of O'Hara in gold oval, signed "Schreiber"] | [white] [script] The | [roman] DOCTOR'S SON | [script] and other stories'. Spine lettered on black, light gold, and gold panels: '[gold] JOHN | O'HARA | [script] The | [roman] DOCTOR'S | SON | [black] HARCOURT, BRACE | AND COMPANY'. Back has excerpts from 6 reviews of *AIS*. Front flap has blurb for *DS*. Back flap has photo of O'Hara and biographical sketch.

*Publication:*  Unknown number of copies of the first printing. Published 21 February 1935. $2.50. Copyright #A79860.

*Printing:*  Set, printed, and bound by Quinn & Boden, Rahway, N.J.

*Locations:*  LC (FEB 28 1935); MJB (dj); PSt.

*Review copy:*  A copy of the first printing is blindstamped on the back cover: 'COMPLIMENTARY | PROFESSIONAL | COPY'. Location: MJB.

Dust jacket for A3.1.a

A 3.1.b
*Second printing:* New York: Harcourt, Brace, [1935].

On copyright page: 'Second printing, February, 1935'.

A 3.2
*Second edition:* New York: New Avon Library, [1943].

#31. 28 stories. Noted with variant wrappers; probably 2 printings.

A 3.3
*Third edition:* New York: Editions for the Armed Services, [1946?].

#979. 28 stories. Location: MJB.

A 3.4
*Fourth edition:* New York: Avon, [   ].

#T511. 35¢. 28 stories.

A 3.5
*Fifth edition: The Great Short Stories of John O'Hara Stories from The Doctor's Son and Other Stories and Files on Parade.* New York: Bantam, [1956].

See AA 4.

*Note:* See *All the Girls He Wanted,* AA 2.

A 4 BUTTERFIELD 8

A 4.1.a
*First edition, first printing (1935)*

# Butterfield 8

## A NOVEL BY JOHN O'HARA

Starting on December 16, a distinguishing
numeral will be added to, and become part of,
each central office name in New York City.
For example:

HANover will become HAnover 2

[ *From an advertisement of the New York* ]
[ *Telephone Company, December 8, 1930.* ]

### HARCOURT, BRACE AND COMPANY

### NEW YORK

A 4.1.a: 5³/₈″ × 8″

[i–iv] [1–2] 3–310 [311–316]

[1–20]⁸

*Contents:* p. i: half title; p. ii: *'Other books by John O'Hara';* p. iii: title; p. iv: copyright; p. 1: half title; p. 2: blank; pp. 3–310: text, headed '1'; pp. 311–316: blank.

*Typography and paper:* Caslon Old Face, $11\frac{1}{2}$ point on 13. 6″ (6¹/₄″) × 3¹¹/₁₆″; 31 lines per page. No running heads. Wove paper.

*Binding:* Black varnished V cloth (smooth). Spine goldstamped: 'BUTTER- | FIELD 8 | *John O'Hara* | *Harcourt, Brace* | *and Company'.* All edges trimmed. White wove calendered endpapers.

*Dust jacket:* Front lettered on black and gray buildings: [vertically up, reddish orange] BUTTERFIELD 8 | [horizontally] [white] JOHN O'HARA | [reddish orange] AUTHOR OF | APPOINTMENT | IN SAMARRA | [signature of designer]'. Spine lettered on black background: '[white] O'HARA | [vertically up, reddish orange] BUTTERFIELD 8 | [horizontally, white] HARCOURT, BRACE | AND COMPANY'. Back: 'OTHER BOOKS BY JOHN O'HARA'. Front flap has blurb for *BU 8.* Back flap has biographical note on O'Hara.

*Publication:* Unknown number of copies of the first printing. Published 17 October 1935. $2.50. Copyright #A86975.

*Printing:* Set, printed, and bound by Quinn & Boden, Rahway, N.J.

*Locations:* LC (OCT 24 1935), Lilly (dj), MJB (dj), PSt.

*Review copies:* Noted with gray paper label tipped on free front endpaper: 'ADVANCE COPY | FROM HARCOURT, BRACE AND COMPANY | Please note the release date for review and the price | [rubber-stamped] OCT 17 1935 $2.50'. Location: MJB.
   Also copy rubber-stamped on free front endpaper: 'REVIEW COPY | PUBLICATION DATE | OCT 17 1935   PRICE $2.50'. Location: MJB.

*Note:* 500 sets of sheets for *Butterfield 8* were bound in the cases for a life of John Wesley (*The Pleasures of Publishing,* III [15 June 1936]).

BY JOHN O'HARA

BUTTERFIELD 8

$2.50

Readers of "Appointment in Samarra" will certainly not be disappointed in John O'Hara's extraordinary new novel. Once more this able and hard-hitting writer has told a story that registers with terrific force. And once again he exposes the roots of strange patterns in the behaviour of everyday Americans.

This time O'Hara tells about a girl in New York, a girl who is leading a cruelly paced, un-normal existence in the feverish atmosphere of mid-Manhattan's early 1930's. The thing this girl, who caused a sensation in New York, most wanted has been hardest to secure. "It would be easy enough," writes the author, "to say any one of a lot of things about Gloria, and many things were said. It could be said that she was a person who in curious ways—some of them peculiar—had the ability to help other people, but lacked the ability to help herself. Someone could write a novel about Gloria without ever going very far from that thesis."

## John O'Hara

John O'Hara's meteoric rise was one of the literary events of 1934. His first novel, "Appointment in Samarra," was more widely read and more widely discussed than any other first novel of the year. As McClain said in the *New York Sun* recently: "John O'Hara hauled off last year and did the thing every newspaper man is going to do tomorrow—he wrote 'the great American novel.'

*Appointment in Samarra* turned out to be a long-run best seller, which is both great and novel in the lives of most writers, American or not."

John O'Hara followed up with a book of short stories and, although books of short stories usually have short and unhappy lives, "The Doctor's Son and Other Stories" went swiftly through three printings, with a fourth in sight as the publication date of the new novel draws near.

Before he sat down to the typewriter to write books, O'Hara had spent almost ten years in newspaper work, on such publications as the *Daily Mirror*, the *Morning Telegraph*, *Editor and Publisher*, *Time*, *The New Yorker*. He has also press-agented for the movies, contributed stories to half a dozen of the leading magazines, and edited a newspaper.

He was married once. He now lives in New York. He is thirty years old.

OTHER BOOKS BY JOHN O'HARA

### Appointment in Samarra

DOROTHY PARKER: "*Appointment in Samarra* is a fine and serious American novel, of shrewd and inevitable pattern and almost unbelievable pace. This swift, savage story of Julian English's life and the lives of those who crowd his way, set down as sharp and deep as if the author had used steel for paper, is, it seems to me, of high importance both as a work of American letters and a document of American history. The novelist has included, in his telling of English's short years, a record of the ways and mores of English's times—our times. Mr. O'Hara's eyes and ears have been spared nothing; but he has kept in his heart a curious, bitter mercy."

CLIFTON FADIMAN, *The New Yorker*: "Oh, most sheerly readable novel within miles . . . it is something we cannot lay down."

JOHN CHAMBERLAIN, *The New York Times*: "There is no doubt about it, Mr. O'Hara is possessed by the America he has known, and he is able to communicate that possession simply and remarkably."

ERNEST HEMINGWAY, *Esquire*: "If you want to read a book by a man who knows what he is writing about and has written it marvellously well, read *Appointment in Samarra* by John O'Hara."

$2.50

### The Doctor's Son and Other Stories

*Time Newsmagazine*: "As straight a reporter of U.S. dialect as the late great Ring Lardner and straighter than Hemingway, O'Hara writes without bitterness, without pity."

EDITH H. WALTON, *New York Times*: "O'Hara is a superbly gifted observer, shrewd, savage, merciless and apparently fertile in ideas. . . . Trenchant all of these stories, usually ironic, often a little cruel, they display precisely the same qualities as *Appointment in Samarra*."

LEWIS GANNETT, *New York Herald Tribune*: "O'Hara has the Hemingway touch with the American language and the O. Henry gift of the sharp ending."

$2.50

Harcourt, Brace and Company
383 MADISON AVENUE, NEW YORK

BUTTERFIELD 8

JOHN O'HARA

AUTHOR OF APPOINTMENT IN SAMARRA

HARCOURT BRACE AND COMPANY

Dust jacket for A 4.1.a

A 4.1.b
*Second printing:* New York: Harcourt, Brace, [1935].

On copyright page: *'Second printing, October, 1935'.*

A 4.1.c
*Third printing:* New York: Grosset & Dunlap, [1937?].

A 4.1.d
*Fourth printing:* New York: Modern Library, [1952?].

#323. $1.95. 4 printings.

A 4.1.e
*Fifth printing:* New York: Modern Library, [1957?].

#P32. Paperbound. 95¢. 5 printings.

A 4.1.f
*Sixth printing:* New York: Vintage Books, [1957?].

#V-49. Paperbound. 95¢. 2 printings.

A 4.2
*Second edition:* New York: Editions for the Armed Services, [1945?].

#799. Locations: MJB, PSt.

A 4.3
*Third edition: Here's O'Hara.* New York: Duell, Sloan & Pearce, [1946].

See AA 1.

A 4.4.a
*Fourth edition, Avon printings:* New York: Avon, [1946].

#94. 25¢. 9 printings: May 1946, April 1947, April 1948, November 1948, September 1949, November 1951, June 1955, July 1957, May 1959.

A 4.4.b
*Fourth edition, Shakespeare printing:* New York: Shakespeare House, [1951].

A 4.5.a
*First English edition, first printing (1951)*

JOHN O'HARA

BUTTERFIELD

8

LONDON
THE CRESSET PRESS
1951

A 4.5.a: 4$^{13}$/$_{16}$″ × 7$^{3}$/$_{16}$″

*Copyright page:* 'First published 1951 | by The Cresset Press, Ltd, 11 *Fitzroy Square, London, W.* 1, *and printed in Great Britain | by the Pitman Press, Bath'.*

[i–ii] [1–7] 8–268 [269–270]

[1–4] 5–17⁸

*Contents:* pp. i–ii: blank; p. 1: half title; p. 2: *'By the same Author';* p. 3: title; p. 4: copyright; p. 5: epigraph; p. 6: blank; pp. 7–268: text, headed 'CHAPTER 1'; pp. 269–270: blank.

*Typography and paper:* 34 lines per page. Wove paper.

*Binding:* Vivid red (#11) V cloth (smooth). Spine goldstamped: 'BU | TTER- | FIELD | 8 | JOHN | O'HARA | CRESSET | PRESS'. All edges trimmed. White wove calendered endpapers.

*Dust jacket:* Front and spine lettered in white on black. Front: 'BU TTERFIELD | 8 | JOHN O'HARA | AUTHOR OF "A RAGE TO LIVE" '. Spine: 'JOHN | O'HARA | BU | TTER- | FIELD | 8 | CRESSET | PRESS'. Back cover: 'By the same author'. Front flap: blurb for *BU 8.* Back flap blank.

*Publication:* Unknown number of copies of the first printing. Published September 1951. 12s. 6d.

*Locations:* BL (10 AUG 51), Bod (16 AUG 1951), Lilly (dj), MJB (dj), PSt (dj).

*Note:* Chatto & Windus set galleys for a London edition of *Butterfield 8,* possibly in 1936. Although the text was probably expurgated, it was not published because of the publisher's concern about action by the Lord Chamberlain.

A 4.5.b
*Second printing:* London: Barrie & Rockliff The Cresset Press, [1969].

A 4.5.c
*Third printing:* [London]: Barrie & Jenkins, [1975].

A 4.6.a
*Sixth edition, Bantam printings:* New York: Bantam, [1960].

#H 2104. 60¢. 26 printings, September 1960–1970.

A 4.6.b
*Sixth edition, Popular printing:* New York: Popular Library, [1976].

#445-08445-175. $1.75.

A 4.7
*Seventh edition:* [Harmondsworth]: Penguin, [1960].

#1469. 2s. 6d. Reprinted 1961, 1962, 1964.

A 4.8
*Eighth edition: Appointment in Samarra—Butterfield 8—Hope of Heaven.* New York: Random House, [1968].
See AA 6.

A 4.9
*Ninth edition:* London: Hodder Paperback, 1971.

Not seen.

*Note*

Abridged in the *New York Post:* 28 November 1949, 3, 29; 29 November, 3, 39; 30 November, 3, 59; 1 December, 3, 41; 2 December, 3, 57; 4 December, 1S–7S; 5 December, 29; 6 December, 41; 7 December, 53; 8 December, 51; 9 December, 63; 11 December, 1S–7S.

A 5 HOPE OF HEAVEN

A 5.1.a
*First edition, first printing (1938)*

# HOPE of HEAVEN

## BY JOHN O'HARA

Harcourt, Brace and Company    New York

A 5.1.a: 5³/₈″ × 8″

COPYRIGHT, 1938, BY
HARCOURT, BRACE AND COMPANY, INC.

*All rights reserved, including*
*the right to reproduce this book*
*or portions thereof in any form.*

*first edition*

*Typography by Robert Josephy*
PRINTED IN THE UNITED STATES OF AMERICA
BY QUINN & BODEN COMPANY, INC., RAHWAY, N. J.

[i–iv] [1–2] 3–182 [183–188]

[1–12]$^8$

*Contents:*  p. i: half title; p. ii: *'Books by John O'Hara'*; p. iii: title; p. iv: copyright; p. 1: half title; p. 2: blank; pp. 3–182: text, headed '1'; pp. 183–188: blank.

*Typography and paper:*  Caslon, 12 point on 16. 5$^3$/$_4$" (6") × 3$^5$/$_8$"; 26 lines per page. No running heads. Wove paper.

*Binding:*  Black V cloth (smooth). Spine goldstamped: 'HOPE OF | HEAVEN | *John O'Hara* | *Harcourt, Brace* | *and Company*'. All edges trimmed. White wove calendered endpapers.

*Dust jacket:*  Front and spine have illustration in shades of blue of signpost for corner of Vine St. and Hollywood Blvd. Front: '[white] [script] Hope of | [roman] HEAVEN | [light blue script] by | [white roman] JOHN O'HARA'. Spine lettered in white: '[script] Hope of | [roman] HEAVEN | [light blue star] | O'HARA | [script] Harcourt, Brace | and Company'. Back: 'OTHER BOOKS BY JOHN O'HARA'. Front flap has blurb for *HOH*. Back flap has biographical sketch of O'Hara.

*Publication:*  Unknown number of copies of the first printing. Published 17 March 1938. $2. Copyright #A115548.

*Printing:*  Printed and bound by Quinn & Boden, Rahway, N.J.

*Locations:*  BL (10 MAR 38), LC (MAR 23 1938), Lilly (dj), MJB (dj), PSt.

*Review copy:*  Rubber-stamped on free front endpaper: 'REVIEW COPY | PUBLICA-TION DATE | MAR 17 1938 | PRICE $2.00'. Location: MJB.

A 5.1.b
*Second printing:* New York: Harcourt, Brace, [1938].

On copyright page: 'Second printing, March 1938'.

## John O'Hara

John O'Hara's meteoric rise has been one of the literary events of recent years. His first novel, "Appointment in Samarra," was more widely read and more widely discussed than any other first novel of the year. As McClish said in the *New York Sun* at the time: "John O'Hara hauled off and did the thing every newspaper man is going to do tomorrow—he wrote 'the great American novel.'" "Appointment in Samarra" turned out to be a long-term best seller, which is both great and novel in the lives of most writers, American or not.

John O'Hara followed it up with a book of short stories, "The Doctor's Son and Other Stories." Then, in 1935, came a second novel, "Butterfield 8," a hard hitting story about a New York girl in the speakeasy epoch.

Before he set down to the typewriter to write two books, O'Hara had spent almost ten years in newspaper work, on such publications as the *New York Herald Tribune*, the *Daily Mirror*, the *Morning Telegraph*, *Editor and Publisher*, *Time*, *The New Yorker*. He has also press-agented for the movies, contributed stories to half a dozen of the leading magazines, and edited a newsmagazine.

HARCOURT, BRACE AND COMPANY
383 Madison Avenue, New York

## OTHER BOOKS BY JOHN O'HARA

### Butterfield 8

JOHN CHAMBERLAIN, *New York Times*: "Butterfield 8 has literary power. Mr. O'Hara can write like a streak ... the swift O'Hara pace, the clever dove-tailing of incident, the skillful manipulation of the flash-back, are all here."

RICHARD WATTS, *New York Herald Tribune*: "The quality of Mr. O'Hara which demands first consideration is his great gift for the drama. A brilliant observer of how people speak and look, he possesses a knowledge of the dramatic possibilities of dialogue as well as the proper ear for its manipulation. In addition, he knows how to build up a scene of striking power and how to make it vibrate with significance and emotion. He knows characterization and dramatic movement and narrative vividness."

HARRY HANSEN, *New York World-Telegram*: "Taking New York's speakeasy life in stride, John O'Hara makes a moving history. For those who have followed the chronicles of manners and morals written by Dorothy Parker, Ernest Hemingway, and Dashiell Hammett, Butterfield 8 is a must book."

$2.50

### The Doctor's Son and Other Stories

*Time Newsmagazine*: "As straight a reporter of U. S. dialect as the late great Ring Lardner and straighter than Hemingway, O'Hara writes without bitterness, without pity."

EDITH H. WALTON, *New York Times*: "O'Hara is a superbly gifted observer, shrewd, savage, merciless and apparently fertile in ideas ... Trenchant, all of these stories, usually ironic, often a little cruel, they display precisely the same qualities as Appointment in Samarra."

LEWIS GANNETT, *New York Herald Tribune*: "O'Hara has the Hemingway touch with the American language and the O. Henry gift of the sharp ending."

$2.50

HARCOURT, BRACE & CO.
383 Madison Avenue, New York

## HOPE OF HEAVEN
### by John O'Hara

There is only one John O'Hara. And of the many compelling reasons for reading this new book (his third novel), it is hard to say which is the most persuasive.

Is it that John O'Hara (age 33) is one of the few most accomplished craftsmen American literature has recently produced? Is it because his stories have powerful symbolism? Or because he is so amazing and careful a reporter? Or because his writing is fast-paced and sustained, always? Or is it, essentially, that John O'Hara is one of those gifted writers who can really tell a story and not fake it?

In any event, here it is: the compassionate story of a man and a girl—and of a weird crisscrossing of the lines of life—of passion spent and hope of heaven. Its California setting is something new in the work of O'Hara, its technique is equally fascinating, and its characters are as memorably alive as any you will find in the revealing shadow-world of letters.

HARCOURT, BRACE AND COMPANY
383 Madison Avenue New York

Dust jacket for A5.1.a

A 5.2.a
*First English edition, first printing (1939)*

# HOPE OF HEAVEN

and other stories

by

JOHN O'HARA

Faber and Faber Limited
24 Russell Square
London

A 5.2.a: 4³/₄″ × 7³/₈″

*Copyright page:* 'First published in February Mcmxxxix | by Faber and Faber Limited | 24 Russell Square, London, W.C.1 | Printed in Great Britain by | Western Printing Services Ltd., Bristol | All Rights Reserved'.

[1–6] 7–8 [9–10] 11–19 [20] 21–25 [26] 27–39 [40] 41–45 [46] 47–53 [54] 55–223 [224] 225–229 [230] 231–237 [238] 239–243 [244] 245–253 [254] 255–263 [264] 265–269 [270] 271–275 [276] 277–281 [282] 283–297 [298] 299–309 [310] 311–315 [316] 317–321 [322] 323–347 [348] 349–387 [388]

[A] B–I K–U X–Z⁸ 2A¹⁰

*Contents:*  pp. 1–2: blank; p. 3: half title; p. 4: 'by the same author'; p. 5: title; p. 6: copyright; pp. 7–8: 'Contents'; p. 9: half title; p. 10: blank; pp. 11–387: text, headed 'The Public Career of | Mr. Seymour Harrisburg'; p. 388: blank.

*Includes* Hope of Heaven *and 36 stories:* "The Public Career of Mr. Seymour Harrisburg," "Sidesaddle,"* "Saffercisco,"* "Price's Always Open,"* "Hotel Kid," "Of Thee I Sing, Baby," "In the Morning Sun," "Can You Carry Me?"* "Lunch Tuesday,"* "Shave,"* "Portisan on the Portis,"* "The Cold House,"* "Days,"* "Are We Leaving Tomorrow?"* "Salute a Thoroughbred," "Sportsmanship," "Dr. Wyeth's Son," "Over the River," "Pleasure," "Alone," "Frankie," "The Gentleman in the Tan Suit,"* "Most Gorgeous Thing,"* "It Must Have Been Spring," "I Could Have Had a Yacht,"* "Olive,"* "Ice Cream,"* "Brother,"* "By Way of Yonkers,"* "My Girls,"* "No Sooner Said,"* "Good-bye, Herman,"* "Give and Take,"* "Peggy,"* "Straight Pool," "The Doctor's Son." Asterisks indicate previously uncollected stories; this volume was published before *Files on Parade.* "Can You Carry Me?" was published here before it appeared in *The New Yorker.*

*Typography and paper:*  34 lines per page. Wove paper.

*Binding:*  Yellow brown (#76) V cloth (smooth). Spine stamped in blue: 'HOPE | OF | HEAVEN | [wavy rule] | JOHN | O'HARA | FABER AND | FABER'. All edges trimmed. White wove endpapers.

*Dust jacket:*  Same illustration as American dust jacket. Front: '[white] [script] Hope of | [roman] HEAVEN | AND OTHER STORIES | [light blue] [script] by | [white] [roman] JOHN O'HARA'. Spine lettered in white: '[script] Hope of | [roman] HEAVEN | [light blue star] | O'HARA | *Faber* | *and Faber*'. Back: 'NEW FICTION'. Front flap has blurb for *HOH.* Back flap: '*Also by John O'Hara*'.

*Publication:*  3,050 copies of the first printing. Published 9 February 1939. 7s. 6d.

*Locations:*  BL (9 FEB 1939), Bod (FEB 17 1939), MJB (dj).

A 5.2.b
*Second printing:* London: Faber & Faber, [1953].

On copyright page: '*Reprinted lithographically in Great Britain Mcmliii | at the University Press, Oxford | by Charles Batey, Printer to the University*'. Remaindered with yellow wrap-around band: 'JOHN O'HARA | Hope of Heaven | *NOW 6/6ᵈ net*'. Location: A. Erskine.

A 5.3
*Third edition: Hope of Heaven and Other Stories.* New York: Avon, [1946].

Avon Modern Short Story Monthly #29. 25¢. Omits final chapter. With 4 stories: "Platform," "A Purchase of Some Golf Clubs," "Too Young," "Where's the Game."

A 5.4

*Fourth edition: Here's O'Hara.* New York: Duell, Sloan & Pearce, [1946].

See AA 1.

A 5.5

*Fifth edition:* New York: Avon, [1947].

#144. 25¢. Omits final chapter. Reprinted 1950.

A 5.6

*Sixth edition:* [Toronto]: News Stand Library, [1948].

Omits final chapter. Reprinted 1949.

A 5.7

*Seventh edition:* New York: Bantam, [1956].

#1422. 25¢. 13 printings: January 1956 (2 printings), July 1960, August 1960, September 1960, March 1961, July 1961, February 1962, September 1962, October 1963 (2 printings), August 1964, January 1966.

A 5.8

*Eighth edition:* [London]: Panther, [1960].

#1086. 3s. 6d. With 36 stories. 6 printings: 1960, 1963, 1964, 1966, 1968, 1972.

A 5.9

*Ninth edition: Appointment in Samarra—Butterfield 8—Hope of Heaven.* New York: Random House, [1968].

See AA 6.

A 5.10

*Tenth edition:* New York: Popular Library, [1973].

#445-00149-125. $1.25. Reprinted.

A6 FILES ON PARADE

A6.1.a₁
*First edition, first printing, first state (1939)*

---

# FILES on
# PARADE

## BY JOHN O'HARA

Harcourt, Brace and Company    New York

---

A6.1.a: 5⁵/₁₆″ × 8″

[i–vi] vii–viii [ix–x] [1–2] 3–277 [278]

[1]⁸ (±1₄) [2–18]⁸; foreword tipped in.

*Contents:* p. i: half title; p. ii: 'Also by John O'Hara'; p. iii: title; p. iv: copyright; p. v: 'TO | KATHARINE DELANEY O'HARA | WHOSE SON I AM'; p. vi: acknowledgment; pp. vii–viii: 'Foreword'; pp. ix–x: 'Contents'; p. 1: half title; p. 2: blank; pp. 3–277: text, headed 'Price's Always Open'; p. 278: blank.

*35 stories:* "Price's Always Open," "Trouble in 1949," "The Cold House," "Days," "Are We Leaving Tomorrow?" "Portisan on the Portis," "Lunch Tuesday," "Shave," "Sidesaddle," "No Mistakes," "Brother," "Saffercisco," "Ice Cream," "Peggy," "And You Want a Mountain," "Pal Joey," "Ex-Pal," "How I Am Now in Chi," "Bow Wow," "Give and Take," "The Gentleman in the Tan Suit," "Good-by, Herman," "I Could Have Had a Yacht," "Richard Wagner: Public Domain?" "Olive," "It Wouldn't Break Your Arm," "My Girls," "No Sooner Said," "Invite," "All the Girls He Wanted," "By Way of Yonkers," "Most Gorgeous Thing," "A Day Like Today," "The Ideal Man," "Do You Like It Here?" All stories previously published. See A 5.2.a.

*Typography and paper:* Caslon, 12 point on 15. 5⁵/₁₆″ (5¹³/₁₆″) × 3⁵/₈″; 25 lines per page. Running heads: rectos and versos, story titles. Wove paper.

*Binding:* Vivid blue (#176) varnished V cloth (smooth). Spine goldstamped: 'FILES | ON PARADE | & | OTHER STORIES | John O'Hara | Harcourt, Brace | and Company'. All edges trimmed. Top edge stained yellow. White wove calendered endpapers.

*Dust jacket:* Front and spine lettered on gray background. Front: '[white] JOHN | [following 2 lines in script on dark blue panel] Files on | Parade | O'HARA'. Spine: '[white] JOHN | O'HARA | [following 2 lines in dark blue script] Files on | Parade | [white] HARCOURT, BRACE | AND COMPANY'. Back: 'OTHER BOOKS BY JOHN O'HARA'. Front flap has blurb for *FOP*. Back flap has biographical note on O'Hara.

*Publication:* Unknown number of copies of the first printing. Published 21 September 1939. $2.50. Copyright #A132361.

*Printing:* Printed and bound by Quinn & Boden, Rahway, N.J.

*Locations:* LC (SEP 27 1939), MJB (dj), PSt.

*Review copy:* Rubber-stamped on free front endpaper: 'REVIEW COPY | PUBLICA-TION DATE | SEP 21 1939 PRICE $2.50'. Location: MJB.

A 6.1.a₂
*Second state*

[1–18]⁸

$2.50

# Files on Parade
### by JOHN O'HARA

JOHN O'HARA

Files on Parade

O'HARA

Files on Parade

HARCOURT, BRACE AND COMPANY

HARCOURT, BRACE AND COMPANY
383 MADISON AVENUE, NEW YORK

## OTHER BOOKS BY JOHN O'HARA

### Butterfield 8

JOHN CHAMBERLAIN, *New York Times*: "Butterfield 8 has literary power. Mr. O'Hara can write like a streak . . . the swift O'Hara pace, the clever dovetailing of incident, the skillful manipulation of the flash-back, are all here."

RICHARD WATTS, *New York Herald Tribune*: "The quality of Mr. O'Hara which demands first consideration is his great gift for the drama. A brilliant observer of how people speak and look, he possesses a knowledge of the dramatic possibilities of dialogue as well as the proper ear for its manipulation. In addition, he knows how to build up a scene of striking power and how to make it vibrant with significance and emotion. He knows characterization and dramatic movement and narrative vividness."

HARRY HANSEN, *New York World-Telegram*: "Taking New York's literary life in stride, John O'Hara makes a moving history . . . better than who have followed the chronicles of manners and morals written by Dorothy Parker, Ernest Hemingway, and Dashiel Hammett, Butterfield 8 is a must book."

$2.50

### The Doctor's Son and Other Stories

*Time Newsmagazine*: "As straight a reporter of U. S. dialect as the late great Ring Lardner and straighter than Hemingway, O'Hara writes without bitterness, without pity."

EDITH H. WALTON, *New York Times*: "O'Hara is a superbly gifted observer, shrewd, savage, merciless, and apparently fertile in ideas . . . Trenchant all of these stories, usually ironic, often a little cruel, they display precisely the same qualities as Appointment in Samarra."

LEWIS GANNETT, *New York Herald Tribune*: "O'Hara has the Hemingway touch with the American language and the O. Henry gift of the sharp ending."

HARCOURT, BRACE AND COMPANY
383 Madison Avenue, New York

## John O'Hara

John O'Hara's first novel, "Appointment in Samarra," was more widely read and more widely discussed than any other first novel of the year. As McClain said in the *New York Sun* at the time: "John O'Hara handed off and did the thing every newspaper man is going to do someday—he wrote 'the great American novel.' 'Appointment in Samarra' turned out to be a long-run best seller, which is both great and novel in the lives of most writers, American or not."

John O'Hara followed up with a book of short stories, "The Doctor's Son and Other Stories." Then, in 1935, came a second novel, "Butterfield 8," a hard hitting story about a New York girl in the speakeasy era. In 1938 he wrote his companionate story of a man and a girl in the California of today—"Hope of Heaven."

Before he sat down to the typewriter to write books, John O'Hara had spent almost ten years in newspaper work, on such publications as the *New York Herald Tribune*, the *Daily Mirror*, the *Morning Telegraph*, *Editor and Publisher*, *Time*, *The New Yorker*. He has also press-agented for the movies, reported stories to half a dozen of the leading magazines, and edited a newspaper.

HARCOURT, BRACE AND COMPANY
383 Madison Avenue, New York

The regularity with which such young writers are conquered to John O'Hara is evidence of his commanding place in American letters. No one else has to the same degree that ear for the American language, that unerring eye for human foibles and mischiefs, combined with a sense of structure, that make his short stories complete as many long novels are never complete.

It has been almost five years since he last collection of stories, "The Doctor's Son," was published. In those years he has, on talent, have opened and deepened. Without abating the merciless of his observation, the quality of compassion is now more frequent, his diction more varied, the pace swifter.

Ranging in subject from music days to mobsters, from bowling houses to the haunts of café society, this new collection is another milestone in the development of the author of "Appointment in Samarra," "Butterfield 8," and "Hope of Heaven."

HARCOURT, BRACE AND COMPANY
383 MADISON AVENUE, NEW YORK

Dust jacket for A 6.1.a

*Note:* The 'Foreword' leaf is integral in the second state; the text is identical with that of the inserted leaf in the first state.

*Location:* PSt (black, dj).

A 6.1.b
*Second printing:* New York: Harcourt, Brace, [1939].

On copyright page: 'Second printing, September, 1939'.

A 6.1.c
*Third printing:* New York: Harcourt, Brace, [1939].

On copyright page: 'Third printing, October, 1939'.

A 6.2
*Second edition:* New York: Avon, [1943].

Avon Modern Short Story Monthly #2. 25¢.

A 6.3
*Third edition: The Great Short Stories of John O'Hara Stories From The Doctor's Son and Other Stories and Files on Parade.* New York: Bantam, [1956].

See AA 4.

A 7 PAL JOEY

A 7.1.a
*First edition, first printing (1940)*

# PAL JOEY

## BY JOHN O'HARA

Duell, Sloan and Pearce     New York

A 7.1.a: 5³/₈″ × 8″

[1–8] 9–18 [19–20] 21–29 [30–32] 33–46 [47–48] 49–61 [62–64] 65–75 [76–78] 79–93 [94–96] 97–105 [106–108] 109–118 [119–120] 121–127 [128–130] 131–142 [143–144] 145–156 [157–158] 159–168 [169–170] 171–181 [182–184] 185–195 [196–200]

[1–12]⁸ [13]⁴

*Contents:* p. 1: half title; p. 2: *'Books by John O'Hara'*; p. 3: title; p. 4: copyright; p. 5: 'Contents'; p. 6: blank; p. 7: half title; p. 8: blank; pp. 9–195: text, headed 'Pal Joey'; pp. 196–200: blank.

*14 stories:* "Pal Joey," "Ex-Pal," "How I Am Now in Chi," "Bow Wow," "Avast and Belay," "Joey on Herta," "Joey on the Cake Line," "The Erloff," "Even the Greeks," "Joey and the Calcutta Club," "Joey and Mavis," "A New Career," "A Bit of a Shock,"* "Reminiss?"* Asterisks indicate previously unpublished stories.

*Typography and paper:* Caslon, 12 point on 15. 5⁷/₁₆″ (5³/₄″) × 3¹/₂″; 22 lines per page. Running heads: rectos and versos, 'PAL JOEY'. Wove paper.

*Binding:* Black varnished V cloth (smooth). Spine goldstamped: 'PAL | JOEY | *John O'Hara* | DUELL, SLOAN | AND PEARCE'. All edges trimmed. Off-white calendered wove endpapers.

*Dust jacket:* Front and spine lettered on pattern of horizontal white rules on red at top and vertical white rules against gray below. Front: '[white] PAL JOEY | [red on thick white rule] BY | [red] *John | O'Hara*'. Spine: '[white] PAL JOEY | *by | John | O'Hara* | [red] DUELL, SLOAN | AND PEARCE'. Back has toned photo of O'Hara with biographical sketch. Front flap has blurb for *PJ.* Back flap lists 6 O'Hara titles. Original dust jacket replaced by jacket with photo of Gene Kelly and 2 chorus girls on front.

*Publication:* Unknown number of copies of the first printing. Published 23 October 1940. $2. Copyright #A146979.

*Printing:* Printed and bound by Quinn & Boden, Rahway, N.J.

*Locations:* MJB (both jackets), PSt (both jackets).

*Note:* The "Pal Joey" material was used for the book of a musical show in 1940 and published in 1952. See A 12.

*Review copy:* First-printing sheets bound in wrappers made from first dust jacket. Location: MJB.

PAL JOEY
by
John O'Hara

PAL JOEY

BY

John O'Hara

A new book by the celebrated author of APPOINTMENT IN SAMARRA and BUTTERFIELD 8:

PAL JOEY
by
JOHN O'HARA

If Pal Joey had his way, this book would be called, *Of a Man and His Mouse*. Trouble is that while Joey stays the same man, the Mouse is always a different Mouse.

A night-club singer—Joey calls himself a poor man's Bing Crosby—stranded in the provinces, he has fallen into the habit of talking his troubles to Friend Ted, back in New York with his bigtime band. Joey makes no secret that he is plenty sick of singing and scatting for coffee & cakes in one crib after another on the South Side of Chi. Meantime he keeps alive, of course, and not always by one of the vocal cords. As he might say, he is not adverse to a little larceny, blackmail, or borrowing for keeps from any reasonably attractive babe.

Joey is unmistakable, funny and terrifying—an American characterization in whose creation Mr. O'Hara's unerring eye, ear, and wit have been used with devastating precision.

Duell, Sloan and Pearce

This is...
JOHN O'HARA
author of
PAL JOEY

of whom Louis Kronenberger once wrote in the New York Times, "Very few other writers have achieved one . . . zipper style, a matter punch." A waiter-wise style . . . Among them, one of the outstanding modern American novelists, Mr. O'Hara worked as an engineer, a boat steward, secretary in a briquetting plant, a railway freight clerk, a soda jerker, a guest-room maker, a laborer in a steel mill, secretary to Heywood Broun, and played a minor part in the motion picture *The General Died at Dawn*.

Duell, Sloan & Pearce, Inc.
270 Madison Avenue • New York

Duell, Sloan and Pearce have the honor to announce that they are now the publishers of the following books by:

JOHN O'HARA

APPOINTMENT IN SAMARRA
"This book is a brilliant piece of work, its style is vivid, laconic, and unfailingly clear." $2.50
—New Statesman and Nation

BUTTERFIELD 8
"It will carry you along with the tide of its swiftly rising tension until you feel you can stand no more, but you'll be wrong, because you will stand more, and when you have finished it you will not forget it." $2.50
—Herald Tribune BOOKS

HOPE OF HEAVEN
"It is a fragment from his life in the cafés, poignant most of it, a General reminiscence, in spite of its tension like a whip." $2.00
—The New Republic

THE DOCTOR'S SON
"His reporting of conversation is as good as that of Lewis or Lardner." $2.50
—N. Y. Herald Tribune

FILES ON PARADE
"No one, with the possible exception of Ring Lardner or Ernest Hemingway, has so well succeeded in summing up a lifetime in an instant." $2.50
—Partisan Press, Saturday Review

PAL JOEY $2.00

DUELL, SLOAN & PEARCE, Inc.
270 Madison Avenue • New York

Dust jacket for A 7.1.a

A 7.1.b
*Second printing:* New York: Duell, Sloan & Pearce, [1940].

On copyright page: 'Second printing, October, 1940'. Noted in Kelly dust jacket and in original jacket with Grosset & Dunlap imprint. No Grosset & Dunlap binding noted. Presumably Grosset & Dunlap distributed remainder copies of second Duell, Sloan & Pearce printing.

A 7.2.a
*Second edition, first printing:* New York: Editions for the Armed Services, [1945?].

#817. Locations: MJB, PSt.

A 7.2.b
*Second edition, second printing:* New York: Editions for the Armed Services, [1946].

#1147. Location: MJB.

A 7.3
*Third edition:* New York: Penguin, [1946].

#580. 25¢.

A 7.4
*Fourth edition: Here's O'Hara.* New York: Duell, Sloan & Pearce, [1946].

See AA 1.

A 7.5
*Fifth edition:* New York: Dell, [1951?].

#24. 10¢.

A 7.6.a
*First English edition, first printing (1952)*

JOHN O'HARA

# Pal Joey

LONDON
THE CRESSET PRESS
MCMLII

A 7.6.a: $4^{13}/_{16}"$ × $7^{1}/_{4}"$

*Copyright page:* 'Published in 1952 by | The Cresset Press, Ltd., 11 Fitzroy Square, London, W. 1 | and printed in Great Britain by | Butler & Tanner Ltd., Frome, Somerset'.

[1–4] 5 [6] 7–124 [125–128]; last page of each story unnumbered

[A] B–H⁸

*Contents:* p. 1: half title; p. 2: *'By the same author';* p. 3: title; p. 4: copyright; p. 5: 'CONTENTS'; p. 6: blank; pp. 7–125: text, headed 'Pal Joey'; pp. 126–128: blank.

Contains 14 stories.

*Typography and paper:* 28 lines per page. Wove paper.

*Binding:* Deep red (#13) paper-covered boards with B grain (linen). Spine gold-stamped: 'PAL | JOEY | ★ | JOHN | O'HARA | CRESSET | PRESS'. All edges trimmed. White wove endpapers.

*Dust jacket:* Front and spine lettered in white on black. Front: 'JOHN O'HARA | Pal | Joey | BY THE | AUTHOR OF ⟨⟨ A RAGE TO LIVE ⟩⟩ '. Spine: 'JOHN | O'HARA | Pal | Joey | CRESSET | PRESS'. Back has blurbs for *Butterfield 8.* Front flap has blurb for *PJ.* Back flap blank.

*Publication:* Unknown number of copies of the first printing. Published 10 November 1952.

*Locations:* Bod (4 NOV 1952), Lilly (dj), MJB (dj).

A 7.6.b
*Second printing:* London: Barrie & Rockliff / The Cresset Press, [1969].

A 7.7
*Seventh edition:* New York: Bantam, 1957.

25¢. 4 printings: November 1957, December 1957, January 1965, 4th printing.

A 7.8
*Eighth edition:* [London]: Panther, [1960].

#1115. 2s. 6d. 5 printings: September 1960, April 1964, March 1965, 1968, 1971.

A 7.9
*Ninth edition:* New York: Popular Library, [1976].

#445-03151-150. $1.50. Contains the stories, libretto, and lyrics. See A 12.2.

A 8 PIPE NIGHT

A 8.1.a
*First edition, first printing (1945)*

# PIPE

# NIGHT

## BY JOHN O'HARA

### WITH A PREFACE BY WOLCOTT GIBBS

### DUELL, SLOAN AND PEARCE
NEW YORK

A 8.1.a: 5$^1$/$_8$″ × 7$^5$/$_{16}$″

A WARTIME BOOK

THIS COMPLETE EDITION IS PRODUCED IN FULL COMPLIANCE WITH THE GOVERN-MENT'S REGULATIONS FOR CONSERVING PAPER AND OTHER ESSENTIAL MATERIALS.

COPYRIGHT, 1939, 1940, 1941, 1942, 1943, 1944, 1945
BY JOHN O'HARA

PRINTED IN THE UNITED STATES OF AMERICA
AMERICAN BOOK–STRATFORD PRESS, INC., NEW YORK

[i–viii] ix–xi [xii] xiii–xiv [1–2] 3–205 [206–210]

[1]⁸ [2–7]¹⁶ [8]⁸

*Contents:* p. i: half title; p. ii: 'Books by | John O'Hara'; p. iii: title; p. iv: copyright; p. v: *'To Belle'*; p. vi: blank; p. vii: acknowledgment; p. viii: blank; pp. ix–xi: 'Preface' by Wolcott Gibbs; p. xii: blank; pp. xiii–xiv: 'Table of | Contents'; p. 1: half title; p. 2: blank; pp. 3–205: text; pp. 206–210: blank.

*31 stories:* "Walter T. Carriman," "Now We Know," "Free,"* "Can You Carry Me?" "A Purchase of Some Golf Clubs,"* "Too Young," "Joey and the Calcutta Club," "Summer's Day," "Radio," "Nothing Missing," "The King of the Desert," "Bread Alone," "Reunion Over Lightly," "Memo to a Kind Stranger," "The Erloff," "Patriotism,"* "A Respectable Place," "The Magical Numbers," "On Time," "Graven Image," "Adventure on the Set," "Platform,"* "Civilized," "Revenge," "Fire!"* "The Lieutenant," "The Next-to-Last Dance of the Season," "Leave," "The Handler,"* "Where's the Game,"* "Mrs. Whitman." Asterisks follow previously unpublished stories.

*Typography and paper:* Baskerville, 11 point on 13. 5³/₈″ (5⁵/₈″) × 3⁷/₁₆″; 30 lines per page. Running heads: rectos, story titles; versos, 'Pipe Night'.

*Binding:* Black or vivid red (#11) V cloth (smooth). Spine goldstamped: 'PIPE | NIGHT | JOHN | O'HARA | DUELL | SLOAN | AND | PEARCE'. Top and bottom edges trimmed; fore edge rough trimmed. Off white endpapers.

*Dust jacket:* Front lettered on orange background: '[white] PIPE | [black] JOHN O'HARA | [white] NIGHT | [designer's signature]'. Spine lettered on black background: '[orange] PIPE | NIGHT | [vertically, white] JOHN O'HARA | [horizontally, orange] DUELL, SLOAN | AND PEARCE'. Back has photo of O'Hara by Katherine Young. Front flap has blurb for *PN*. Back flap has reviews of *Pal Joey*.

*Publication:* Unknown number of copies of the first printing. Published 14 March 1945. $2.50. Copyright #A187094.

*Printing:* Manufactured by American Book-Stratford Press, New York.

Dust jacket for A 8.1.a

*Locations:* LC (2 copies in black cloth, MAR 19 1945), MJB (red cloth in dj and black cloth), PSt (red cloth, dj).

*Review copy:* Unbound signatures. Location: MJB.

A 8.1.b
*Second printing:* New York: Duell, Sloan & Pearce, 1945?

Not seen.

A 8.1.c
*Third printing:* New York: Duell, Sloan & Pearce, 1945?

Not seen.

A 8.1.d
*Fourth printing:* New York: Duell, Sloan & Pearce, 1945?

Not seen.

A 8.1.e
*Fifth printing:* New York: Duell, Sloan & Pearce, 1945?

Not seen. The second, third, fourth, and fifth printings were probably not differentiated on copyright page.

A 8.1.f
*Sixth printing:* New York: Duell, Sloan & Pearce, [1945?].

On copyright page: 'SIXTH PRINTING'.

A 8.1.g
*Seventh printing:* Cleveland & New York: World, [1946].

On copyright page: 'FORUM BOOKS EDITION | *First Printing September 1946*'.

A 8.2
*Second edition:* New York: Editions for the Armed Services, [1945?].

#741. Locations: MJB, PSt.

A 8.3.a
*First English edition, first printing (1946)*

# PIPE NIGHT

*John O'Hara*

*Faber and Faber*
24 Russell Square
London

A 8.3.a: 4³/₄″ × 7³/₈″

*Copyright page:* 'First published in Mcmxlvi | by Faber and Faber Limited | 24 Russell Square London W.C.1 | Printed in Great Britain by | Western Printing Services Limited Bristol | All rights reserved'.

[1–6] 7–11 [12] 13–194 [195–196]

[A] B–I K–L⁸ M¹⁰

*Contents:* p. 1: half title; p. 2: *'by the same author'*; p. 3: title; p. 4: copyright; p. 5: dedication; p. 6: acknowledgments; pp. 7–8: contents; pp. 9–11: 'Preface' by Wolcott Gibbs; p. 12: blank; pp. 13–194: text; pp. 195–196: blank.

Contains 31 stories.

*Typography and paper:* 35 lines per page. Wove paper.

*Binding:* Pale blue (#185) V cloth (smooth). Spine goldstamped: '[thick and thin rules] | Pipe- | Night | [thin and thick rules] | *Short* | *Stories* | *by* | *John* | *O'Hara* | *Faber'.* White wove endpapers.

*Dust jacket:* Front and spine lettered on yellow background. Front: '[red rule] | [outlined in black] PIPE | NIGHT | [red rule] | [red] Short Stories | by [black] John O'Hara | [red rule] | [black] *FABER'.* Spine: '[vertically] [red rule] [black] PIPE NIGHT [red rule] [black] by John O'Hara [red rule] [black] F & F'. Back: 'NEW FICTION'. Front flap has blurb for *PN.* Back flap blank.

*Publication and printing:* 5,000 copies of the first printing. Published 2 August 1946. 7s. 6d.

*Locations:* BL (1 AUG 46), Bod (7 AUG 1946), MJB (dj).

A 8.3.b
*Second printing:* London: Faber & Faber, [1946].

On copyright page: *'Second impression November Mcmxlvi'.*

A 8.4
*Fourth edition: Stories of Venial Sin from Pipe Night.* New York: Avon, [1947?].

26 Stories. #661. 25¢. On copyright page: *'Third Avon Printing'.*

A 8.5
*Fifth edition: Stories of Venial Sin from Pipe Night.* New York: Avon, 1949?

Avon Modern Short Story Monthly #39. Not seen.

A 8.6
*Sixth edition: Stories of Venial Sin from "Pipe Night".* New York: Avon, [1952].

26 stories. Avon special. 35¢.

A 8.7.a
*Seventh edition, Mayflower printings:* London: Mayflower-Dell, 1963.

Not seen. Reprinted 1966.

A 8.7.b
*Seventh edition, NEL printing:* [London]: New English Library, [1969].

#2380. 5s.

A 8.8.a
*Eighth edition, Bantam printings:* New York: Bantam, [1966].

H3104. 60¢. 3 printings.

A 8.8.b
*Eighth edition, Popular printing:* New York: Popular Library, [1974].

#445-00202-125. $1.25.

A 9 HELLBOX

A 9.1.a
*First edition, first printing (1947)*

# HELLBOX

*John O'Hara*

*Random House · New York*

A 9.1.a: 4$^{15}$/$_{16}$″ × 7$^{5}$/$_{16}$″

[i–x] [1–3] 4–210 [211–214]; first page of each story unnumbered

[1–7]$^{16}$

*Contents:*  pp. i–ii: blank; p. iii: half title; p. iv: blank; p. v: title; p. vi: copyright; p. vii: '*To Wylie O'Hara* | FROM HER FATHER'; p. viii: blank; p. ix: contents; p. x: blank; p. 1: half title; p. 2: blank; pp. 3–210: text, headed '*Common Sense Should Tell You*'; pp. 211–214: blank.

*26 stories:* "Common Sense Should Tell You," "Pardner," "Someone to Trust," "Horizon," "Like Old Times," "Ellie," "Life Among These Unforgettable Characters," "War Aims," "Clara," "Secret Meeting," "Drawing Room B," "The Decision," "Somebody Can Help Somebody,"* "The Pretty Daughters," "Everything Satisfactory," "The Moccasins," "Doctor and Mrs. Parsons," "Wise Guy," "The Three Musketeers," "Other Women's Households," "Transaction,"* "Miss W.," "Time To Go,"* "A Phase of Life,"* "The Chink in the Armor,"* "Conversation in the Atomic Age." Asterisks follow previously unpublished stories.

*Typography and paper:*  Bodoni, 12 point on 14. 5$^9$/₁₆″ (5$^{13}$/₁₆″) × 3$^{13}$/₁₆″; 29 lines per page. Running heads: rectos, story titles; versos, '*Hellbox*'. White wove paper.

*Binding:*  Black with V cloth grain (smooth). Front: '[silver stamped within 2-sided blue frame] HELLBOX'. Spine: '[vertically, stamped in silver] *John O'Hara* [blue rule] [silver] *HELLBOX* [blue] *Random House*'. All edges trimmed. Top edge stained bluish gray. White wove calendered endpapers.

*Dust jacket:*  Front and spine lettered on reddish orange background. Front: '[white] Hellbox | [black] BY JOHN O'HARA | [Random House device] A RANDOM HOUSE BOOK'. Spine: '[vertically, black] HELLBOX BY JOHN O'HARA RANDOM HOUSE'. Back has comments on O'Hara by Thomas Sugrue, Lionel Trilling, and Kenneth Fearing; continued on back flap. Front flap has blurb for *Hellbox*.

*Publication:*  7,500 copies of the first printing. Published 9 August 1947. $2.50. Copyright #A15335.

*Printing:*  Set, printed, and bound by H. Wolff, New York.

*Locations:*  Lilly (dj), MJB (dj), PSt (dj).

*Review copy:*  Proof bound in blue wrappers, with white label on front: '*Uncorrected Proof from* | RANDOM HOUSE | [Random House device] | [tapered rule] | HELLBOX | John O'Hara | [tapered rule with "Aug 4, 1947" and "$2.50" written above in ink] | *for* ADVANCE *readers*'. Location: MJB.

$2.50

# HELLBOX

Nowhere does John O'Hara's hard, diamond-like brilliance show to better advantage than in his short stories. Of his most recent lot, twenty-six are included in this volume.

Writing in *The New York Times* of Mr. O'Hara's previous collection, *Pipe Night*, Lionel Trilling noted that: "John O'Hara occupies a unique position in our contemporary literature. He stands alone not by reason of his literary skill, although that is considerable, but by reason of the subject: he is the only American writer to whom America presents itself as a social scene in the way it once presented itself to Henry James, or France to Proust."

For many years John O'Hara's stories have been outstanding features of *The New Yorker*, in which magazine most of the present collection have appeared. His novels—*Appointment in Samarra, Butterfield 8,* and *Hope for Heaven*—and his famous play, *Pal Joey,* have done much to establish his reputation as one of today's top writing talents.

*Hellbox*—a printer's receptacle for broken type

A RANDOM HOUSE BOOK

---

# Hellbox

## BY JOHN O'HARA

A RANDOM HOUSE BOOK

---

## WHAT THE CRITICS HAVE SAID ABOUT

## JOHN O'HARA

THOMAS SUGRUE in the *Saturday Review of Literature:* "... Almost any *Celt* can tell a story which, whatever the plot, will contain characters of interest and persuasion. John O'Hara has developed this racial ability for observation and deduction into a high and subtle art, and he has chosen to apply it where it will do the most good—among the evolving social classes of America.

"O'Hara has no use for the easy touches—the very rich and the very poor. He like a middle ground, where the shadows are mixed and the chiaroscuro is a test for his powers. Primarily he is occurred with man against man, rather than man against the world; his characters move against each other rather than against circumstance or fate. They are little people, all of them, whatever their economic situation; they are cruelly formed entities, unskilled in the use of themselves. Now and then a sensitive soul drifts in, but only for contrast."

LIONEL TRILLING in the *New York Times:* "More than anyone now writing, O'Hara understands the complex, contradictory, asymmetrical society in which we live. He has the

*(continued on back flap)*

---

*(continued from back of jacket)*

most precise knowledge of the content of our subtlest snobberies, of our points of social honor and dishonor—minutiae of personal prestige. He knows, and persuades us to believe, that life's deepest intentions may be expressed by the angle at which a hat is worn, the pattern of a necktie, the size of a monogram, the pitch of a voice, the turn of a phrase of slang, a gesture of courtesy and the way it is received."

KENNETH FEARING in the *New York Herald Tribune:* "The author's technique should earn for these swift portraitures some other word than 'stories,' for each is only the beginning, the middle, or the end of a complete story, the rest of which is, nevertheless, clearly shadowed and in fact the essential part of the tale. Some of the fragments are heartbreakd anecdotes, while others are compressed myth.... The percentage of those that seem to read themselves through, almost of their own accord, is extraordinarily high."

HELLBOX
John O'Hara
Random House

A 9.1.b
*Second printing:* New York: Random House, [1947].

On copyright page: 'SECOND PRINTING'.

A 9.2
*Second edition:* New York: Avon, [1949].

Avon Modern Short Story Monthly #45. 35¢.

A 9.3
*Third edition:* New York: Avon, [1950].

#293. 25¢. Reprinted once.

A 9.4
*First English edition, first printing (1952)*

# John O'Hara

# HELLBOX

**FABER AND FABER**
24 Russell Square
London

A 9.4: 5$^1$/$_8$″ × 7$^7$/$_8$″

*Copyright page:* 'First published in mcmlii | by Faber and Faber Limited | 24 Russell Square London W.C. 1 | Printed in Great Britain by | Purnell and Sons Limited | Paulton (Somerset) and London | All rights reserved'.

[1–8] 9–199 [200]

[A] B–I K⁸ L¹² M⁸

*Contents:* 1–2: blank; p. 3: half title; p. 4: blank; p. 5: title; p. 6: copyright; p. 7: dedication; p. 8: 'ACKNOWLEDGEMENT'; pp. 9–10: contents; pp. 11–200: text.

Contains 26 stories.

*Typography and paper:* 33 lines per page. Wove paper.

*Binding:* Strong red (#12) V cloth (smooth). Spine goldstamped: '[beveled rule] | HELL | BOX | [beveled rule] | JOHN | O'HARA | FABER'. All edges trimmed. White wove calendered endpapers.

*Dust jacket:* Front and spine lettered on red background. Front: '[outlined in shaded blue lettering on white panel with black shadows] HELL | BOX | [white] JOHN | O'HARA | [black] Author of *Appointment in Samarra* | *Butterfield 8* and *A Rage to Live*'. Spine: '[outlined in shaded blue lettering on white panel with black shadows] HELL | BOX | [black] 26 | Short | Stories | by | JOHN | O'HARA | Faber | and | Faber'. Back: 'NEW FICTION'. Front flap has blurb for *Hellbox*. Back flap has blurbs for *Appointment in Samarra* and *Pipe Night*.

*Publication and printing:* 4,000 copies of the first printing. Published 1 September 1952. 12s. 6d.

*Locations:* BL (14 AUG 52), Bod (4 SEP 1952), MJB (dj), PSt (dj).

A 9.5
*Fifth edition:* New York: Bantam, [1961].

#A2230. 35¢. Reprinted January 1967.

A 9.6.a
*Sixth edition, Mayflower printings:* [London]: Mayflower-Dell, [1963].

Not seen. Reprinted 1966.

A 9.6.b
*Sixth edition, NEL printing:* [London]: New English Library, [1969].

#2379. 5s.

A 9.7
*Seventh edition:* New York: Popular Library, [1975].

#445-00233-125. $1.25.

A 10 A RAGE TO LIVE

A 10.1.a
*First edition, first printing (1949)*

> To Toast our wants and wishes, is her way;
> Nor asks of God, but of her Stars, to give
> The mighty blessing, "while we live, to live."
> Then all for Death, that Opiate of the soul!
> Lucretia's dagger, Rosamonda's bowl.
> Say, what can cause such impotence of mind?
> A Spark too fickle, or a Spouse too kind.
> Wise wretch! with Pleasures too refin'd to please;
> With too much Spirit to be e'er at ease;
> With too much Quickness ever to be taught;
> With too much thinking to have common Thought:
> You purchase Pain with all that Joy can give,
> And die of nothing but a Rage to live.
>               —Epistle to a Lady BY ALEXANDER POPE

# A RAGE TO LIVE

*John O'Hara*

RANDOM HOUSE · NEW YORK

A 10.1.a: title line in deep red orange (#36); 5$^7$/₁₆″ × 8$^1$/₄″

```
┌─────────────────────────────────────────────────────────────────┐
│                    FIRST  PRINTING                                │
│    ^^^^^^^^^^^^^^^^^^^^^^^^^^^^^^^^^^^^^^^^^^^^^^^^^^^^^^^^^^^^^^   │
│                 COPYRIGHT, 1949, BY JOHN O'HARA                    │
│                                                                   │
│            ALL RIGHTS RESERVED UNDER INTERNATIONAL                 │
│            AND PAN-AMERICAN COPYRIGHT CONVENTIONS                  │
│      PUBLISHED IN NEW YORK BY RANDOM HOUSE, INC., AND SIMULTANEOUSLY│
│       IN TORONTO, CANADA, BY RANDOM HOUSE OF CANADA, LIMITED.      │
│                                                                   │
│            MANUFACTURED IN THE UNITED STATES OF AMERICA            │
│             BY KINGSPORT PRESS, INC., KINGSPORT, TENNESSEE         │
└─────────────────────────────────────────────────────────────────┘
```

[i–viii] [1–2] 3–246 [247–248] 249–353 [354–356] 357–455 [456–458] 459–590 [591–592]

[1]¹² [2–19]¹⁶

*Contents:* p. i: half title; p. ii: 'Books by John O'Hara'; p. iii: title; p. iv: copyright; p. v: *'To Belle';* p. vi: blank; p. vii: *'NOTE';* p. viii: blank; p. 1: 'BOOK ONE'; p. 2: blank; pp. 3–590: text, headed '1'; pp. 591–592: blank.

*Typography and paper:* Electra, 10 point on 12. 6⁷/₈″ (7¹/₈″) × 4¹/₈″; 41 lines per page. No running heads. Wove paper.

*Binding:* Black V cloth (smooth), with dust-jacket illustration blindstamped on lower front and spine. Front: '[red facsimile of O'Hara's signature] | [gold] A RAGE TO LIVE'. Spine: '[red] JOHN | O'HARA | [gold] A | RAGE | TO | LIVE | [red] RANDOM | HOUSE'. All edges trimmed. Top edge stained red. White wove sized endpapers.

*Dust jacket:* Illustration of vehicles along country road by John O'Hara Cosgrave II across bottom of front, spine, and back. Front: '[black] A | RAGE | to LIVE | A NOVEL BY | JOHN O'HARA'. Spine: '[black] A | RAGE | TO | LIVE | JOHN | O'HARA | RANDOM | HOUSE'. Back: 10-line statement by Clifton Fadiman. Front and back flaps have blurb for *ARTL.*

*Publication:* Unknown number of copies of the first printing. Published 16 August 1949. $3.75. Copyright #A34607.

*Printing:* Set, printed, and bound by Kingsport Press, Kingsport, Tenn.

*Locations:* LC (JUL 22 1949), Lilly (dj), MJB (dj), PSt.

*Presentation binding:* Unknown number of copies of first printing goldstamped on front cover: *'PRESENTATION EDITION'.* Distributed to booksellers. Locations: MJB, PSt.

*Review copy:* Proofs, in unprinted paper blue covers, tied at top. Title page: 'TITLE, PUBLICATION DATE, AND PRICE TENTATIVE | PLEASE CHECK WITH RANDOM HOUSE | BEFORE PUBLISHING REVIEW | [short tapered rule] | *Uncorrected Proof from* | RANDOM HOUSE | [Random House device] | [tapered rule] | A RAGE TO LIVE | [tapered rule] | *for* ADVANCE *readers'.* Location: MJB.

*Note*

Abridged in *Omnibook,* XII (January 1950), 1–47.

A 10.1.b
*Second printing:* New York: Random House, [1949].

On copyright page: 'SECOND PRINTING'.

A
RAGE
TO
LIVE

A
RAGE
to LIVE

A NOVEL BY
JOHN O'HARA

JOHN
O'HARA

RANDOM
HOUSE

"I think it a remarkably able novel, readable from first word to last, written with extraordinary crispness and honesty. I know of no finer presentation in our recent fiction of the culture of the rich Americans of our medium-sized towns. Mr. O'Hara's eyes and ears have never worked with such merciless accuracy."
— Clifton Fadiman

(Continued from front flap)

violent extra-marital affairs, scandal, disaster and her own kind of triumphs to the fulfillment of a life-pattern determined by her nature and background.

Idealists and libertines, public-spirited and self-seeking citizens, officials and tradesmen and crusaders, men of violence and good-will, and women of fierce possessiveness and tenderness form the pageant of memorable characters who vitalize this novel. It is a full-canvas portrait of a city and its people, done with a zest for color and light and movement. Precise in detail, it is always suggestive of the entire organism of a city and the people who give it meaning and life.

Exactly fifteen years after the publication of his penetrating first novel, APPOINTMENT IN SAMARRA, John O'Hara maintains his enviable place in the first rank of American novelists with A RAGE TO LIVE.

RANDOM HOUSE, INC.
*Publishers of The American College Dictionary and The Modern Library*

His first novel in eleven years, A Rage to Live is by far the most ambitious work yet undertaken by John O'Hara. It is a large-scale social chronicle of America, localized in Central Pennsylvania, but it moves by forceful implication onto the larger stage of an entire society in the manifold processes of change.

A heterogeneous community comes alive in a typical American city. Its social stratification, its politics, its puritanism, its commerce, its prejudices and pretensions and passions are revealed with naked candor and insight. Fort Penn, Pennsylvania, is a city with a dynamic history, both public and personal.

The Caldwells are its leading family, and Grace Caldwell Tate is the dramatic symbol of their dominance. She is a woman with the courage of her instincts. Never counting costs, the most obey her own impulses in defiance of the mores of her group, and never know the meaning of shame. Her avidity for life carries her through an impetuous childhood, through marriage,

(Continued on back flap)

Jacket painting by Jean O'Hara Cosgrave

Dust jacket for A 10.1.a

A 10.1.c
*Third printing:* New York: Random House, [1949].

On copyright page: 'THIRD PRINTING'.

A 10.1.d
*Fourth printing:* New York: Random House, [1949].

On copyright page: 'FOURTH PRINTING'.

A 10.1.e
*Fifth printing:* New York: Random House, [1949].

On copyright page: 'FIFTH PRINTING'.

A 10.1.f
*Sixth printing:* New York: Random House, [1949].

On copyright page: 'SIXTH PRINTING'.

A 10.1.g
*Seventh printing:* New York: Random House, 1949.

Not seen.

A 10.1.h
*Eighth printing:* New York: Random House, [1949].

On copyright page: 'EIGHTH PRINTING'.

A 10.1.i
*Ninth printing:* New York: Grosset & Dunlap, [1950].

Stiff paper covers. 75¢.

A 10.1.j
*First edition, first English printing (1950)*

# JOHN O'HARA

# A
# RAGE TO LIVE

LONDON ·
THE CRESSET PRESS
1950

A 10.1.j: 5³/₈" × 8¹/₂"

*Copyright page:* 'First published 1950 | by Cresset Press Ltd., 11 *Fitzroy Square, London, W.* 1 | *and printed in Great Britain by* | L. *van Leer & Co. Ltd., London'.*

Same pagination as Random House first printing.

[1–18]¹⁶ [19]⁸ [20]⁴

*Contents:* p. i: half title; p. ii: *'By the same author';* p. iii: title; p. iv: dedication and printing information; p. v: epigraph; p. vi: blank; p. vii: *'NOTE';* p. viii: blank; p. 1: 'BOOK ONE'; p. 2: blank; pp. 3–590: text; pp. 591–592: blank.

*Typography and paper:* 41 lines per page. Wove paper.

*Binding:* Vivid red (#11) B cloth (linen) stamped in black. Front: 'A RAGE TO LIVE'. Spine: 'A RAGE | TO LIVE | JOHN O'HARA | CRESSET | PRESS'. All edges trimmed. White wove calendered endpapers.

*Dust jacket:* Front and spine lettered in white on black background. Front: 'JOHN O'HARA | A | Rage | to | Live | t'. Spine: 'A | Rage | to | Live | JOHN | O'HARA | CRESSET | PRESS'. Back: 'By | ELLIOT PAUL'. Front flap has blurb for *ARTL.* Back flap blank.

*Publication:* Unknown number of copies of the first printing. Published November 1950. 15s.

*Locations:* BL (6 NOV 50), Bod (22 NOV 1950), Lilly (dj), MJB (dj), PSt (dj).

A 10.1.k
*Second Cresset printing:* London: Cresset Press, 1951.

A 10.1.l
*Eleventh printing:* New York: Random House, 1964.

Not seen.

*Note*

*A Rage to Live* was also distributed by The Book Find Club in 1949–1950.

A 10.2
*Second edition:* New York: Bantam, [1951].

#F935. 50¢. 3 printings: October 1951, December 1951, February 1952.

A 10.3
*Third edition:* London: Cresset Press, 1953.

"Cheap edition." 7s. 6d.

A 10.4.a
*Fourth edition, Bantam printings:* New York: Bantam, [1957].

#F 1583. 50¢. 27 printings 1957–1969.

A 10.4.b
*Fourth edition, Popular printings:* New York: Popular Library, [1974].

#445-03025-150. $1.50. Reprinted.

A 10.5
*Fifth edition:* [London]: Panther, [1960].

#1051. 5s. Reprinted 1963, 1964, 1965 (twice), 1966, 1967, 1971, 1973.

A 11 THE FARMERS HOTEL

A 11.1.a
*First edition, first printing (1951)*

A NOVEL BY JOHN O'HARA

## The Farmers Hotel

RANDOM HOUSE  NEW YORK

A 11.1.a: 5³/₈″ × 8″

[i–vi] [1–2] 3–85 [86–88] 89–134 [135–136] 137–153 [154]

[1–5]¹⁶

*Contents:* p. i: half title; p. ii: 'Books by John O'Hara'; p. iii: title; p. iv: copyright; p. v: 'PHILIP BARRY | 1896–1949 | REQUIESCAT IN PACE'; p. vi: blank; p. 1: *'Part One';* p. 2: blank; pp. 3–153: text; p. 154: blank.

*Typography and paper:* Baskerville, 11 point on 14. 5⁷/₁₆″ (6″) × 3⁵/₈″; 25 lines per page. Running heads: rectos and versos, 'The Farmers Hotel'. Wove paper.

*Binding:* Medium blue (#182) V cloth (smooth). Front blackstamped with facsimile of O'Hara's signature. Spine goldstamped on black panel: 'JOHN | O'HARA | The | Farmers | Hotel | RANDOM | HOUSE | [Random House device below panel]'. All edges trimmed. Top edge stained grayish blue.

*Dust jacket:* Night scene of hotel by J. O'H. Cosgrave II across front and spine: Front: [yellow] 'THE | Farmers | Hotel | A NOVEL BY *John O'Hara'.* Spine lettered in yellow: 'THE | Farmers | Hotel | *John* | *O'Hara* | [white] RANDOM | HOUSE'. Back: blurbs for *A Rage to Live.* Front flap: blurb for *FH.* Back flap: books by O'Hara.

*Publication:* 20,375 copies of the first printing. Published 8 November 1951. $2. Copyright #A60721.

*Printing:* Manufactured by H. Wolff, New York.

*Locations:* LC (NOV-5 1951), Lilly (dj), MJB (dj), PSt, (dj).

*Note:* Published in play form in *Five Plays* (1961). See A 19.

A 11.1.b
*Second printing:* New York: Random House, [1951].

On copyright page: 'SECOND PRINTING'.

A 11.2
*Second edition:* New York: Bantam, [1952].

#1046. 25¢. Reprinted 1953.

$2.50

The new novel by the author of *A Rage to Live* is a surprising departure in style and mood and purpose. John O'Hara now turns to a parable of our times, told with disarming simplicity but with overtones that give it accumulating dramatic tension. *The Farmers Hotel* is a story that projects itself far beyond the simple frame in which it is concentrated and contains implications as wide as the reader's own imagination. The locale is the Pennsylvania country made familiar by *A Rage to Live* and *Appointment in Samarra* and the time our own.

A RANDOM HOUSE BOOK

---

Books by
JOHN O'HARA

APPOINTMENT IN SAMARRA

* * *

BUTTERFIELD 8

* * *

THE DOCTOR'S SON
AND OTHER STORIES

* * *

HOPE OF HEAVEN

* * *

FILES ON PARADE

* * *

PAL JOEY

* * *

PIPE NIGHT

* * *

HELLBOX

* * *

A RAGE TO LIVE

* * *

THE FARMERS HOTEL

---

Acclaim for John O'Hara's
*A Rage to Live*

"A remarkably able novel, readable from first word to last. I know of no finer presentation in our recent fiction of the culture of the rich Americans of our medium-sized towns. Mr. O'Hara's eyes and ears have never worked with such merciless accuracy."
—CLIFTON FADIMAN

"A major event of this new season. This is a true novel, capacious and real."
—*New York Herald Tribune*

"A big, comprehensive, startlingly memorable piece of work. It would be hard to find any work done more soundly and impressively and honestly."
—*Chicago Sunday Tribune*

"The best O'Hara has ever done. For sheer readability, it just reminds us again that nobody writing today is O'Hara's peer."
—*Philadelphia Inquirer*

"A distinguished, brilliant novel, powerful, solid, thoughtful, enormously readable."
—*New York Post*

A 11.3.a
*First English edition, clothbound printing (1953)*

# John O'Hara

# THE
# FARMERS HOTEL

LONDON
THE CRESSET PRESS
MCMLIII

A 11.3.a: 4⁷/₈″ × 7³/₁₆″

*Copyright page:* 'First published in 1953 by | The Cresset Press Ltd., 11 Fitzroy Square, London, W. 1 | Made and printed in Great Britain by C. Tinling & Co. Ltd. | Liverpool, London and Prescot'.

[1–8] 9–92 [93–94] 95–140 [141–142] 143–158 [159–160]

[A] B–I K⁸

*Contents:*  p. 1: half title; p. 2: *'By the same Author';* p. 3: title; p. 4: copyright; p. 5: 'TO PHILIP BARRY | 1896–1949 | REQUIESCAT IN PACE'; p. 6: blank; p. 7: *'Part One';* p. 8: blank; pp. 9–159: text; p. 160: blank.

*Typography and paper:*  26 lines per page. Laid paper with vertical chains.

*Binding:*  Vivid red (#11) paper-covered boards with B grain (linen). Spine gold-stamped: 'THE | FARMERS | HOTEL | JOHN | O'HARA | CRESSET | PRESS'. All edges trimmed. White wove endpapers.

*Dust jacket:*  Front and spine have winter scene in white, black, yellow, and gray. Front: '[white, outlined in yellow] THE | FARMERS | HOTEL | [black] JOHN O'HARA | Author of "A Rage to Live" '. Spine: '[yellow] THE | FARMERS | HOTEL | BY | JOHN | O'HARA | [black] CRESSET | PRESS'. Back lists books by O'Hara. Front flap has blurb for *FH*. Back flaps blank.

*Publication:*  Unknown number of copies of the first printing. Published 19 October 1953. 8s. 6d.

*Locations:*  BL (5 OCT 53), Bod (23 OCT 1953), MJB (dj).

*Note:*  Published simultaneously with Guild Original printing. See next entry.

A 11.3.b
*First English edition, paperbound printing (1953)*

John O'Hara

# THE
# FARMERS HOTEL

*Published for*
The British Publishers Guild Limited
*by The Cresset Press Ltd.,*
*11 Fitzroy Square, London, W.1*

A 11.3.b: 4⁷/₁₆″ × 6⁷/₈″

*Copyright page:* 'FIRST PUBLISHED IN 1953 | *Made and printed in Great Britain by C. Tinling & Co. Ltd.* | *Liverpool, London and Prescot'.*

Same pagination as clothbound printing.

[A] B–E¹⁶

*Contents:* p. 1: blurb; p. 2: 'by the same author—'; p. 3: title; p. 4: copyright; p. 5: dedication; p. 6: blank; p. 7: *'Part One';* p. 8: blank; pp. 9–159: text; p. 160: blank.

*Typography and paper:* 26 lines per page. Wove paper.

*Binding:* Paper covers. Front lettered against panels of blue and dull gold: '[white] *A Guild Original* | [blue] The | FARMERS | HOTEL | [black] JOHN O'HARA | a dramatic new novel by | a masterly story-teller | [white swash] A [black outlined in white] NEW [white swash] Book | [black] *LIMITED IN THIS EDITION* | *TO A SALE OF 15000 COPIES* | [in lower right corner against gold circle; black] 2/- | NET'. Spine lettered on gold: '[vertically] [black] JOHN O'HARA [blue] THE FARMERS HOTEL *Guild'.* Back has 3-paragraph statement about Guild program: 'A Guild Original is a brand-new book which is published *at the same time* as the publisher's normal edition, but at the price of a reprint. The sale of the Guild Edition is to be definitely limited to 15,000 copies within the first two years of original publication.'

*Publication:* Published simultaneously with Cresset printing. See "Binding." 2s.

*Locations:* MJB, PSt.

A 11.3.c
*Third Printing:* London: Barrie & Rockliff The Cresset Press, [1969].

A 11.4
*Fourth edition:* New York: Bantam, [1957].

#1594. 25¢. 16 printings: April 1957 (twice), July 1957, July 1960, August 1960, September 1960, March 1961, July 1961, February 1962, September 1962, July 1963, October 1963, June 1964, January 1966, August 1966, June 1969.

A 11.5
*Fifth edition:* [London]: Panther, [1961].

#1186. 2s. 6d. 5 printings: 1961, 1963, 1964, 1967 (twice).

A 11.6
*Sixth edition:* New York: Popular Library, [1973].

#445—00161—125. $1.25.

A 12 PAL JOEY LIBRETTO

A 12.1.a
*First edition, first printing (1952)*

# THE LIBRETTO AND LYRICS

# PAL JOEY

☆

## By JOHN O'HARA

☆

## Lyrics by LORENZ HART

☆

## Music by RICHARD RODGERS

☆

## RANDOM HOUSE · NEW YORK

A 12.1.a: 5⁵/₁₆″ × 7¹⁵/₁₆″

[i–viii] [1–2] 3–17 [18] 19–37 [38] 39–53 [54] 55–69 [70–72] 73–135 [136]

[1–4]¹⁶ [5]⁸; frontispiece and 2 leaves of photos inserted between pp. 72 and 73.

*Contents:* p. i: half title; p. ii: blank; p. iii: title; p. iv: copyright; p. v: 'HISTORICAL NOTE' signed *'J.O'H.'*; pp. vi–vii: 'THE CAST'; p. viii: 'SCENES'; p. 1: 'ACT ONE'; p. 2: blank; pp. 3–135: text; p. 136: blank.

*Typography and paper:* Garamond, 11 point on 13. 5⁷/₁₆″ (6¹/₁₆″) × 3⁵/₈″. Running heads: rectos and versos, 'PAL JOEY'. Wove paper.

*Binding:* Yellowish gray (#93) V cloth (smooth). Front: photo of Joey and Vera within reddish brown quintuple-rules frame surmounted by goldstamped Random House device on square reddish brown panel. Spine, vertically: '[reddish brown] O'HARA [star] HART [star] RODGERS [goldstamped on reddish brown rectangular panel within single-rule gold frame] THE LIBRETTO AND LYRICS | PAL JOEY [outside panel in reddish brown] RANDOM HOUSE'. All edges trimmed. Top edge stained reddish brown. White wove endpapers.

*Dust jacket:* Beige. Front: '[gray single-rule frame] [reddish brown single-rule frame] [the following in beige on gray panel] THE LIBRETTO & LYRICS | PAL | JOEY | BY John O'Hara | LYRICS BY Lorenz Hart | MUSIC BY Richard Rogers | A RANDOM HOUSE PLAY [reddish-brown Random House device on lower right corner of panel]'. Spine: '[gray rule] | [reddish brown rule] | [gray] Pal | Joey | ★ | O'Hara | ★ | Hart | ★

Dust jacket for A12.1.a

**Front cover:**

THE LIBRETTO & LYRICS

PAL JOEY

BY John O'Hara

LYRICS BY Lorenz Hart

MUSIC BY Richard Rodgers

A RANDOM HOUSE PLAY

**Spine:**

Pal
Joey
*
O'Hara
*
Hart
*
Rodgers

RANDOM HOUSE

**Front flap:**

$2.50

THE LIBRETTO AND LYRICS

PAL JOEY

BY JOHN O'HARA

LYRICS BY LORENZ HART

MUSIC BY RICHARD RODGERS

"A masterpiece!"
ROBERT COLEMAN, New York Daily Mirror

"The best and most exciting new musical play of the season. A genuine treat, brilliant, fresh, delightful, great fun. John O'Hara's book is biting, rich, and filled with its author's celebrated gift for recognizable talk and character. Very definitely an authentic work of art."
RICHARD WATTS, JR., New York Post

"A great hit, lost and funny."
MC CLAIN, New York Journal-American

"One of the shrewdest, toughest, and most literate books ever written for musical comedy."
KERR, New York Herald Tribune

"Pal Joey may turn out to be as much of a Broadway classic as Show Boat."
Life Magazine

"An exuberant new hit."
Newsweek Magazine

**Back flap:**

RANDOM HOUSE

BOOKS ON THE DRAMA

In the past, Random House has published the texts of more outstanding play successes than all other trade publishers in America combined. The following is only a partial list of the celebrated dramatists whose plays are published in the United States under the Random House imprint: Eugene O'Neill, Lindsay and Crouse, Kaufman and Hart, S. N. Behrman, Sidney Kingsley, John van Druten, Joshua Logan, F. Hugh Herbert and Rodgers and Hammerstein.

One of the most important publications on the Random House drama list is a superb edition of The Complete Greek Drama. It is issued in two stately volumes, with a complete glossary.

THE COMPLETE GREEK DRAMA
2 vols., boxed $8.50

A companion set to the Greek Drama is The Complete Roman Drama, containing the thirty-six plays of Plautus, Terence, and Seneca.
THE COMPLETE ROMAN DRAMA
2 vols., boxed $10.00

A popular Random House publication is The Theatre Guild Anthology, containing fourteen Guild successes, including Strange Interlude and Saint Joan.
THE THEATRE GUILD ANTHOLOGY
$4.75

Recent Random House Play Hits

THE KING AND I
by Rodgers and Hammerstein

I AM A CAMERA
by John van Druten

POINT OF NO RETURN
by Paul Osborn

THE MOON IS BLUE
by F. Hugh Herbert

DARKNESS AT NOON
by Sidney Kingsley

SOUTH PACIFIC
by Rodgers and Hammerstein

BAREFOOT IN ATHENS
by Lindsay and Crouse

A new and beautiful three-volume edition of The Plays of Eugene O'Neill presents the work of America's foremost dramatist in the form in which it is intended.
THE PLAYS OF EUGENE O'NEILL
3 vols., boxed $15.00

THE PLAYS AND POEMS OF W. S. GILBERT
$3.50

THE COMPLETE WORKS OF J. M. SYNGE
$3.95

Play lists of the new season will be published by Random House at frequent intervals. Your bookseller or the publisher will be glad to keep you posted.

RANDOM HOUSE · NEW YORK

**Back cover:**

RECENT

RANDOM HOUSE PLAY

SUCCESSES

*

The Shrike
(The Pulitzer Prize Play for 1951)
BY JOSEPH KRAMM
$2.50

I Am a Camera
BY JOHN VAN DRUTEN
$2.50

Point of No Return
BY PAUL OSBORN
$2.50

Jane
BY S. N. BEHRMAN
$2.50

The Grass Harp
BY TRUMAN CAPOTE
$2.50

| Rogers | [reddish brown Random House device] | [gray] RANDOM | HOUSE | [reddish brown rule] | [gray rule]'. Back: *'RANDOM HOUSE | BOOKS ON THE DRAMA'*. Front flap has blurbs for the play. Back flap: 'RECENT | RANDOM HOUSE PLAY | SUCCESSES'.

*Publication:*   2,500 copies of the first printing. Published 16 August 1952. $2.50. Copyright #DP1160.

*Locations:*   LC (SEP 18 1952), PSt (dj), Lilly (dj), MJB (dj).

*Note 1:*   Based on the character in the "Pal Joey" stories. The show opened at the Ethel Barrymore Theatre in New York on 25 December 1940 and ran for 374 performances. It was revived on Broadway in 1952 and ran for 540 performances.

*Note 2:*   Mimeographed play script at Lilly Library.

A 12.1.b
*Second printing:* New York: Random House, [1952].

Dust jacket: 'FIRESIDE THEATRE BOOK CLUB EDITION'.

A 12.2
*Second edition:* New York: Popular Library, [1976].

#445-03151-150. $1.50. Contains the stories, libretto, and lyrics. See A 7.9.

A 13 SWEET AND SOUR

A 13.1.a
*First edition, first printing (1954)*

A 13.1.a: 5³/₈" × 8"

[i–x] [1–3] 4–8 [9] 10–14 [15] 16–20 [21] 22–26 [27] 28–32 [33] 34–38 [39] 40–44
[45] 46–50 [51] 52–56 [57] 58–62 [63] 64–68 [69] 70–74 [75] 76–80 [81] 82–86 [87]
88–92 [93] 94–97 [98] 99–103 [104] 105–109 [110] 111–115 [116] 117–121 [122]
123–127 [128] 129–133 [134] 135–139 [140] 141–145 [146] 147–150 [151] 152–156
[157] 158–162 [163–166]

[1–11]⁸

*Contents:*   p. i: half title; p. ii: blank; p. iii: 'BOOKS BY JOHN O'HARA'; pp. iv–v: title;
p. vi: copyright; p. vii: *'to Winifred Wylie Gardiner';* p. viii: blank; pp. ix–x: *'Foreword';*
p. 1: half title; p. 2: blank; pp. 3–162: text, headed *'1.';* p. 163: 'ABOUT THE AUTHOR';
pp. 164–166: blank.

Columns from the Trenton *Times-Advertiser.* See E 3.

*Typography and paper:*   Caledonia, 11 point on 14. 6″ (6¹/₄″) × 3¹/₂″; 29 lines per
page. Running heads: rectos only, 'SWEET *and* SOUR'. Wove paper.

*Binding:*   Boards covered with reddish brown and black marbled paper; brown V
cloth (smooth) spine. Spine: '[pink] SWEET | [orange] and | [yellow] SOUR | [light
blue] JOHN O'HARA | RANDOM | HOUSE | [blindstamped Random House device]'.
All edges trimmed. Top edge stained gray. Pale yellow (#89) laid endpapers of
heavier stock than text paper.

*Dust jacket:*   Front and spine lettered on brown and yellow background. Front:
'[black] John O'Hara | [yellow type decoration] | [white] SWEET | AND | SOUR |
[yellow type decoration] | [black] Comments | on Books and People'. Spine: '[hori-
zontally, black] John | O'Hara | [vertically, white] SWEET AND SOUR | [horizontally,
black] [Random House device] | Random | House'. Back has photo of O'Hara. Front
flap has blurb for *S&S.* Back flap: 'About the author'.

*Publication:*   7,500 copies of the first printing. Published 23 October 1954. $3. Copy-
right #A155650.

*Printing:*   Manufactured by H. Wolff, New York.

*Locations:*   LC (OCT 11 1954), Lilly (dj), MJB (dj), PSt (dj).

SWEET
AND
SOUR

John O'Hara

SWEET
AND
SOUR

Comments on Books and People

Random House

SWEET AND SOUR

John O'Hara

---

SWEET
AND
SOUR
by JOHN O'HARA

In the only pages of this book, Mr. O'Hara offers his opinions on everything from Ernest Hemingway to publishers' blurbs, from George Washington to plagiarism.

This is a publisher's blurb, but no one had the temerity to ask Mr. O'Hara's opinion of it before setting the type. On the back of this wrapper is a photograph of Mr. O'Hara—and this was a risk, too, for to these pages he has his say about authors' photographs—as well as about book critics, how to handle publisher, and other equally controversial literary matters.

Then, too, you will find comments here about The Bobbsey Twins at the Ice Carnival, duplication of books at Christmas time, the Stork Bearcat, Joe H. Palmer, country stores, St. Patrick's Day, honors for writers, Frank Sullivan's Christmas poems, neglected classics, novels about Time magazine, Aldous Huxley, the by-products of writing, and Wolcott Gibbs.

End of publisher's blurb. We hope the author—and his readers—will approve.

---

About the author

JOHN O'HARA's first novel was Appointment in Samarra, published in 1934 and now available in The Modern Library. Ever since its appearance he has been a major figure on the American literary scene and has been on intimate terms with publishers, authors and critics.

Son of a doctor and the eldest of eight children, Mr. O'Hara was born in Pottsville, Pennsylvania, in 1905. After graduating from Niagara Prep School, he worked as a ship steward, railway freight clerk, soda clerk and press agent. For a time he was secretary to the late Heywood Broun.

O'Hara's career as a reporter was equally varied. He worked first for two Pennsylvania papers and then, for three in New York, where he covered everything from sports to religion. He also was on the staff of Newsweek and Time.

His two recent novels were A Rage to Live (1949) and The Farmers Hotel (1951). He was also the author of the smash-hit musical comedy, Pal Joey, for which Lorenz Hart wrote the lyrics and Richard Rodgers the musical score.

Heretofore, "Appointment with O'Hara," is a regular feature in Collier's magazine, and each Sunday he writes another column ("Sweet and Sour") for the Trenton Times-Advertiser. Mr. O'Hara lives in Princeton, New Jersey.

RANDOM HOUSE, INC.
457 Madison Avenue, New York 22, New York
Publishers of The American College Dictionary and The Modern Library

John O'Hara

Dust jacket for A.13.1.a

A 13.1.b
*First edition, first English printing (1955)*

**John O'Hara**

# SWEET AND SOUR

**LONDON**
**THE CRESSET PRESS**
**MCMLV**

A 13.1.b: 5$^{1}/_{16}$″ × 7$^{11}/_{16}$″

*Copyright page:* 'First published in 1955 by The Cresset Press Ltd., | 11 *Fitzroy Square, London, W. 1* | *and printed in Great Britain by* | *Lowe & Brydone (Printers) Ltd., London, N.W. 10.'*

[i–viii] [1–3] 4–162 [163–168]; first page of each chapter unnumbered.

[A] B–I K–L⁸ (-L₆)

*Contents:* p. i: half title; p. ii: *'By the same Author';* p. iii: title; p. iv: copyright; p. v: *'to Winifred Wylie Gardiner';* p. vi: blank; pp. vii–viii: *'Foreword';* p. 1: half title; p. 2: blank; pp. 3–162: text, headed *'1.';* pp. 163–164: canceled; pp. 165–168: blank.

*Typography and paper:* 29 lines per page. Wove paper.

*Binding:* Dark blue (#183) paper-covered boards with B grain (linen). Spine gold-stamped: 'SWEET | AND | SOUR | JOHN | O'HARA | CRESSET'. All edges trimmed. Off-white wove calendered endpapers.

*Dust jacket:* Front lettered on light blue background with quills and ink bottles: '[black] SWEET | AND | SOUR | [white] JOHN [black] O'HARA | [white] Author of [black] A Rage to Live'. Spine: '[horizontally, black] John | O'Hara | [vertically, white] SWEET and SOUR | [horizontally, black] CRESSET | PRESS'. Back has blurbs for *A Rage to Live, Butterfield 8,* and *Pal Joey.* Front flap has blurb for *S&S.* Back flap blank.

*Publication:* Unknown number of copies of the first English printing. Published 23 January 1955. 12s. 6d.

*Locations:* BL (11 JAN 56), Bod (21 JAN 1956), MJB (dj), PSt (dj).

A 13.2
*Second edition:* [London]: Panther, [1968].

#2395X. 5s.

A 13.3
*Third edition:* New York: Popular Library, [1974].

#445-00215-125. $1.25.

A 14 TEN NORTH FREDERICK

A 14.1.a
*First edition, first printing (1955)*

A 14.1.a: nameplate is strong yellow (#84); 5¹/₂″ × 8¹/₈″

[i–vi] [1–2] 3–389 [390–392] 393–408 [409–410]

[1–13]¹⁶

*Contents:*   p. i: half title; p. ii: 'BOOKS BY JOHN O'HARA'; p. iii: title; p. iv: copyright; p. v: '*To K. B. O'H.*'; p. vi: 'FOREWORD'; p. 1: 'PART ONE'; p. 2: blank; pp. 3–408: text; p. 409: blank; p. 410: 'ABOUT THE AUTHOR'.

*Typography and paper:*   Electra, 11 point on 12. 6⁵/₈″ (6¹⁵/₁₆″) × 4³/₁₆″; 40 lines per page. No running heads. Wove paper.

*Binding:*   Medium blue (#182) V cloth (smooth). Spine: '[blue against gold panel] TEN NORTH | FREDERICK | [goldstamped on gray panel] [script] John | O'Hara | [Random House device] | [roman] RANDOM | HOUSE'. All edges trimmed. Top edge stained light yellow. Dark gray (#266) grained endpapers.

*Dust jacket:*   Front and spine lettered against gray and white illustration of doorway. Front: '[red] Ten North | Frederick | [purple] *John O'Hara*'. Spine: '[red] John | O'Hara | Ten | North | Frederick | [purple] [Random House device] | RANDOM | HOUSE'. Back has photo of O'Hara. Front flap has blurb for *TNF.* Back flap: '*About the Author.*'

*Publication:*   Unknown number of copies of the first printing. Published 24 November 1955. $3.95. Copyright #A209968.

*Printing:*   Manufactured by H. Wolff, New York.

*Locations:*   LC (NOV 21 1955), Lilly (dj), MJB (dj), PSt (dj).

*Review copy:*   Sewn unbound sheets in dust jacket. Locations: MJB, PSt.


A 14.1.b
*Second printing:* New York: Random House, [1955].

On copyright page: 'SECOND PRINTING'. November.


A 14.1.c
*Third printing:* New York: Random House, [1955].

On copyright page: 'THIRD PRINTING'. December.


A 14.1.d
*Fourth printing:* New York: Random House, [1956].

January. Not seen.

Dust jacket for A14.1.a

A 14.1.e
*Fifth printing:* New York: Random House, [1956].

March. Not seen.

A 14.1.f
*Sixth printing:* New York: Random House, 1956.

April. Not seen.

A 14.1.g
*Seventh printing:* New York: Random House, 1956?

Not seen.

A 14.1.h
*Eighth printing:* New York: Random House, 1956?

Not seen.

A 14.1.i
*Ninth printing:* New York: Random House, 1956?

Not seen.

A 14.1.j
*Tenth printing:* New York: Random House, [1956?].

On copyright page: *'Tenth Printing'*.

A 14.1.k
*Unidentified printing:* Sears Readers Club & Sears Selective Readers Service, 1956.

Not seen.

A 14.1.l
*Unidentified printing:* Grosset & Dunlap, [1957].

On copyright page: *'Sixth Printing'*.

A 14.1.m
*Unidentified printing:* New York: Random House, [    ].

On dust-jacket flap: 'BOOK CLUB EDITION'.

*Note*

Also published in *Books Abridged* (April 1956). Not seen.

A 14.2.a
*First English edition, first printing (1956)*

JOHN O'HARA

# Ten
# North Frederick

LONDON

THE CRESSET PRESS

1956

A 14.2.a: $5^3/8'' \times 8^1/2''$

*Copyright page:*   'First published in Great Britain in 1956 | by The Cresset Press Ltd., 11 Fitzroy Square, London, W.1 | and printed in Great Britain | by the Shenval Press, London, Hertford and Harlow'.

[i–vi] 1–400 [401–402]

[A] B–H [I] K$^{16}$ L$^{12}$ M–N$^{16}$

*Contents:*   p. i: half title; p. ii: *'By the same Author:';* p. iii: title; p. iv: copyright and dedication; p. v: 'FOREWORD'; p. vi: blank; pp. 1–401: text; p. 402: blank.

*Typography and paper:*   40 lines per page. Wove paper.

*Binding:*   Vivid red (#11) paper-covered boards, stamped in B grain (linen). Spine goldstamped: 'TEN | NORTH | FREDERICK | JOHN | O'HARA | CRESSET | PRESS'. All edges trimmed. White wove calendered endpapers.

*Dust jacket:*   Front and spine lettered in white on black. Front: 'JOHN O'HARA | [script] Ten | North | Frederick'. Spine: '[script] Ten | North | Frederick | [roman] JOHN | O'HARA | CRESSET | PRESS'. Back: *'BY THE SAME AUTHOR'.* Front flap has blurb for *TNF.* Back flap blank.

*Publication:*   Unknown number of copies of the first printing. Published 28 June 1956. 16s.

*Locations:*   BL (6 JUN 56), Bod (28 JUN 1956), Lilly (dj), MJB (dj), PSt (dj).

A 14.2.b
*Second printing:* London: Cresset, 1956.

Not seen.

A 14.2.c
*Third printing:* London: Barrie & Rockliff The Cresset Press, [1969].

A 14.3.a
*Third edition, Bantam printings:* New York: Bantam, [1957].

#F 1554. 50¢. January 1957. 35 Bantam printings, 1957–1970.

A 14.3.b
*Third edition, Popular printings:* New York: Popular Library, [1975].

#445-08364-195. $1.95. Reprinted.

A 14.4
*Fourth edition:* [London]: Panther, [1959].

#959. 5s. October 1959. 12 printings, 1959–1967.

A 15 A FAMILY PARTY

A 15.1.a
*First edition, first printing (1956)*

---

*John O'Hara*

# A Family Party

*RANDOM HOUSE · NEW YORK*

---

A 15.1.a: 5³/₈″ × 8″

First Printing

© Copyright, 1956, by John O'Hara

All rights reserved under International and Pan-American Copyright Conventions. Published in New York by Random House, Inc. and simultaneously in Toronto, Canada, by Random House of Canada, Limited.

Library of Congress Catalog Card Number: 56-10932

[i–x] [1–2] 3–64 [65–70]

[1]¹⁶ [2]⁸ [3]¹⁶

*Contents:* pp. i–ii: pastedown endpaper; pp. iii–iv: free endpaper; p. v: half title; p. vi: 'Books by John O'Hara'; p. vii: title; p. viii: copyright; p. ix: *'To Verna Delaney'*; p. x: blank; p. 1: half title; p. 2: blank; pp. 3–64: text, headed 'Stenographic Report'; p. 65: 'ABOUT THE AUTHOR'; p. 66: blank; pp. 67–68: free endpaper; pp. 69–70: pastedown endpaper.

*Typography and paper:* Scotch, 12 point on 15. 5³/₁₆″ (5³/₄″) × 3⁵/₁₆″; 20 or 21 lines per page. Running heads: rectos and versos; 'A Family Party'. Wove paper.

*Binding:* Gray green (#150) paper-covered boards, with black and light gray pattern. Light gray (#264) V cloth (smooth) shelfback, stamped vertically: '[reddish brown] JOHN O'HARA [black] A FAMILY PARTY | [reddish brown Random House device] [reddish brown] RANDOM | HOUSE'. All edges trimmed. Top edge stained dark gray. White wove sized endpapers around sheets.

*Dust jacket:* Front lettered on off-white: '[black] A | FAMILY | PARTY | [reddish brown] JOHN | O'HARA'. Spine: '[vertically] [black] *A Family Party:* [reddish brown] *John O'Hara* [horizontal black Random House device] [vertical] [black] *Random House'*. Back has excerpts from 3 reviews of *Ten North Frederick.* Front flap has blurb for *FP.* Back flap: 'ABOUT THE | AUTHOR'.

*Publication:* 8,000 copies of the first printing. Published 16 August 1956. $1.95.

*Locations:* Lilly (dj), MJB (dj), PSt (dj).

*Note:* "A Family Party" was originally published in *Collier's* (2 March 1956). See C 234.

$3.95

A FAMILY
PARTY

BY JOHN O'HARA

A delightful and heart-warming novelette about small-town America — by the author of *Ten North Frederick* and *Appointment in Samarra*.

The story develops from a family party — a testimonial dinner — in honor of Dr. Sam Merritt's first forty years of service to his community, Lyons, Pennsylvania.

This short novel is Mr. O'Hara's first book since he won the 1955 National Book Award for fiction.

RANDOM HOUSE, INC.

*Publishers of* THE MODERN LIBRARY &
THE AMERICAN COLLEGE DICTIONARY
*457 Madison Avenue · New York 22, N.Y.*

*A Family Party: John O'Hara*   Random House

A
FAMILY
PARTY

JOHN
O'HARA

The Critics Praise
JOHN O'HARA
*and*
TEN NORTH FREDERICK

ST. CLAIR MCKELWAY, *The New Yorker* "What happens to most people when they start reading a book by John O'Hara is going to happen to them once again on the first page of Part One of his long, strong new novel . . . I think this is the feeling that you are in the hands of a born novelist. Since he published *Appointment in Samarra*, twenty years ago, O'Hara's fiction has, I think, never failed to give that impression . . . O'Hara decided he was ready to write about a subject larger and fuller than he had undertaken in the past, and sat down and did so."

JAMES KELLY, *Saturday Review* "Mr. O'Hara sees, hears, and writes as truly as ever within the pre-selected viewpoint of a social historian. He gives us visual journalism rather than mental or emotional flight. His characters spring to life, however briefly he touches them, and in the supporting cast of this story there are staggering numbers . . ."

ROBERT GORHAM DAVIS, *New York Times* "There are two kinds of impelling truth, nevertheless, in John O'Hara's fiction: truth about the nature of much social behavior, and truth about the nature of much of our concern with other people's lives."

ABOUT THE
AUTHOR

JOHN O'HARA's first novel was *Appointment in Samarra*, published in 1934 and now available in The Modern Library. Ever since its appearance he has been a major figure on the American literary scene.

His three recent novels were *A Rage to Live* (1949), *The Farmers Hotel* (1951) and *Ten North Frederick* — which won for its author the 1955 National Book Award for fiction. He was the author of the smash-hit musical comedy, *Pal Joey*, for which Lorenz Hart wrote the lyrics and Richard Rodgers the musical score.

His column, "Appointment with O'Hara," is now a regular feature in *Collier's* magazine. In 1954 Random House published *Sweet and Sour*, a series of weekly columns he wrote for the *Trenton Times-Advertiser*. Mr. O'Hara lives in Princeton, New Jersey.

Printed in U.S.A.

Dust jacket for A 15.1.a

A 15.1.b
*Second printing:* New York: Random House, [1956].

Not seen.

A 15.1.c
*Third printing:* New York: Random House, [1956].

On copyright page: 'Third Printing,'.

A 15.1.d
*Fourth printing:* New York: Random House, [1956].

On copyright page: 'Fourth Printing'.

A 15.1.e
*First edition, first English printing (1957)*

### John O'Hara

# A FAMILY
# PARTY

LONDON : THE CRESSET PRESS : MCMLVII

A 15.1.e: 4³/₄″ × 7¹/₄″

*Copyright page:* 'First published in Great Britain in 1957 by | The Cresset Press, 11 Fitzroy Square, London, W. 1 | and printed in Great Britain by | Lowe & Brydone (Printers) Ltd., London, N.W. 10'.

[i–iv] [1–2] 3–63 [64]

[A] B–C⁸ D¹⁰

*Contents:* p. i: half title; p. ii: '*By the same author:*'; p. iii: title; p. iv: copyright; p. 1: dedication; p. 2: blank; pp. 3–64: text, headed 'Stenographic Report'.

*Typography and paper:* 20 or 21 lines per page. Wove paper.

*Binding:* Light greenish gray (#154) paper-covered boards, with B grain (linen). Spine goldstamped vertically: 'A FAMILY PARTY ★ John O'Hara ★ Cresset'. All edges trimmed. Off-white wove endpapers, sized.

*Dust jacket:* Front lettered on blue background: '[white on 2 black pennants] A Family | Party | [black on 2 white pennants] John | O'Hara'. Spine: '[vertically, white] A FAMILY PARTY JOHN O'HARA Cresset'. Back: 'ALSO BY JOHN O'HARA'. Front flap has blurb for *FP*. Back flap blank.

*Publication:* Unknown number of copies of the first printing. Published 23 September 1957. 8s. 6d.

*Locations:* BL (27 AUG 1957), Bod (30 AUG 1957), MJB (dj), PSt (dj).

A 15.1.f
*Second Cresset printing:* London: Cresset, 1957.

Not seen.

A 15.2
*Second edition: Reader's Digest Condensed Books,* I (Winter 1957). Pleasantville, N.Y.: Reader's Digest. [1957].

On copyright page: 'FIRST EDITION'.

A 15.3
*Third edition:* New York: Bantam, [1957].

#1640. 25¢. Reprinted January 1965.

A 15.4
*Fourth edition:* Amsterdam: Meulenhoff, 1962.

12 pages of stapled notes by C. F. M. Weijers inserted. Locations: MJB, PSt.

A 15.5
*Fifth edition:* [London]: Panther, [1968].

#2398. 3s. 6d. See AA 8.

A 16 FROM THE TERRACE

A 16.1.a
*First edition, first printing (1958)*

# FROM
# THE
# TERRACE

**A NOVEL** *by*

# John O'Hara

**RANDOM HOUSE · NEW YORK**

A 16.1.a: device is deep reddish orange (#36): 5³/₄″ × 8¹/₂″

[i–vi] [1–2] 3–897 [898]

[1]⁴ [2–29]¹⁶

*Contents:*   p. i: half title; p. ii: '*Books by* JOHN O'HARA'; p. iii: title; p. iv: copyright; p. v: '*TO:* | MISS KATIE CARPENTER | *GOD BLESS HER';* p. vi: blank; p. 1: half title; p. 2: blank; pp. 3–897: text; p. 898: blank.

*Typography and paper:*   Times Roman, 10 point on 12. 7¹/₄″ (7¹/₂″)″) × 4³/₈″; 47 lines per page. No running heads. Wove paper.

*Binding:*   Dark blue (#183) V cloth (smooth). Front goldstamped with facsimile of O'Hara's signature. Spine goldstamped: '[on black panel within double-rules frame and surmounted by Random House device] FROM | THE | TERRACE | John O'Hara | [on blindstamped panel] RANDOM HOUSE'. Top and bottom edges trimmed; fore edge rough trimmed. Top edge stained blue. Red and yellow bands at top and bottom. Light yellowish brown (#76) endpapers.

*Dust jacket:*   Front and back lettered in white on blue background with black grain. Front: 'A NOVEL | BY JOHN O'HARA | From the | Terrace | A RANDOM HOUSE BOOK [Random House device]'. Spine: 'JOHN | O'HARA | [short rule] | From | the | Terrace | [short rule] | [Random House device] | RANDOM | HOUSE'. Back has photo of O'Hara. Front flap has blurb for *FTT.* Back flap: 'Books by | JOHN O'HARA'.

*Publication:*   Unknown number of copies of the first printing. Published 27 November 1958. $6.95. Copyright #A373088.

*Printing:*   Manufactured by Colonial Press, Clinton, Mass.

*Locations:*   Lilly (dj), MJB (dj), PSt (dj).

*Textual note:*   The first printing reads 'Mary' at 618.30; corrected to 'Natalie' in second printing.

*Review copy:*   Unbound sewn sheets. Location: MJB.

A 16.1.b
*Second printing:* New York: Random House, [1958].

On copyright page: 'SECOND PRINTING'.

Dust jacket for A16.1.a

A 16.1.c
*First edition, first English printing (1959)*

JOHN O'HARA

---

# *From The*

# *Terrace*

LONDON

THE CRESSET PRESS

1959

A 16.1.c: $5^7/_{16}'' \times 8^1/_2''$

*Copyright page:* '© *Copyright* 1958, *by John O'Hara* | *First published in Great Britain in* 1959 | *by The Cresset Press,* 11 *Fitzroy Square, London, W.* 1 | *and printed in Holland* | *by L. Van Leer & Co. N.V.'*.

[i–vi] [1–2] 3–897 [898]

[1]⁴ [2–29]¹⁶

*Contents:*  p. i: half title; p. ii: blank; p. iii: dedication; p. iv: blank; p. v: title; p. vi: copyright; p. 1: blurb for *FTT;* p. 2: '*By the same Author:*'; pp. 3–897: text; p. 898: blank.

*Typography and paper:*  47 lines per page. Wove paper.

*Binding:*  Strong red (#12) paper-covered boards with B grain (linen). Spine gold-stamped: 'FROM | THE | TERRACE | JOHN | O'HARA | CRESSET | PRESS'. All edges trimmed. White wove calendered endpapers.

*Dust jacket:*  Front and spine lettered in white on black background. Front: 'JOHN O'HARA | [script] From | the | Terrace'. Spine: '[script] From | the | Terr= | ace | JOHN | O'HARA | CRESSET | PRESS'. Back: 'BY THE SAME AUTHOR'. Front flap has blurb for *FTT.* Back flap blank.

*Publication:*  Unknown number of copies of the first printing. Published 12 October 1959. 25s.

*Locations:*  BL (16 SEP 59), Bod (23 NOV 1959), MJB (dj), PSt (dj).


A 16.2.a
*Second edition, Bantam printings:* [New York: Bantam, 1960].

#N2026. 95¢. 32 printings: January 1960 (4 printings), February 1960, March 1960 (2 printings), May 1960, July 1960 (2 printings), August 1960, September 1960 (3 printings), January 1961, March 1961, September 1961, March 1962, September 1962, February 1963, March 1963, August 1964, October 1965 (2 printings), February 1966, August 1966, May 1967, November 1967 (2 printings), March 1968, January 1969, 32nd printing.


A 16.2.b
*Second edition, Popular printing:* New York: Popular Library, [1974].

#445-08247-175. $1.75.


A 16.3
*Third edition:* [London]: Panther, [1961].

1251. 6s. Reprinted 1967 (twice), 1971 (twice), 1972.

A 17 OURSELVES TO KNOW

A 17.1.a
*First edition, first printing (1960)*

# OURSELVES TO KNOW

A NOVEL *by*

## John O'Hara

RANDOM HOUSE · NEW YORK

A 17.1.a: device is dark yellow green (#137); 5³/₄″ × 8⁷/₁₆″

First Printing

© Copyright, 1960, by John O'Hara

All rights reserved under International and Pan-American Copyright
Conventions. Published in New York by Random House, Inc., and
simultaneously in Toronto, Canada, by Random House of Canada, Limited.

Library of Congress Catalog Card Number: 60–5528

Manufactured in the United States of America
by H. Wolff Book Mfg. Co., Inc.

[i–vi] [1–2] 3–408 [409–410]

[1–13]$^{16}$

*Contents:*  p. i: half title; p. ii: '*Books by* JOHN O'HARA'; p. iii: title; p. iv: copyright; p.
v: epigraph; p. vi: blank; p. 1: half title; p. 2: blank; pp. 3–408: text; pp. 409–410:
blank.

*Typography and paper:*  Times Roman, 10 point on 12. 7$^1$/$_8$" (7$^3$/$_8$") × 4$^3$/$_{16}$"; 42 or 43
lines per page. No running heads. Wove paper.

*Binding:*  Dark red (#16) V cloth (smooth). Front goldstamped with O'Hara's signa-
ture. Spine goldstamped on two red panels: '[top panel] [Random House device] | [2
rules] | OURSELVES | TO | KNOW | John O'Hara | [2 rules] | [lower panel] RANDOM
HOUSE'. Top and bottom edges trimmed; fore edge rough trimmed. Top edge stained
red. Red and yellow bands at top and bottom. Light brown (#57) endpapers.

*Dust jacket:*  Front and spine lettered in white on red curtain. Front: 'Ourselves | To
Know | A NOVEL BY | JOHN | O'HARA | A RANDOM HOUSE BOOK'. Spine: 'Our- |
selves | To | Know | JOHN | O'HARA | [Random House device ] | | RANDOM
HOUSE'. Back: 'Books by John O'Hara'. Front and back flaps have blurbs for *OTK*.

*Publication:*  Unknown number of copies of the first printing. Published 27 February
1960. $4.95. Copyright #A434989.

*Printing:*  Manufactured by H. Wolff, New York.

*Locations:*  LC (MAR 21 1960), Lilly (dj), MJB (dj), PSt.

*Note:*  Galley proofs are at PSt and MJB; page proofs at PSt.

*Review copy:*  Spiral-bound proofs with blue paper covers. Front: 'OURSELVES TO
KNOW | And all our Knowledge is ourselves to know. | ALEXANDER POPE: *An Essay
on Man* | John O'Hara'. Location: MJB.


A 17.1.b
*Second printing:* New York: Random House, [1960].

On copyright page: 'Second Printing'.

A 17.1.c
*Pirated printing*

Offset reprint of first edition, probably printed in Taiwan, ca. 1960. Location: MJB.

Ourselves To Know

A NOVEL BY

JOHN O'HARA

A RANDOM HOUSE BOOK

RANDOM HOUSE

Ourselves To Know

JOHN O'HARA

Ourselves
To Know
BY
John O'Hara

Robert Millhouser, prominent citizen of Lyons, Pennsylvania, shot and killed his young wife Hedda in 1908. That fact is revealed by Gerald Higgins in the early part of his account of Robert Millhouser's life, which began in Lyons in 1855 and ended, for Millhouser, with his wife's death, although he lived on for more than a quarter of a century. When Gerald was a small boy he first became aware of Mr. Millhouser and the fact that there was some mystery about him. At the age of sixteen, Gerald made the acquaintance of this man whose life history he began writing in 1927, with the full co-operation of the subject.

(continued on back flap)

## Books by John O'Hara

Appointment in Samarra*
The Doctor's Son and Other Stories
Butterfield 8†
Hope of Heaven
Files on Parade
Pal Joey
Pipe Night
Hellbox
A Rage to Live
The Farmers Hotel
Sweet and Sour
Ten North Frederick
A Family Party
Selected Short Stories of John O'Hara*
From the Terrace
Ourselves To Know

*Available in the Modern Library
†Available in Modern Library Paperbacks

RANDOM HOUSE, INC. 457 Madison Avenue, New York 22, N.Y.
Publishers of The American College Dictionary and The Modern Library

Printed in U.S.A.

(continued from front flap)
The mystery of Robert Millhouser lay not in the facts of the affair. The facts were known, or easily discoverable, and they are recorded in this chronicle exactly as they happened. Gerald Higgins' purpose was not primarily to reconstruct a crime but, through that reconstruction, to reveal a man. Through his painstaking explorations of Millhouser's heritage, his one close friendship, and his relationships with his parents, his servants and the members of his community, Gerald found him to be a man of intelligence, charm, integrity, good will. And in this man's conscious decision to destroy by killing lay a far more fundamental mystery about the inner forces by which mankind is betrayed.

That one of the greatest of contemporary novelists should write superbly in a form he has not used before is hardly surprising. Yet it must be said that John O'Hara's mastery in adapting his chosen medium to his own high purpose makes Ourselves To Know a brilliant achievement.

Dust jacket for A 17.1.a

A 17.1.d
*First edition, first English printing (1960)*

# JOHN O'HARA

---

# *Ourselves to Know*

LONDON
THE CRESSET PRESS
1960

A 17.1.d: $5^{3}/_{8}'' \times 8^{1}/_{2}''$

*Copyright page:* '© Copyright 1960, by John O'Hara | First published in Great Britain in 1960 by | The Cresset Press, 11, Fitzroy Square, London, W. 1. | *Printed in Great Britain by | Charles Birchall and Sons, Ltd., Liverpool and London.*'

Pagination same as American first printing.

[A] B–I K–N¹⁶

*Contents:* p. i: blurb for *OTK;* p. ii: *'By the same Author';* p. iii: title; p. iv: copyright; p. v: epigraph; p. vi: blank; p. 1: half title; p. 2: blank; pp. 3–408: text; pp. 409–410: blank.

*Typography and paper:* 42 or 43 lines per page. Wove paper.

*Binding:* Vivid red (#11) paper-covered boards, with B grain (linen). Spine gold-stamped: 'OURSELVES | TO | KNOW | JOHN | O'HARA | CRESSET | PRESS'. All edges trimmed. Cream calendered endpapers.

*Dust jacket:* Front and spine lettered in white on dark red background. Front: 'JOHN O'HARA | Our | Selves | to | Know'. Spine: 'JOHN | O'HARA | Our | Selves | to | Know | CRESSET | PRESS'. Back: 'BY THE SAME AUTHOR'. Front flap: blurb for *OTK*. Back flap blank.

*Printing and publication:* Unknown number of copies of the first printing. Published 21 November 1960. 21s.

*Locations:* BL (14 NOV 60), Bod (12 DEC 1960), MJB (dj).

A 17.1.e
*Second Cresset printing:* London: Cresset, 1961.

On copyright page: 'Second Impression, 1961'.

A 17.2.a
*Second edition, Bantam printings:* New York: Bantam, [1961].

#S2213. 75¢. 16 Printings: March 1961 (2 printings), April 1961, August 1961, October 1961, August 1962 (2 printings), October 1962, April 1963, April 1964, November 1964, January 1966, August 1966, November 1967, October 1968, January 1969.

A 17.2.b
*Second edition, Popular printing:* New York: Popular Library, [1973].

#445-00143-125. $1.25.

A 17.3
*Third edition:* [London]: Panther, [1962].

#1415. 5s. 9 printings: September 1962, December 1963, April 1964, July 1964, July 1965, 1966, 1967, 1971, 1974.

A 18 SERMONS AND SODA-WATER

A 18.1.a
*First edition, first printing (1960)*

*Volume I:   The Girl on the Baggage Truck*

---

# JOHN O'HARA

---

## SERMONS AND
## SODA-WATER

I         The Girl on the
          Baggage Truck

 RANDOM HOUSE · NEW YORK

---

A 18.1.a, vol. I: 5⁵/₁₆″ × 8″

[A–D] [i–viii] ix–xi [xii] [1–2] 3–106 [107–112]

[1–8]⁸; first 2 leaves and last 2 leaves are endpapers

*Contents:* pp. A–B: pastedown endpaper; pp. C–D: free endpaper; p. i: half title; p. ii: blank; p. iii: 'OTHER BOOKS BY JOHN O'HARA'; p. iv: blank; p. v: title; p. vi: copyright; p. vii: *'Foreword to* | SERMONS AND SODA-WATER'; p. viii: blank; pp. ix–xi: foreword; p. xii: blank; p. 1: half title; p. 2: blank; pp. 3–106: text; p. 107–108: blank; pp. 109–110: free endpaper; pp. 111–112: pastedown endpaper.

*Typography and paper:* Caledonia, 11 point on 14. 5³/₄″ (6″) × 3¹¹/₁₆″; 28 lines per page. Running heads: rectos, *'The Girl on the Baggage Truck'*; versos, 'SERMONS AND SODA-WATER'. Wove paper.

*Binding:* V cloth (smooth). Front lettered on brilliant yellow (#83): '[gray Random House device] | [blue] JOHN | O'HARA'. Spine: '[vertically, on dark gray panel, within blue frame] [white] JOHN O'HARA [yellow] SERMONS AND SODA-WATER | [light gray] The Girl on the Baggage Truck [yellow] I | [black rules on white] [horizontally, black] RANDOM | HOUSE'. Back lettered on light gray: '[white] SERMONS | AND SODA- | WATER | [yellow] I'. All edges trimmed. Top edge stained dark gray. White wove calendered endpapers (see "Contents").

*Box:* 3 volumes in one box. Black top and bottom with printed paper front, spine, and back. Front lettered on blue background: '[black] SERMONS | AND [yellow] SODA- | WATER'. Spine: '[the following on black panel within blue single-rule frame] [yellow] JOHN | O'HARA | [white] SERMONS | AND | SODA-WATER | I | [light gray] THE GIRL | on the | Baggage Truck | [white] II | [light gray] Imagine | Kissing Pete | [white] III | [light gray] We're Friends | Again | [outside frame, vertical black rules on white] [gray Random House device] | [gray] RANDOM HOUSE'. Back lettered on blue: '[white] JOHN | [yellow] O'HARA'. Blue rectangular price tab pasted on box.

*Publication:* Unknown number of copies of the first printing. Published 4 November 1960. $5.95. Copyright #A492722.

*Printing:* Manufactured by Haddon Craftsmen, Scranton, Pa.

*Locations:* LC (both deposit copies are second printings: MAR 27 1961), MJB (boxed), PSt.

SERMONS AND SODA-WATER

JOHN O'HARA

JOHN O'HARA

SERMONS AND SODA-WATER

I
The Girl on the Baggage Truck

II
Imagine Kissing Pete

III
We're Friends Again

RANDOM HOUSE

# JOHN O'HARA

## SERMONS AND SODA-WATER

II    Imagine Kissing Pete

RANDOM HOUSE • NEW YORK

[i–x] [1–2] 3–112 [113–118]

[1–8]⁸; first 2 leaves and last 2 leaves are endpapers.

*Contents:*  pp. i–ii: pastedown endpaper; pp. iii–iv: free endpaper; p. v: half title; p. vi: blank; p. vii: 'OTHER BOOKS BY JOHN O'HARA'; p. viii: blank; p. ix: title; p. x: copyright; p. 1: half title; p. 2: blank; pp. 3–112: text; pp. 113–114: blank; pp. 115–116: free endpaper; pp. 117–118: pastedown endpaper.

*Typography and paper:*  See Volume I. Running heads: rectos, *'Imagine Kissing Pete'*; versos, 'SERMONS AND SODA-WATER'.

*Binding:*  See Volume I. Spine: 'Imagine Kissing Pete II' substituted. Back lettered against white; 'II' substituted.

*Box:*  See Volume I.

*Publication:*  See Volume I.

*Printing:*  See Volume I.

*Locations:*  See Volume I.

*Note:*  First published in *The New Yorker,* 17 September 1960. See C 236.

# JOHN O'HARA

## SERMONS AND SODA-WATER

### III   We're Friends Again

RANDOM HOUSE • NEW YORK

[i–x] [1–2] 3–110 [111–118]

[1–8]⁸; first 2 leaves and last 2 leaves are endpapers

*Contents:*  pp. i–ii: pastedown endpaper; pp. iii–iv: free endpaper; p. v: half title; p. vi: blank; p. vii: 'OTHER BOOKS BY JOHN O'HARA'; p. viii: blank; p. ix: title; p. x: copyright; p. 1: half title; p. 2: blank; pp. 3–110: text; pp. 111–114: blank; pp. 115–116: free endpaper; pp. 117–118: pastedown endpaper.

*Typography and paper:*  See Volume I. Running heads: rectos, '*We're Friends Again*'; versos, 'SERMONS AND SODA-WATER'.

*Binding:*  See Volume I. Spine: 'We're Friends Again III' substituted. Back lettered against strong blue (#178); 'III' substituted.

*Box:*  See Volume I.

*Publication:*  See Volume I.

*Printing:*  See Volume I.

*Locations:*  See Volume I.

*Note:*  Galley proofs and page proofs for *Sermons and Soda-Water* are at PSt.

*Review copy:*  Spiral-bound proofs, bound in blue paper covers. Front: 'TITLE, PUBLI-CATION DATE, AND PRICE TENTATIVE | PLEASE CHECK WITH RANDOM HOUSE | BEFORE PUBLISHING REVIEW | [tapered rule] | *Uncorrected Proof from* | RANDOM HOUSE | [Random House device] | [tapered rule] | Sermons and Soda-Water | By | John O'Hara | [tapered rule] | *for* ADVANCE *readers'*. Location: MJB.

A 18.1.a*
*Signed issue*

An unknown number of copies have a blank leaf signed by O'Hara tipped in between the free front endpaper and the half title of volume I: [1]⁸ (1₂ + 1) [2–8]⁸.

*Location:*  MJB.

A 18.1.b
*Second printing:* New York: Random House, [1960].

3 vols. On copyright page: 'Second Printing'.

A 18.1.c
*Third printing:* New York: Random House, [1960].

3 vols. On copyright page: 'Third Printing'.

A 18.1.d
*Fourth printing:* New York: Random House, [   ].

1 vol. On copyright page: 'Third printing'. On dust jacket: 'MARBORO BOOK CLUB EDITION'.

A 18.1.e
*Pirated printing*

Offset reprint of the first printing, probably printed in Taiwan, ca. 1961. 1 vol. On copyright page: 'First Printing'. Location: MJB.

A 18.2
*English limited edition* (1961)

Volume I:   *The Girl on the Baggage Truck*

SERMONS AND SODA-WATER

# *The Girl on the Baggage Truck*

BY

JOHN O'HARA

LONDON : THE CRESSET PRESS : MCMLXI

A 18.2, vol. I: volume title lines in dark gray (#266); 5″ × 7³/₄″

*Copyright page:* 'Copyright ©, *1960, by John O'Hara* | *Published in Great Britain in 1961 by* | *The Cresset Press, 11 Fitzroy Square, London W. 1* | *Printed in Great Britain by Richard Clay and Company, Ltd.,* | *Bungay, Suffolk'*.

[i–xii] 1–96

[A]⁶ B–G⁸

*Contents:* pp. i–ii: blank; p. iii: *'This edition printed on* | *mould made paper and signed* | *by the author is limited to* | *525 copies* | THE NUMBER OF THIS COPY | IS [number] | [signature]'; p. iv: blank; p. v: half title; p. vi: blank; p. vii: title; p. viii: copyright; pp. ix–x: blank; p. xi: half title; p. xii: blank; pp. 1–96: text. Omits O'Hara's "Foreword."

*Typography and paper:* 5⁹/₁₆″ (6¹/₈″) × 3¹¹/₁₆″; 31 lines per page. Running heads: rectos, *'The Girl on the Baggage Truck';* versos, *'Sermons and Soda-Water'*. Laid paper with vertical chain lines.

*Binding:* Boards covered with dark gray green (#151) and white marbled paper. White paper spine separated from marbled paper by vertical gold stripe. Spine gold-stamped: '[horizontally] O'HARA | [vertically, on dark gray green panel within single-rule gold frame] *The Girl on the Baggage Truck* | [horizontally] CRESSET'. Red and white band at top only. All edges trimmed. Top edge stained green. White wove calendered endpapers.

*Box:* 3 volumes in one box. Boards covered with gray and white marbled paper. Printed white paper label on spine: '[within double-rules frame] SERMONS | AND SODA-WATER | [star] | JOHN | O'HARA | [star] | Cresset'. Each volume in unprinted cellophane dust jacket.

*Publication:* 525 copies of limited printing. Published 28 September 1961. 63s. Published simultaneously with trade edition.

*Locations:* Lilly, MJB, PSt.

SERMONS AND SODA-WATER

# *Imagine Kissing Pete*

BY

JOHN O'HARA

LONDON : THE CRESSET PRESS : MCMLXI

A 18.2, vol. II: volume title lines in dark gray (#266); 5″ × 7³/₄″

[i–xii] 1–86 [87–88]

[A]⁶ B–D⁸ E¹² F⁸

*Contents:*   pp. i–ii: blank; p. iii: 'THE NUMBER OF THIS COPY | IS [number]'; p. iv: blank; p. v: half title; p. vi: blank; p. vii: title; p. viii: copyright; pp. ix–x: blank; p., xi: half title; p. xii: blank; pp. 1–86: text; pp. 87–88: blank.

*Typography and paper:*   See Volume I. Running heads: rectos, *'Imagine Kissing Pete';* versos, *'Sermons and Soda-Water'.*

*Binding:*   See Volume I. Spine: *'Imagine Kissing Pete'* substituted.

*Box:*   See Volume I.

*Publication:*   See Volume I.

*Locations:*   See Volume I.

SERMONS AND SODA-WATER

## *We're Friends Again*

BY

JOHN O'HARA

LONDON : THE CRESSET PRESS : MCMLXI

A 18.2, vol. III: volume title lines in dark gray (#266): 5″ × 7³/₄″

[i–xii] 1–81 [82–84]

[A]$^6$ B–D$^8$ E$^{10}$ F$^8$

*Contents:*    pp. i–ii: blank; p. iii: 'THE NUMBER OF THIS COPY | IS [number]'; p. iv: blank; p. v: half title; p. vi: blank; p. vii: title; p. viii: copyright; pp. ix–x: blank; p. xi: half title; p. xii: blank; pp. 1–81: text; pp. 82–84: blank.

*Typography and paper:*    See Volume I. Running heads: rectos, *'We're Friends Again';* versos, *'Sermons and Soda-Water'.*

*Binding:*    See Volume I. Spine: *We're Friends Again'* substituted.

*Box:*    See Volume I.

*Publication:*    See Volume I.

*Locations:*    See Volume I.

A 18.3
*English trade edition (1961)*

JOHN O'HARA

# SERMONS
# AND
# SODA-WATER

LONDON : THE CRESSET PRESS : 1961

A 18.3: 5″ × 7³/₄″

*Copyright page:* '© *Copyright, 1960, by John O'Hara* | *First published in Great Britain in 1961 by* | *The Cresset Press, 11 Fitzroy Square, London W.1* | *Printed in Great Britain by Richard Clay and Company, Ltd.,* | *Bungay, Suffolk'.*

[i–vi] [1–2] 3–94 [95–96] 97–182 [183–184] 185–265 [266]

[A] B–I K–R⁸

*Contents:*   p. i: ad for *S&SW;* p. ii: *'By the same Author:';* p. iii: title; p. iv: copyright; p. v: *'Contents';* p. vi: blank; p. 1: 'THE GIRL ON THE BAGGAGE TRUCK'; p. 2: blank; pp. 3–265: text; p. 266 blank. Omits O'Hara's "Foreword."

*Typography and paper:*   31 or 32 lines per page. Wove paper.

*Binding:*   Dark yellow green (#137) paper-covered boards with B grain (linen). Spine goldstamped: 'SERMONS | AND | SODA-WATER | [star] | JOHN | O'HARA | CRES-SET'. White wove endpapers.

*Dust jacket:*   Front and spine lettered in white on gray. Front: 'JOHN O'HARA | [script] SeRMons | & | Soda | WateR'. Spine: 'JOHN | O'HARA | [script] SERMONS | AND | Soda | WateR | CRESSET | PRESS'. Back: 'BY THE SAME AUTHOR'. Front flap has blurb for *S&SW.* Back flap blank.

*Publication:*   Unknown number of copies of the first trade printing. Published 28 September 1961. Published simultaneously with limited edition.

*Locations:*   BL (7 SEP 61), Bod (18 OCT 1961), MJB (dj).

A 18.4.a
*Fourth edition, Bantam printings:* New York: Bantam, [1962].

#2338. 75¢. 9 printings: January 1962 (2 printings), February 1962, April 1964, January 1965 (2 printings), October 1965, May 1967, December 1969.

A 18.4.b
*Fourth edition, Corgi printings:* [London]: Corgi, 1963.

Reprinted in 1965, 1966, 1967.

A 19 FIVE PLAYS

A 19.1
*First edition, only printing (1961)*

# FIVE PLAYS

## JOHN O'HARA

*Random House*   *New York*

A 19.1: 4⁷/₁₆″ × 7⁷/₁₆″

[A–B] [i–viii] ix–xiv [1–2] 3–51 [52] 53–85 [86–88] 89–182 [183–184] 185–231 [232] 233–275 [276] 277–302 [303–304] 305–415 [416–418] 419–449 [450] 451–473 [474–480]

[1–17]¹⁶ [8–9]¹² [10–16]¹⁶

*Contents:*   pp. A–B: blank; p. i: half title; p. ii: *'by John O'Hara'*; p. iii: title; p. iv: copyright; p. v: *'To | Robert Charles Benchley (1889–1945) | The Best of Company'*; p. vi: blank; p. vii: 'CONTENTS'; p. viii: blank; pp. ix–xiv: 'FOREWORD'; p. 1: 'THE | FARMERS | HOTEL'; p. 2: blank; pp. 3–473: text, headed 'ACT ONE'; pp. 474–480: blank.
   *Plays:*   The Farmers Hotel, The Searching Sun, The Champagne Pool, Veronique, The Way It Was.

*Typography and paper:*   Electra, 10 point on 11. 5¹¹/₁₆″ (6″) × 3⁵/₁₆″; varying number of lines per page. Running heads: rectos and versos, title of play. Wove paper.

*Binding:*   Black V cloth (smooth). Front stamped in dark green with facsimile of O'Hara's signature. Spine: '[gold] FIVE | PLAYS | [rule] | [dark green] JOHN | O'HARA | [gold Random House device] | [gold] Random House'. All edges trimmed. Top edge stained light yellow. Green and yellow bands at top and bottom. Off-white wove endpapers of heavy stock.

*Dust jacket:*   Front printed in black on olive brown (#95) background: 'Five Plays | [white rule] | The Farmers Hotel | The Searching Sun | The Champagne Pool | Veronique | The Way It Was | [white rule] | With a Foreword by the Author [vertically up, in green on white along left margin] JOHN O'HARA'. Spine: '[black] Five | Plays | by | [green] JOHN | O'HARA | [white Random House device] | [black] RANDOM HOUSE'. Back: photo of O'Hara. Front flap: blurb for *FP*. Back flap: books by O'Hara.

*Publications:*   6,090 copies of the first printing. Published 11 August 1961. $5.00. Copyright #A543991.

*Printing:*   Manufactured by Colonial Press, Clinton, Mass.

*Locations:*   LC (FEB 13 1962), Lilly (dj), MJB (dj), PSt.

*Note 1:*   Galley proofs and page proofs are at PSt.

*Note 2:*   The Farmers Hotel was produced at the Cecilwood Theatre, Fishkill, N.Y., 1954. It was published as a novel in 1951. See A 11. The Searching Sun was produced by the Theatre Intime and Community Players, Princeton, N.J., 1952.

Five
Plays
by
**JOHN
O'HARA**

Five Plays

The Farmers Hotel

The Searching Sun

The Champagne Pool

Veronique

The Way It Was

With a Foreword by the Author

**JOHN O'HARA**

Five
Plays
by
**JOHN
O'HARA**

RANDOM HOUSE

Five
Plays
by
**JOHN
O'HARA**

John O'Hara proved himself a master in the dramatic medium with *Pal Joey*. The five plays in this book, never previously published and never produced on Broadway, offer eloquent confirmation of his talent as a playwright. O'Hara has written a foreword to the collection, which is, by itself, a valuable contribution to dramatic commentary. The plays are: *The Farmers Hotel, The Searching Sun, The Champagne Pool, Veronique,* and *The Way It Was.*

Books
by
**JOHN
O'HARA**

Appointment in Samarra
The Doctor's Son
and Other Stories
Butterfield 8
Hope of Heaven
Files on Parade
Pal Joey
Pipe Night
Hellbox
A Rage to Live
The Farmers Hotel
Sweet and Sour
Ten North Frederick
A Family Party
Selected Short Stories
From the Terrace
Ourselves to Know
Sermons and Soda-Water

Photograph of John O'Hara by Ann Zane Shanks

Dust jacket for A 19.1

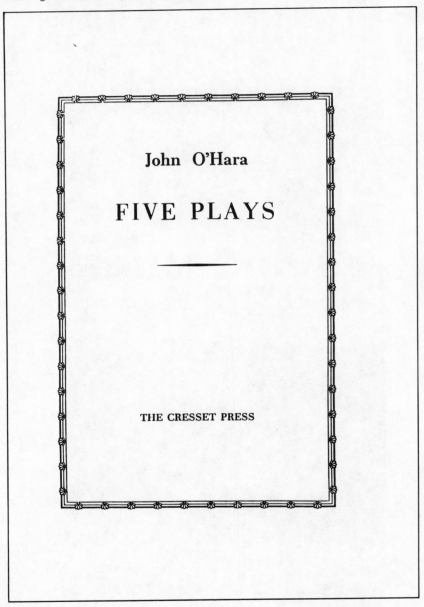

John  O'Hara

# FIVE PLAYS

——

**THE CRESSET PRESS**

A 19.2: frame and title line in deep red (#13); $5^3/_8''$ × $8^7/_{16}''$

*Copyright page:* '© *Copyright, 1935, 1961, by John O'Hara | First published in Great Britain in 1962 by | The Cresset Press, 11 Fitzroy Square, London, W. 1 | Printed in Great Britain by Ebenezer Baylis & Son, Ltd. | The Trinity Press, Worcester, and London*'.

[i–vi] vii [viii] ix–xiii [xiv] [1–2] 3–67 [68–70] 71–144 [145–146] 147–236 [237–238] 239–325 [326–238] 329–369 [370]

[A] B–I K–M¹⁶

*Contents:* p. i: half title; p. ii: books by O'Hara; p. iii: title; p. iv: copyright; p. v: 'To | ROBERT CHARLES BENCHLEY | (1889–1945) | The Best of Company'; p. vi: blank; p. vii: 'CONTENTS'; p. viii: blank; pp. ix–xiii: 'FOREWORD'; p. xiv: blank; p. 1: section title; p. 2: blank; pp. 3–369: text, headed 'ACT ONE'; p. 370: blank.

*Typography and paper:* 39 lines per page. Wove paper.

*Binding:* Dark green (#146) boards with 8 grain (linen). Spine goldstamped: '[following 5 lines on black panel within double-rules frame] FIVE | PLAYS | [star] | John | O'Hara | [below panel] CRESSET'. All edges trimmed. White wove endpapers.

*Dust jacket:* Front and spine lettered on red background. Front: '[following 3 lines in blue on white panel; framed by white wavy double rules] JOHN O'HARA | [tapered rule] | Five Plays | [white] THE FARMERS HOTEL | THE SEARCHING SUN | THE CHAMPAGNE POOL | VERONIQUE | THE WAY IT WAS'. Spine: '[following 5 lines in blue on white panel framed by white wavy double rules] JOHN | O'HARA | [tapered rule] | Five | Plays | [below frame] [white] The | Cresset | Press'. Back lists works by O'Hara. Front flap has blurb for *FP*. Back flap blank.

*Publication:* Unknown number of copies of the first printing. Published 26 February 1962. 30s.

*Locations:* BL (13 FEB 62), Bod (16 MAR 1962), MJB (dj).

*Review copy:* Title page: '[all the following within red decorated frame and red single-rule frame] [black] John O'Hara | [red] FIVE PLAYS | [black tapered rule] | [black] LONDON: THE CRESSET PRESS: 1962'. Page proof, bound in tan wrappers. Front: same as title page, all in black. Spine: '[vertically up] Cresset Press FIVE PLAYS'. Location: MJB.

A 19.3
*Acting script*

THE CHAMPAGNE POOL | [underline] | by John O'Hara | Return to: | MERMAID THEATRE | 422 West 42nd Street | New York, New York | LA 4-3646.

Mimeographed typescript bound in red paper covers. Front goldstamped: 'THE CHAMPAGNE POOL | by John O'Hara | the studio duplicating service | 434 west 43rd street, n.y.c. | LO 3-1225'.

*Location:* MJB.

A 20 ASSEMBLY

A 20.1.a
*First edition, first printing (1961)*

# JOHN O'HARA

# ASSEMBLY

*My task, which I am trying to achieve, is, by the power of the written word, to make you feel—it is, before all, to make you see. That—and no more. And it is everything.*                         JOSEPH CONRAD

RANDOM HOUSE • NEW YORK

A 20.1.a: title line, imprint line, and device in dark reddish brown (#44); 5⁹/₁₆″ × 8⁵/₁₆″

[i–xiv] [1–3] 4–429 [430–434]; first page of each story unnumbered

[1–14]¹⁶

*Contents:* pp. i–ii: blank; p. iii: half title; p. iv: 'BOOKS BY JOHN O'HARA'; p. v: title; p. vi: copyright; p. vii: *'to* | WOLCOTT GIBBS | *(March 15, 1902–August 16, 1958)* | *"Many fetes" '*; p. viii: blank; pp. ix–x: 'Contents'; pp. xi–xiii: 'Foreword'; p. xiv: blank; p. 1: half title; p. 2: blank; pp. 3–429: text, headed 'Mrs. Stratton of Oak Knoll'; pp. 430–434: blank.

*26 stories:* "Mrs. Stratton of Oak Knoll,"* "The Weakness," "The Man with the Broken Arm," "The Lighter When Needed,"* "The Pioneer Hep-Cat,"* "The Sharks,"* "The Girl from California," "A Cold Calculating Thing,"* "You Can Always Tell Newark,"* "The High Point,"* "Call Me, Call Me," "It's Mental Work," "In the Silence,"* "First Day in Town,"* "Exactly Eight Thousand Dollars Exactly," "Mary and Norma," "The Cellar Domain," "The Properties of Love,"* "Reassurance,"* "The Free,"* "The Compliment,"* "Sterling Silver," "The Trip," "In a Grove,"* "The Old Folks,"* "A Case History."* Asterisks follow previously unpublished stories.

*Typography and paper:* Times Roman, 11 point on 13. 6¹¹/₁₆" (7") × 4¹/₁₆"; 37 lines per page. Running heads: rectos, story titles; versos, *'Assembly'*. Wove paper.

*Binding:* Yellow gray (#93) V cloth (smooth). Front goldstamped: 'JOHN O'HARA'. Spine goldstamped on three red panels: '[top panel] *John O'Hara* | [middle panel] ASSSEMBLY | [bottom panel] *Random* | *House* | [Random House device stamped in red below panels]'. Top and bottom edges trimmed; fore edge rough trimmed. Top edge stained light reddish orange. Red and yellow bands at top and bottom. Yellow gray (#93) endpapers.

*Dust jacket:* Front and spine lettered on cream. Front: '[red] ASSEMBLY | [black] A | COLLECTION | OF 26 NEW | STORIES BY | [red] JOHN | O'HARA | [black] A RANDOM HOUSE BOOK'. Spine: '[black] ASSEMBLY | [red] JOHN | O'HARA | [red Random House device] | [black] RANDOM HOUSE'. Back has photo of O'Hara. Front flap has blurb for *Assembly*. Back flap lists books by O'Hara.

*Publication:* Unknown number of copies of the first printing. Published 23 November 1961. $5.95. Copyright #556964.

*Printing:* Manufactured by H. Wolff, New York.

*Locations:* LC (APR 17 1962), MJB (dj), PSt.

*Note:* Galley proofs and page proofs are at PSt.

Dust jacket for A20.1.a

A 20.1.b
*Second printing:* New York: Random House, [1961].

On copyright page, *'Second Printing'*.

A 20.1.c
*Third printing:* New York: Random House, [1961].

Not seen.

A 20.1.d
*Fourth printing: 49 stories.* New York: Modern Library. [1963].

#MLG88. Includes *Assembly* and *The Cape of Cod Lighter.* Introduction by John K. Hutchens. See AA 5.

A 20.1.e
*Pirated printing*

Offset reprint of the first edition, probably printed in Taiwan, ca. 1962. On copyright page: *'Second Printing'*. Location: MJB.

A 20.2.a
*First English edition, first printing (1962)*

JOHN O'HARA

# ASSEMBLY

*My task, which I am trying to achieve, is, by the power of the written word, to make you feel — it is, before all, to make you see. That — and no more. And it is everything.*

JOSEPH CONRAD

LONDON
THE CRESSET PRESS
1962

A 20.2.a: $5^5/_{16}'' \times 8^1/_4''$

*Copyright page:* '© *Copyright 1960, 1961, by John O'Hara | First published in Great Britain in 1962 by | The Cresset Press, 11 Fitzroy Square, London W. 1 | Printed in Great Britain by Ebenezer Baylis & Son, Ltd. | The Trinity Press, Worcester, and London'.*

[i–iv] v–vii [viii] 1–408

[1] 2–13$^{16}$

*Contents:* p. i: half title; p. ii: *'Other books by John O'Hara';* p. iii: title; p. iv: copyright and dedication; pp. v–vi: 'FOREWORD'; p. vii: *'Contents';* p. viii: blank; pp. 1–408: text, headed 'MRS. STRATTON OF OAK KNOLL'. 26 stories.

*Typography and paper:* 38 lines per page. Wove paper.

*Binding:* Vivid green (#139) paper-covered boards with V grain. Spine gold-stamped: '[thick rule] | [following 4 lines on brown panel] ASSEMBLY | [*] | JOHN | O'HARA | [thick rule] | CRESSET | PRESS'. All edges trimmed. White wove endpapers.

*Dust jacket:* Front has design of orange and green boxes on white background: '[blue] Assembly | JOHN O'HARA | 26 New Stories'. Spine: '[blue] JOHN | O'HARA | [orange box] | [vertically, blue] ASSEMBLY | [green box] | [blue] CRESSET | PRESS'. Back lists books by O'Hara. Front flap has blurb for *Assembly.* Back flap blank.

*Publication:* Unknown number of copies of the first printing. Published 7 May 1962. 21s.

*Locations:* BL (2 MAY 62), Lilly (dj), MJB (dj).

*Review copy:* Title page: 'John O'Hara | [decorated tapered rule] | ASSEMBLY | LONDON | THE CRESSET PRESS | 1962'. Page proof, bound in brown wrapers. Front: same as title page. Spine: '[vertically up] Cresset Press ASSEMBLY'. Location: MJB.

A 20.2.b
*Second printing:* [London]: Corgi, [1964].

#XN 7266. 6s. Reprinted 1965, 1966, 1967.

A 20.3.a
*Third edition, Bantam printings:* New York: Bantam, [1963].

#S2506. 75¢. 10 printings: January 1963 (3 printings), February 1963, March 1963, May 1963, March 1964, January 1965, 9th printing, 10th printing.

A 20.3.b
*Third edition, Popular printing:* New York: Popular Library, [1973].

#445-00169-125. $1.25.

A 21.1
*First edition, only printing (1962)*

# THE
# BIG LAUGH

A NOVEL *by*

# John O'Hara

RANDOM HOUSE · NEW YORK

A 21.1: 5³/₄″ × 8¹/₄″

[i–viii] [1–2] 3–308 [309–312]

[1–10]¹⁶

*Contents:*   pp. i–ii: blank; p. iii: half title; p. iv: '*Books by* | JOHN O'HARA'; p. v: title; p. vi: copyright; p. vii: 'TO | *David Lewelyn Wark Griffith* | (1874–1948) | *Rudolph Alphonso Guglielmi di Valentino* | *d'Antonguiela* | (1895–1926) | *Greta Louisa Gustafsson* | (1905–   ) | *Roscoe Arbuckle* | (1887–1933)'; p. viii: blank; p. 1: half title; p. 2: blank; pp. 3–308: text; pp. 309–312: blank.

*Typography and paper:*   Caledonia, 12 point on 15. 6¼″ (6¾″) × 4″; 30 lines per page. Running heads: rectos, 'THE BIG LAUGH'; versos, 'JOHN O'HARA'. Wove paper.

*Binding:*   Black V cloth (smooth). Front goldstamped with facsimile of O'Hara's signature. Spine goldstamped on 2 red panels: '[top panel] [Random House device] | [thick and thin rules] | THE | BIG LAUGH | John O'Hara | [thin and thick rules] | [lower panel] RANDOM HOUSE'. Top and bottom edges trimmed; fore edge rough trimmed. Top edge stained red. Yellow and red bands at top and bottom. Reddish orange (#36) endpapers.

*Dust jacket:*   Front and spine lettered on white background. Front: '[blue] THE | BIG | LAUGH | [in white on thick black rule] *a novel by* | [red] JOHN | O'HARA'. Spine: '[vertically] [blue] THE BIG LAUGH [horizontal black rule] [vertically] [red] JOHN | O'HARA | [horizontal black Random House device]'. Back has photo of O'Hara by Ann Zane Shanks. Front flap has blurb for *BL*. Back flap: 'Books by | JOHN O'HARA'.

*Publication:*   Unknown number of copies of the first printing. Published 29 May 1962. $4.95. Copyright #A591432.

*Printing:*   Set, printed, and bound by Colonial Press, Clinton, Mass.

*Locations:*   LC (OCT 31 1962), Lilly (dj), MJB (dj), PSt (dj).

*Note:*   Galley proofs and page proofs are at PSt.

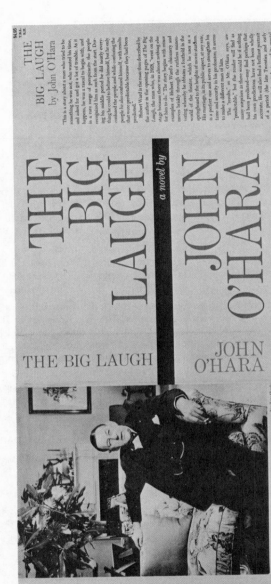

Dust jacket for A 21.1

A 21.2
*First English edition, first printing (1962)*

# THE
# BIG LAUGH

## JOHN O'HARA

## THE CRESSET PRESS

A 21.2: 5$^{1}/_{16}$″ × 7$^{3}/_{4}$″

*Copyright page:* '© *Copyright* 1962, *by John O'Hara* | *First published in Great Britain in* 1962 *by* | *The Cresset Press,* 11 *Fitzroy Square, London, W.* 1 | *Printed in Great Britain by Ebenezer Baylis & Son, Ltd.* | *The Trinity Press, Worcester, and London'.*

[i–vi] 1–250

[1] 2–16⁸

*Contents:* p. i: blurb for *BL;* p. ii: *'Other books by John O'Hara';* p. iii: title; p. iv: copyright; p. v: dedications; p. vi: blank; pp. 1–250: text.

*Typography and paper:* 35 lines per page. Wove paper.

*Binding:* Dark blue (#183) paper-covered boards with V grain. Spine goldstamped: 'THE | BIG | LAUGH | [star] | JOHN | O'HARA | CRESSET'. All edges trimmed. White wove calendered endpapers.

*Dust jacket:* Front and spine lettered in white on dark blue background. Front: 'JOHN O'HARA | The | BIG | Laugh'. Spine: 'JOHN | O'HARA | The | BIG | Laugh | CRESSET | PRESS'. Back: 'BY THE SAME AUTHOR'. Front flap has blurbs for *BL.* Back flap blank.

*Publication:* Unknown number of copies of the first printing. Published 29 October 1962. 18s.

*Locations:* BL (11 OCT 62), Bod (11 Jan 1963), Lilly (dj), MJB (dj), PSt.

A 21.3.a
*Third edition, Bantam printings:* New York: Bantam, [1963].

#S2654. 75¢. 11 printings: October 1963 (twice), November 1963, April 1964, January 1965 (two printings), January 1966, June 1967, April 1968, January 1969, October 1970.

A 21.3.b
*Third edition, Transworld printing:* London: Transworld, [1964].

Corgi #FN7030. 5s.

A 21.3.c
*Third edition, Popular printing:* New York: Popular Library, [1977].

#0-445-04017-3. $1.95.

A 22 THE CAPE COD LIGHTER

A 22.1.a
*First edition, first printing (1962)*

# JOHN O'HARA

# THE CAPE COD LIGHTER

RANDOM HOUSE · NEW YORK

A 22.1.a: $5^5/_8'' \times 8^5/_{16}''$

[A–B] [i–vi] vii–xiii [xiv–xvi] [1–3] 4–425 [426–430]; first page of each story unnumbered.

[1–14]¹⁶

*Contents:*   pp. A–B: blank; p. i: blank; p. ii: 'BOOKS BY JOHN O'HARA'; p. iii: half title; p. iv: blank; p. v: title; p. vi: copyright; pp. vii–xiii: 'FOREWORD'; p. xiv: blank; pp. xv–xvi: 'CONTENTS'; p. 1: half title; p. 2: blank; pp. 3–425: text, headed 'APPEARANCES'; pp. 426–430: blank.

   *23 stories:* "Appearances,"* "The Bucket of Blood," "The Butterfly,"* "Claude Emerson, Reporter,"* "The Engineer,"* "The Father," "The First Day,"* "Jurge Dulrumple,"* "Justice,"* "The Lesson,"* "Money," "The Nothing Machine,"* "Pat Collins,"* "The Professors,"* "A Short Walk from the Station," "Sunday Morning," "The Sun-Dodgers,"* "Things You Really Want,"* "Two Turtledoves," "Winter Dance," "The Women of Madison Avenue," "You Don't Remember Me,"* "Your Fah Neefah Neeface."* Asterisks follow previously unpublished stories.

*Typography and paper:*   Caslon, 12 point on 15. 5¹⁵/₁₆″ (6⁹/₁₆″) × 3³/₄″; 33 lines per page. Running heads: rectos, story titles; versos, 'THE CAPE COD LIGHTER'. Wove paper.

*Binding:*   Vivid red (#11) V cloth (smooth). Front goldstamped: 'JOHN O'HARA '. Spine goldstamped on 3 black panels: '[top panel] *John O'Hara* | [middle panel] THE | CAPE COD | LIGHTER | [bottom panel] *Random* | *House* | [Random House device below panels]'. Top and bottom edges trimmed; fore edge rough trimmed. Top edge stained yellow. Yellow and red bands top and bottom. Dark yellow (#88) endpapers.

*Dust jacket:*   Front and spine lettered on gray background. Front: '[green] THE | CAPE COD | LIGHTER | [black] A | COLLECTION | of 23 NEW | STORIES BY | [green] JOHN | O'HARA | [black] A RANDOM HOUSE BOOK'. Spine: '[green] THE | CAPE COD | LIGHTER | [black] JOHN | O'HARA | [Random House device] | RANDOM HOUSE'. Back has photo of O'Hara by Gordon Parks. Front flap has blurb for *CCL*. Back flap: '*Books by* | JOHN O'HARA'.

*Publication:*   Unknown number of copies of the first printing. Published 29 November 1962. $5.45. Copyright #A616174.

*Printing:*   Set, printed, and bound by H. Wolff, New York.

*Locations:*   LC (MAR 15 1963), MJB (dj), PSt (dj).

*Note:*   Galley proofs and page proofs are at PSt.

THE
CAPE COD
LIGHTER

A
COLLECTION
OF 23 NEW
STORIES BY

JOHN
O'HARA

A RANDOM HOUSE BOOK

THE
CAPE COD
LIGHTER

JOHN
O'HARA

RANDOM HOUSE

The twenty-three short stories and novellas in this volume were written in the year following the completion of Assembly which was published one year earlier.

In his foreword to Assembly Mr. O'Hara referred to his joyful discovery that after neglecting the short story form for eleven years, he had an apparently inexhaustible urge to express an unlimited supply of short story ideas. THE CAPE COD LIGHTER presents abundant evidence that he did not overstate either the impulse or the wealth, for these stories continue to display the diversity of theme, economy of statement and formal excellence that made Assembly such an exciting and important literary event

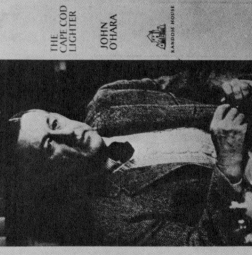

Photograph of John O'Hara by Gordon Parks

Books by
JOHN O'HARA

APPOINTMENT IN SAMARRA
THE DOCTOR'S SON AND OTHER STORIES
BUTTERFIELD 8
HOPE OF HEAVEN
FILES ON PARADE
PAL JOEY
PIPE NIGHT
HELLBOX
A RAGE TO LIVE
THE FARMERS HOTEL
SWEET AND SOUR
TEN NORTH FREDERICK
A FAMILY PARTY
SELECTED SHORT STORIES
FROM THE TERRACE
OURSELVES TO KNOW
SERMONS AND SODA-WATER: A TRILOGY
FIVE PLAYS
ASSEMBLY
THE BIG LAUGH
THE CAPE COD LIGHTER

Random House, Inc.
457 Madison Avenue, New York 22, New York
Publishers of The American College Dictionary
and The Modern Library
PRINTED IN U.S.A.

Dust jacket for A 22.1.a

A 22.1.b
*Second printing:* New York: Random House, [1962].

On copyright page: 'SECOND PRINTING'.

A 22.1.c
*Third printing:* New York: Random House, [1962].

On copyright page: 'THIRD PRINTING'.

A 22.1.d
*Fourth printing:* New York: Random House, [1962].

On copyright page: 'FOURTH PRINTING'.

A 22.1.e
*Fifth printing:* New York: Random House, [1963].

On copyright page: *'Fifth Printing'*.

A 22.1.f
*Sixth printing:* New York: Random House, [1963].

Not seen.

A 22.1.g
*Seventh printing:* New York: Random House, [1963].

On copyright page: *'Seventh Printing'*.

A 22.1.h
*Eighth printing: 49 Stories.* New York: Modern Library, [1963].

#MLG88. *Assembly* and *Cape Cod Lighter.* See AA 5.

A 22.2.a
*First English edition, first printing (1963)*

# THE CAPE COD LIGHTER

BY

## JOHN O'HARA

## THE CRESSET PRESS
### LONDON

A 22.2.a: 5³/₈″ × 8¹/₄″

*Copyright page:* '© Copyright, 1961, 1962, by John O'Hara | *First published in Great Britain in 1963* | *by The Cresset Press* | *Printed in Great Britain* | *by Ebenezer Baylis and Son, Ltd.* | *The Trinity Press, Worcester, and London*'.

[i–iv] v–viii [ix–x] 1–309 [310]

[1] 2–10$^{16}$

*Contents:* p. 1: half title; p. ii: *'Other books by John O'Hara'*; p. iii: title; p. iv: copyright; pp. v–viii: 'FOREWORD'; p. ix: 'CONTENTS'; p. x: blank; pp. 1–309: text, headed 'APPEARANCES'; p. 310: blank.

Contains 23 stories.

*Typography and paper:* 39 lines per page. Wove paper.

*Binding:* Dark olive (#108) paper-covered boards with V grain. Spine goldstamped: '[rule] | [following 5 lines on red panel] THE | CAPE COD | LIGHTER | JOHN | O'HARA | [rule] | CRESSET'. All edged trimmed. White wove calendered endpapers.

*Dust jacket:* Front and spine lettered on green, blue, and white illustration of sea and sky. Front: '[black] [script] John | [roman] O'HARA | [pale green and white] [script] The | *CAPE COD* | *LIGHTER* | [on light green panel] [dark green] *23 New Stories*'. Spine: '[black] [script] John | [roman] O'HARA | [pale green and white] [script] The | *CAPE* | *COD* | *LIGHTER* | [on light green panel] [white] *CRESSET*'. Back: 'BY THE SAME AUTHOR'. Front flap has a blurb for *CCL*. Back flap blank.

*Publication:* Unknown number of copies of the first printing. Published 27 May 1963. 21s.

*Locations:* BL (8 MAY 63), MJB (dj), PSt.

*Review copy:* Title page; 'THE CAPE COD | LIGHTER | BY | JOHN O'HARA | THE CRESSET PRESS | LONDON'. Page proof, bound in light tan wrappers. Front: same as title page. Spine: '[vertically up] Cresset Press THE CAPE COD LIGHTER'. Location: MJB.

A 22.2.b
*Second printing:* London: Barrie & Rockliffe the Cresset Press, [1969].

A 22.3.a
*Third edition, Bantam printings:* New York: Bantam, [1964].

#W2718. 85¢. 3 printings: April 1964 (two printings), June 1969.

A 22.3.b
*Third edition, Corgi printing:* [London]: Corgi, [1965].

#EN 7148. 7s. 6d.

A 22.4
*Fourth edition:* New York: Popular Library, [1973].

#445-00145-125. $1.25.

A 23 ELIZABETH APPLETON

A 23.1.a
*First edition, first printing (1963)*

# ELIZABETH APPLETON

A NOVEL *by*

## John O'Hara

RANDOM HOUSE · NEW YORK

A 23.1.a: 5⁵/₈″ × 8³/₈″

[i–viii] [1–2] 3–310 [311–312]

[1–10]¹⁶

*Contents:*  pp. i–ii: blank; p. iii: half title; p. iv: *'Books by* | JOHN O'HARA'; p. v: title; p. vi: copyright; p. vii: *'To Pat Outerbridge';* p. viii: blank; p. 1: half title; p. 2: blank; pp. 3–310: text, headed 'I'; pp. 311–312: blank.

*Typography and paper:*  Caledonia, 12 point on 13. 6⁷/₈″ (7¹/₈″) × 4″; 38 lines per page. No running heads. Wove paper.

*Binding:*  Deep blue (#179) V cloth (smooth). Front goldstamped with facsimile of O'Hara's signature. Spine goldstamped on two dark blue panels: '[top panel] [Random House device] | [thick and thin rules] | ELIZABETH | APPLETON | John O'Hara | [thin and thick rules] | [lower panel] RANDOM HOUSE'. Top and bottom edges trimmed; fore edge rough trimmed. Top edge stained yellow. Yellow and blue bands top and bottom. Light greenish blue (#172) endpapers.

*Dust jacket:*  Front and spine lettered on light bluish green background. Front: '[orange] ELIZABETH | APPLETON | [brown] A | NOVEL | BY | [green] JOHN | O'HARA | [orange rule] | [green] A RANDOM HOUSE BOOK'. Spine: '[vertically] [green] ELIZABETH APPLETON | [brown, horizontal rule] | [vertically] [orange] JOHN | O'HARA | [horizontally] [green] [Random House device] | RANDOM HOUSE'. Back: *'Books by* JOHN O'HARA'. Front flap has blurb for *EA,* continued on back flap.

*Publication:*  50,101 copies of the first printing. Published 4 June 1963. $4.95. Copyright #A634459.

*Printing:*  Set, printed, and bound by H. Wolff, New York.

*Locations:*  LC (JUN 26 1963), Lilly (dj), MJB (dj), PSt.

*Note:*  Galley proofs are at PSt.

A 23.1.b
*Second printing:* New York: Random House, [1963].

On copyright page: *'Second Printing'.*

A 23.1.c
*Third printing:* New York: Random House, [1963].

On copyright page: *'Third Printing'.*

ELIZABETH APPLETON

A NOVEL BY

JOHN O'HARA

A RANDOM HOUSE BOOK

ELIZABETH APPLETON   JOHN O'HARA

RANDOM HOUSE

Books by JOHN O'HARA

Appointment in Samarra
The Doctor's Son and Other Stories
Butterfield 8
Hope of Heaven
Files on Parade
Pal Joey
Pipe Night
Hellbox
A Rage to Live
The Farmers Hotel
Sweet and Sour
Ten North Frederick
A Family Party
Selected Short Stories
From the Terrace
Ourselves to Know
Sermons and Soda-Water: A Trilogy
Five Plays
Assembly
The Big Laugh
The Cape Cod Lighter
Elizabeth Appleton

Dust jacket for A 23.1.a

A 23.1.d
*Fourth printing:* New York: Random House, [1963].

On copyright page: *'Fourth Printing'*.

A 23.1.e
*Fifth printing:* New York: Random House, 1963.

Not seen.

A 23.1.f
*Pirated printing*

Offset printing of the first edition, probably printed in Taiwan, ca. 1963. On copyright page: 'FIRST PRINTING'. Location: MJB.

A 23.2
*First English edition, first printing (1963)*

JOHN O'HARA

# ELIZABETH APPLETON

**THE CRESSET PRESS**

A 23.2: 5¹/₈″ × 7³/₄″

*Copyright page:* '© *Copyright* 1963 *by John O'Hara* | *First published in Great Britain in 1963 by* | *The Cresset Press, 11 Fitzroy Square, London, W. 1* | *Printed in Great Britain by Ebenezer Baylis & Son, Ltd.* | *The Trinity Press, Worcester, and London'.

[i–vi] [1–2] 3–278 [279–282]

[A] B–I K–P R–T⁸

*Contents:*   p. i: blurb for *EA;* p. ii: *'Other books by John O'Hara';* p. iii: title page; p. iv: copyright; p. v: dedication; p. vi: blank; p. 1: half title; p. 2: blank; pp. 3–279: text, headed 'I'; pp. 280–282: blank.

*Typography and paper:*   37 lines per page. Wove paper.

*Binding:*   Vivid red (#11) paper-covered boards with V grain. Spine goldstamped: 'ELIZABETH | APPLETON | [star] | JOHN | O'HARA | CRESSET'. All edges trimmed. White wove calendered endpapers.

*Dust jacket:*   Front and spine lettered in white on black background. Front: 'JOHN O'HARA | ElizaBeth | Appleton'. Spine: 'JOHN | O'HARA | Eliza | Beth | Apple | ton | CRESSET | PRESS'. Back: 'BY THE SAME AUTHOR'. Front flap has blurb for *EA*. Back flap blank.

*Publication:*   Unknown number of copies of the first printing. Published 4 November 1963. 21s.

*Locations:*   BL (8 OCT 63), Lilly (dj), MJB (dj), PSt.

*Review copy:*   Title page: 'JOHN O'HARA | [decorated tapered rule] | ELIZABETH APPLETON | LONDON : THE CRESSET PRESS : 1963'. Page proof, bound in light gray wrappers. Front: same as title page. Spine: '[vertically up] Cresset Press ELIZA-BETH APPLETON'. Locations: MJB, PSt.

A 23.3.a
*Third edition, Bantam printings:* New York: Bantam, [1964].

#N2787. 95¢. 8 printings: July 1964 (two printings), September 1964, January 1966, November 1966, April 1968, January 1969, December 1969.

A 23.3.b
*Third edition, Corgi printings:* London: Corgi, [1965].

#XN7251. 6s. Reprinted 1966 and 1968.

A 23.3.c
*Third edition, Popular printing:* New York: Popular Library, [1974].

#445-03039-150. $1.50.

A 24 THE HAT ON THE BED

A 24.1.a
*First edition, first printing (1963)*

# JOHN O'HARA

# THE HAT
# ON THE BED

RANDOM HOUSE · NEW YORK

A 24.1.a: 5 $^5/_8''$ × 8 $^3/_8''$

[i–x] [1–3] 4–405 [406]; first page of each story unnumbered

[1–13]¹⁶

*Contents:*   pp. i–ii: blank; p. iii: half title; p. iv: 'BOOKS BY JOHN O'HARA'; p. v: title;
p. vi: copyright; p. vii: *'To William Maxwell';* p. viii: blank; pp. ix–x: 'CONTENTS'; p. 1:
half title; p. 2: blank; pp. 3–405: text, headed 'AGATHA'; p. 406: blank.

  *24 stories:* "Agatha," "Aunt Anna," "Eminent Domain,"* "Exterior: with Figure," "The
Flatted Saxophone," "The Friends of Miss Julia,"* "The Glendale People," "The
Golden,"* "How Can I Tell You?" "I Know That, Roy,"* "John Barton Rosedale, Actors'
Actor," "The Locomobile," "The Manager," "The Man on the Tractor," "The Mayor,"*
"Ninety Minutes Away,"* "Our Friend the Sea," "The Public Dorothy," "The Ride from
Mauch Chunk," "Saturday Lunch," "Teddy and the Special Friends,"* "The Twinkle in
His Eye,"* "The Windowpane Check,"* "Yucca Knolls." Asterisks follow previously
unpublished stories.

*Typography and paper:*   Times Roman, 10 point on 12. 6¹/₂″ (6¹³/₁₆″) × 3¹³/₁₆″; 39
lines per page. Running heads: rectos, story titles; versos, 'THE HAT ON THE BED'.
Wove paper.

*Binding:*   Strong blue green (#160) V cloth (smooth). Front goldstamped: 'JOHN
O'HARA'. Spine goldstamped on three deep blue panels: '[top panel] *John O'Hara* |
[middle panel] THE HAT | ON | THE BED | [bottom panel] *Random* | *House* |
[Random House device below panels]'. Top and bottom edges trimmed; fore edge
rough trimmed. Top edge stained greenish blue. Green and yellow bands top and
bottom. Medium yellow green (#120) endpapers.

*Dust jacket:*   Lettered on light tan background. Front: '[greenish blue] THE HAT ON |
THE BED | [black] A | COLLECTION | OF 24 NEW | STORIES BY | [greenish blue]
JOHN | O'HARA | [black] A RANDOM HOUSE BOOK'. Spine: '[greenish blue] THE |
HAT | ON | THE | BED | [black] JOHN | O'HARA | [greenish blue Random House
device] | [black] RANDOM | HOUSE'. Back: *'Books by* JOHN O'HARA'. Front flap has
blurb for *49 Stories* and *Hat.* Back flap lists books by O'Hara in Modern Library and
Vintage Books.

*Publication:*   47,745 copies of the first printing. Published 28 November 1963. $5.95.
Copyright #A671878.

*Printing:*   Set, printed, and bound by H. Wolff, New York.

*Locations:*   LC (FEB-4 1964), Lilly (dj), MJB (dj), PSt.

*Note:*   Galley proofs and page proofs are at PSt.

THE HAT ON
THE BED
A
COLLECTION
OF 24 NEW
STORIES BY
JOHN
O'HARA

A RANDOM HOUSE BOOK

THE
HAT
ON
THE
BED

JOHN
O'HARA

RANDOM
HOUSE

THE HAT
ON THE BED

John O'Hara

Jacket design by Janque Wong

Dust jacket for A24.1.a

A 24.1.b
*Second printing:* New York: Random House, [1964].

On copyright page: *'Second Printing'*. 6,947 copies.

A 24.1.c
*Third printing:* New York: Random House, 1964.

Not seen. 3,320 copies.

A 24.1.d
*Fourth printing:* New York: Random House, 1964.

Not seen. 2,944 copies.

A 24.2.a
*First English edition, first printing (1964)*

JOHN O'HARA

# THE HAT ON THE BED

LONDON: THE CRESSET PRESS

A 24.2.a: $5^7/_{16}$″ × $8^1/_4$″

*Copyright page:* '© *Copyright* 1962–63, *by John O'Hara* | *First published in Great Britain in* 1964 *by* | *The Cresset Press,* 11 *Fitzroy Square, London, W.* 1. | [3 roman lines] | *Printed in Great Britain* | *by Ebenezer Baylis & Son, Ltd.* | *The Trinity Press, Worcester and London'.*

[i–viii] 1–405 [406–408]

[1] 2–13¹⁶

*Contents:*   p. i: half title; p. ii: *'Other books by John O'Hara';* p. iii: title; p. iv: copyright; p. v: dedication; p. vi: blank; p. vii: *'CONTENTS';* p. viii: blank; pp. 1–405: text, headed 'AGATHA'; pp. 406–408: blank.

Contains 24 stories.

*Typography and paper:*   39 lines per page. Wove paper.

*Binding:*   Deep olive (#108) paper-covered boards with V grain. Spine goldstamped: '[on red panel] [rule] | THE HAT | ON | THE BED | JOHN | O'HARA | [rule] | [below panel] CRESSET'. All edges trimmed. White wove calendered endpapers.

*Dust jacket:*   '[black] JOHN O'HARA | [white] THE HAT ON | THE BED | *24 new stories* | [illustration of bed with hat on red panel]'. Spine: '[vertically] [black] JOHN O'HARA | [red] THE HAT ON | THE BED [black] *24 new stories* | [horizontally] [reduced bed illustration on red panel] | [black] *Cresset Press'.* Back has photo of O'Hara and biographical note. Front flap has blurb for *Hat.* Back flap blank.

*Publication:*   Unknown number of copies of the first printing. Published 27 May 1964. 21s.

*Locations:*   BL (5 MAY 64), Bod (26 JUN 1964), Lilly (dj), MJB (dj), PSt.

A 24.2.b
*Second printing:* London: Barrie & Jenkins, [1973].

A 24.3.a
*Third edition, Bantam printings:* New York: Bantam, [1965].

#N2889. 95¢. 5 printings.

A 24.3.b
*Third edition, Corgi printing:* [London]: Corgi, [1966].

#EN7370. 7s. 6d.

A 24.3.c
*Third edition, Popular printing:* New York: Popular Library, [1975].

#445-03068-150. $1.50.

A 25 THE HORSE KNOWS THE WAY

A 25.1.a
*First edition, trade printing (1964)*

# JOHN O'HARA

# THE HORSE KNOWS THE WAY

*Over the river and through the wood*
*To grandfather's house we'll go;*
*The horse knows the way*
*To carry the sleigh,*
*Through the white and drifted snow.*

—Thanksgiving Day,
by LYDIA MARIA CHILD (1802-1880)

RANDOM HOUSE · NEW YORK

A 25.1.a: 5⅝" × 8⁵/₁₆"

[A–D] [i–v] vi–vii [viii–ix] x [1–3] 4–429 [430–434]; first page of each story unnumbered

[1–14]¹⁶

*Contents:*   pp. A–D: blank; p. i: half title; p. ii: 'BOOKS BY JOHN O'HARA; p. iii: title; p. iv: copyright; pp. v–vii: 'FOREWORD'; p. viii: blank; pp. ix–x: 'CONTENTS'; p. 1: half title; p. 2: blank; pp. 3–429: text, headed 'ALL TIED UP'; pp. 430–434: blank.

   *28 stories:* "All Tied Up," "The Answer Depends," "Arnold Stone," "At the Window," "Aunt Fran," "The Bonfire," "The Brain,"* "Can I Stay Here?" "Clayton Bunter,"* "The Clear Track," "The Gun,"* "The Hardware Man," "His Excellency," "The House on the Corner," "I Can't Thank You Enough,"* "In the Mist,"* "I Spend My Days in Longing," "The Jet Set,"* "The Lawbreaker," "The Madeline Wherry Case," "Mrs. Allanson," "The Pig," "School,"* "The Staring Game," "The Victim,"* "What's the Good of Knowing?" "The Whole Cherry Pie," "Zero." Asterisks follow previously unpublished stories.

*Typography and paper:*   Times Roman, 11 point on 13. 6¹¹⁄₁₆″ (7″) × 4¹⁄₁₆″; 37 lines per page. Running heads: rectos, story titles; versos, 'THE HORSE KNOWS THE WAY'. Wove paper.

*Binding:*   Greenish blue (#169) V cloth (smooth). Front goldstamped: 'JOHN O'HARA'. Spine goldstamped on 3 black panels: '[top panel] *John O'Hara* | [middle panel] THE HORSE | KNOWS | THE WAY | [bottom panel] *Random* | *House* | [goldstamped Random House device below panels]'. Top and bottom edges trimmed; fore edge rough trimmed. Top edge stained gray. Reddish orange (#36) endpapers.

*Dust jacket:*   Front, spine, and back lettered on greenish blue background. Front: '[white] THE HORSE | KNOWS | THE WAY | [black] A | COLLECTION | OF 28 NEW | STORIES BY | [white] JOHN | O'HARA | [black] A RANDOM HOUSE BOOK'. Spine: '[white] THE HORSE | KNOWS | THE WAY | JOHN | O'HARA | [black Random House device] | [white] RANDOM HOUSE'. Back: '*Books by* JOHN O'HARA'. Front flap has blurbs for *Horse.* Back flap lists O'Hara's titles in Modern Library and Vintage Books.

*Publication:*   49,965 copies of the first printing. Published 26 November 1964. $5.95. Copyright #A872369.

*Printing:*   Set, printed, and bound by H. Wolff, New York.

*Locations:*   LC (AUG-8 1966), Lilly (dj), MJB (dj), PSt.

*Note:*   Galley proofs are at PSt.

$5.95
1964

THE HORSE
KNOWS THE WAY

*John O'Hara*

For a while, at least, this will be my last book of short stories. Thus John O'Hara begins his foreword to this volume, the fourth, he has completed since, two years ago, he returned to the short-story form after eleven years of abstinence.

The fruitfulness of that later period part-time attention, for he was doing other work as well, to the short story has been prodigious. *Assembly* (1961), *The Cape Cod Lighter* (1962), *The Hat on the Bed* (1963), and now (1964) *The Horse Knows the Way*. The four volumes contain a total of 101 stories, astonishingly varied in subject and form, and of a degree of excellence unsurpassed in our time. The new volume should extend the critical acclaim and reader acceptance, enjoyed... greater for the second than... for the first, and still greater for the third... than for the second.

It is reassuring that Mr. O'Hara goes on in his foreword to make it clear that though he is refraining from short stories "for a while," he is not for a moment going to refrain from writing.

jacket design by Anita Karl

THE HORSE
KNOWS
THE WAY

A
COLLECTION
OF 28 NEW
STORIES BY

JOHN
O'HARA

A RANDOM HOUSE BOOK

THE HORSE
KNOWS
THE WAY

JOHN
O'HARA

RANDOM HOUSE

*Books by* JOHN O'HARA

Appointment in Samarra
The Doctor's Son and Other Stories
Butterfield 8
Hope of Heaven
Files on Parade
Pal Joey
Pipe Night
Hellbox
A Rage to Live
The Farmers Hotel
Sweet and Sour
Ten North Frederick
A Family Party
Selected Short Stories
From the Terrace
Ourselves to Know
Sermons and Soda-Water: A Trilogy
Five Plays
Assembly
The Big Laugh
The Cape Cod Lighter
Elizabeth Appleton
49 Stories
The Hat on the Bed
The Horse Knows the Way

Books by
JOHN O'HARA

Available in
THE MODERN LIBRARY

Appointment in Samarra, ML 42
Butterfield 8, ML 323
Selected Short Stories, ML 211
49 Stories, G 88

Available in
VINTAGE BOOKS

Butterfield 8, V 49

RANDOM HOUSE, INC.
457 Madison Avenue, New York 22, New York
Publishers of The American College Dictionary
and The Modern Library

PRINTED IN U.S.A.

Dust jacket for A 25.1.a

*Review copy:* Unbound galley proofs. White paper label printed in red on first galley: '[all the following within single-rule frame] ADVANCE PROOFS | [bracket] *UNCORRECTED* [bracket] | TITLE: [typed] THE HORSE KNOWS THE WAY | [printed] AUTHOR: [typed] John O'Hara | [printed] PRICE: [typed] $5.95 | [printed] PUBLICA-TION DATE: [typed] November 26, 1964 | [printed] *All information is tentative. Please check for* | *final details.* | RANDOM HOUSE, INC. | 457 MADISON AVE. | New York 22, N.Y. | [Random House device]'. Location: MJB.

A 25.1.b
*First edition, limited printing*

*Certificate of limitation:* 'Of the first edition of | THE HORSE KNOWS THE WAY | *two hundred and fifty copies have been printed on* | *special paper and specially bound.* | *Each copy is signed by the author and numbered.* | [number] | [rule] | [signature]'.

Same pagination and collation as trade printing.

*Contents:* Same as trade printing, but with certificate of limitation on p. A.

*Paper:* Laid, with vertical chains.

*Binding:* Dark reddish brown (#44) natural finish buckram. Front goldstamped with facsimile of O'Hara's signature. Spine goldstamped on blindstamped oval panel: 'THE | HORSE | KNOWS | THE WAY | [thick rule] | JOHN | O'HARA | [below panel] [Random House device] | [thick rule] | *Random House'*. Top and bottom edges trimmed; fore edge rough trimmed. Top edge stained yellow. Reddish brown (#40) endpapers.

*Dust jacket:* Unprinted glassine dust jacket. No box.

*Publication:* Published simultaneously with trade printing. $10. Priority of printing undetermined.

*Locations:* Lilly, MJB, PSt.

A 25.1.c
*Third printing:* New York: Random House, 1965.

Not seen.

A 25.1.d
*Pirated printing*

Offset reprint of first edition, probably printed in Taiwan, ca. 1965. On copyright page: 'FIRST PRINTING'. Location: MJB.

A 25.2
*First English edition, first printing (1965)*

JOHN O'HARA

# THE HORSE KNOWS THE WAY

*Over the river and through the wood*
*To grandfather's house we'll go;*
*The horse knows the way*
*To carry the sleigh,*
*Through the white and drifted snow.*
—THANKSGIVING DAY,
*by* Lydia Maria Child (1802–1880)

*LONDON*
THE CRESSET PRESS

A 25.2: 5$^7$/$_{16}$″ × 8$^1$/$_4$″

*Copyright page:*  '© *Copyright* 1963, 1964, *by John O'Hara* | *First published in Great Britain in* 1965 *by* | *The Cresset Press,* 11 *Fitzroy Square, London, W.* 1 | [3 lines of roman] | *Printed in Great Britain* | *by Ebenezer Baylis & Son, Ltd.* | *The Trinity Press, Worcester, and London'.*

[i–iv] v–vi [vii–viii] 1–408

[1] 2–13$^{16}$

*Contents:*  p. i: half title; p. ii: books by O'Hara; p. iii: title; p. iv: copyright; pp. v–vi: *'FOREWORD';* p. vii: *'CONTENTS';* p. viii: blank; pp. 1–408: text, headed 'ALL TIED UP'.

Contains 28 stories.

*Typography and paper:*  39 lines per page. Wove paper.

*Binding:*  Dark olive (#108) paper-covered boards with B grain (linen). Spine gold-stamped on red panel: '[rule] | THE HORSE | KNOWS | THE WAY | JOHN | O'HARA | [rule] | [below panel] CRESSET'. All edges trimmed. White wove calendered end-papers.

*Dust jacket:*  Front and spine lettered on red background. Front: '[white] THE HORSE | KNOWS | THE WAY | [black] A COLLECTION OF | 28 NEW STORIES | [white] JOHN | O'HARA'. Spine: '[vertically] [white] JOHN O'HARA [black] THE HORSE | KNOWS THE WAY | [horizontally] CRESSET'. Back lists books by O'Hara. Front flap has note on O'Hara. Back flap blank.

*Publication:*  Unknown number of copies of the first printing. Published 24 May 1965. 21s.

*Locations:*  BL (30 APR 65), Bod (30 JUN 1965), MJB (dj), PSt.

A 25.3.a
*Third edition, Bantam printings:* New York: Bantam, [1966].

#N3103. 95¢. 2 printings.

A 25.3.b
*Third edition, Corgi printings:* [London]: Corgi, [1966].

#EN7438. 7s. 6d. 2 printings.

A 25.3.c
*Third edition, Popular printing:* New York: Popular Library, [1975].

#445-03057-150. $1.50.

A 26 THE LOCKWOOD CONCERN

A 26.1.a
*First edition, trade printing (1965)*

# THE LOCKWOOD CONCERN

A NOVEL *by*

## John O'Hara

RANDOM HOUSE · NEW YORK

A 26.1.a: 5⅝″ × 8⁵⁄₁₆″

*First Printing*

© *Copyright, 1965, by John O'Hara*

All rights reserved under International and Pan-American Copyright
Conventions. Published in New York by Random House, Inc., and
simultaneously in Toronto, Canada, by Random House of Canada
Limited.

*Library of Congress Catalog Card Number: 65-21227*

MANUFACTURED IN THE UNITED STATES OF AMERICA BY

THE HADDON CRAFTSMEN, SCRANTON, PA.

[i–viii] [1–2] 3–269 [270–272] 273–342 [343–344] 345–407 [408]

[1–13]¹⁶

*Contents:*  pp. i–ii: blank; p. iii: half title; p. iv: 'BOOKS BY JOHN O'HARA'; p. v: title;
p. vi: copyright; p. vii: 'TO | *Barklie McKee Henry* | WHO MANY TIMES HAS PROVED
HIMSELF A FRIEND'; p. viii: blank; p. 1: 'BOOK | • 1 • '; p. 2: blank; pp. 3–407: text; p.
408: blank.

*Typography and paper:*  Times Roman, 10 point on 12. 7¹/₈″ (7³/₈″) × 4¹/₈″; 43 lines
per page. No running heads. Wove paper.

*Binding:*  Vivid green (#139) V cloth (smooth). Front goldstamped with facsimile of
O'Hara's signature. Spine goldstamped on 2 red panels: '[top panel] [Random House
device] | [thick and thin rules] | THE | LOCKWOOD | CONCERN | John O'Hara |
[thin and thick rules] | [lower panel] RANDOM HOUSE'. Top edge trimmed and
stained red. Green and yellow bands at top and bottom present in some copies; about
20,000 copies of the first printing lack these bands. Light bluish green (#163) endpapers.

*Dust jacket:*  Front and spine lettered on light green background. Front: '[blue] THE |
LOCKWOOD | CONCERN | [white] A NOVEL BY | [red] JOHN | O'HARA | [white] A
RANDOM HOUSE BOOK'. Spine: '[vertically] [blue] THE LOCKWOOD CONCERN |
[red] JOHN O'HARA | [horizontally, white] [Random House device] | RANDOM |
HOUSE'. Back: '*Books by* JOHN O'HARA'. Front and back flaps have blurbs for *LC*.

*Publication:*  59,652 copies of the first printing. Published 25 November 1965. $5.95.
Copyright #A805667.

*Printing:*  Manufactured by Haddon Craftsmen, Scranton, Pa.

*Locations:*  LC (DEC 20 1965), Lilly (dj), MJB (dj), PSt.

*Note:*  Galley proofs and page proofs are at PSt.

*Textual note:*  276.9–10: 'St.' should read 'St. Mark's'. 375.32: 'of' corrected to 'or' in
fourth printing (A 26.1.d).

*Review copy:*  Spiral-bound proof in blue paper covers, with white label on front
printed in red: '[within single-rule frame] ADVANCE PROOFS | [bracket] *UNCOR-
RECTED* [bracket] | TITLE: [typed] THE LOCKWOOD CONCERN | [printed] AUTHOR:
[typed] John O'Hara | [printed] PRICE: [typed] $5.95 | [printed] PUBLICATION DATE:
[typed] 11/25/65 | [printed] *All information is tentative. Please check for | final details.*
| RANDOM HOUSE, INC. | 457 MADISON AVE. | New York 22, N.Y. | [Random House
device]'. Location: MJB.

THE
LOCKWOOD
CONCERN

A NOVEL BY

JOHN
O'HARA

A RANDOM HOUSE BOOK

THE LOCKWOOD CONCERN
JOHN O'HARA

RANDOM
HOUSE

Moses Lockwood (born 1811)

Abraham Lockwood (born 1840)

George Bingham Lockwood (born 1873)

George Bingham Lockwood II (born 1900)

These are the dominant figures in this major novel, which spans four generations of the Lockwood family of Swedish Haven, Pennsylvania. Before Moses Lockwood, the line was hazy and indefinite; and thus it was Abraham's necessity to look forward rather than back in formulating his plans—plans that Moses could never have dreamed of.

"Abraham Lockwood's plan was more than a plan—which was only a method—and more than an ambition—which was only a desire. It was a Concern . . . the embodiment of a yearning for security, beginning with Moses Lockwood . . ."

The Lockwood Concern was never directly explained by Abraham to his son George, who nevertheless absorbed it and did what he could with his own version, as the George for the third-generation Lockwood, the culmination of the narrative is placed in George Lockwood.

Books by JOHN O'HARA

Appointment in Samarra
The Doctor's Son and Other Stories
Butterfield 8
Hope of Heaven
Files on Parade
Pal Joey
Pipe Night
Hellbox
A Rage to Live
The Farmers Hotel
Sweet and Sour
Ten North Frederick
A Family Party
Selected Short Stories
From the Terrace
Ourselves to Know
Sermons and Soda-Water: A Trilogy
Five Plays
Assembly
The Big Laugh
The Cape Cod Lighter
Elizabeth Appleton
49 Stories
The Hat on the Bed
The Horse Knows the Way
The Lockwood Concern

(Continued from front flap)

of such. And took upon the patrimony of George Bingham Lockwood II.

These Lockwood men were strong-willed, shrewd, aggressive, and each generation gained over the predecessor in self-assurance and attractiveness. But something important was missing in the Lockwoods and in their Concern. What was missing will become apparent to the reader as he follows the intricate and subtle saga whereby this exciting climax is unlocked and resolved.

It should also be apparent that John O'Hara's concern is bigger than the Lockwoods or Eastern Pennsylvania, or even than the century of American social history that comes to life in these pages. This novel about the vanity of human wishes is one of the author's greatest achievements.

JACKET DESIGN BY MURIEL NASSER

Random House, Inc.
457 Madison Avenue, New York 22, New York
Publishers of The American College Dictionary
and The Modern Library
PRINTED IN U.S.A.

A 26.1.b
*Limited printing*

*Certificate of limitation:* 'Of the first edition of | THE LOCKWOOD CONCERN | *three hundred copies have been printed on* | *special paper and specially bound.* | *Each copy is signed by the author and numbered.* | [signature] | [number] | [rule]'.

[i–x] [1–2] 3–269 [270–272] 273–342 [343–344] 345–407 [408]

[1]¹⁶ (1₁+1) [2–13]¹⁶

*Contents:*   Same as trade printing, but with extra leaf tipped in after first leaf; p. iii: certificate of limitation; p. iv: blank.

*Paper:*   Laid, with vertical chains.

*Binding:*   Blackish blue (#188) natural finish buckram. Front goldstamped with O'Hara's signature. Spine goldstamped: '[following 6 lines on blindstamped oval panel] THE | LOCKWOOD | CONCERN | [thick rule] | JOHN | O'HARA | [Random House device] | [thick rule] | *Random House'*. Top edge trimmed; fore and bottom edges rough trimmed. Top edge stained greenish blue. Blue and white bands at top and bottom. Light bluish green (#163) endpapers.

*Dust jacket and box:*   Unprinted cellophane dust wrapper. Unprinted gray box.

*Publication:*   Published simultaneously with the trade printing. $12.50. Priority of printing undetermined.

*Locations:*   Lilly, MJB.

A 26.1.c
*Third printing:* New York: Random House, [1965].

On copyright page: *'Second Printing'.* 7,500 copies.

A 26.1.d
*Fourth printing:* New York: Random House, [1966].

On copyright page: *'Third Printing, February 1966'.*

A 26.1.e
*First edition, first English printing (1966)*

# THE
# LOCKWOOD
# CONCERN

A NOVEL *by*

# John O'Hara

HODDER AND STOUGHTON

A 26.1.e: 5⁷/₁₆″ × 8⁷/₁₆″

*Copyright page:* 'Printed in Great Britain | © Copyright, 1965, by John O'Hara |
Reproduced from the U.S. edition by arrangement with | Random House, New York |
Printed in Great Britain for Hodder and Stoughton Limited | St. Paul's House, Warwick
Lane, London, E.C. 4 | by Billing & Sons Limited, Guildford and London'.

Same pagination as Random House printing

[A] B–I K–N¹⁶

*Contents:* Same as Random House printing.

*Paper:* Wove.

*Binding:* Dark olive green (#126) paper-covered boards with B grain (linen). Spine
goldstamped: '[vertically] THE LOCKWOOD CONCERN | JOHN O'HARA
[horizontally] [Hodder & Stoughton device]'. All edges trimmed. White wove endpapers.

*Dust jacket:* Front, spine, and back lettered on tan. Front has vertical black rules and
vertical white column and 3 figures in nineties costume. Front: '[dark red] JOHN |
O'HARA | [dark tan scrollwork] | [black] THE | LOCKWOOD | CONCERN'. Spine:
'[vertically] [black] THE LOCKWOOD CONCERN | [red] JOHN O'HARA | [horizon-
tally] [black and white Hodder & Stoughton device]'. Back lists books by O'Hara. Front
and back flaps have blurb for *LC*.

*Publication:* 16,000 copies. Published April 1966. 25s.

*Locations:* BL (23 Mar 66), Bod (31 MAR 1966), Lilly (dj), MJB (dj), PSt.

A 26.1.f
*Second printing:* London: Hodder & Stoughton, 1966.

Not seen.

A 26.1.g
*Third printing:* London: Hodder & Stoughton, 1966.

Not seen.

A 26.1.h
*Book Club printing:* London: The Book Club, [1966].

A 26.2
*Second edition:* New York: Signet, [1966].

#Q2876. 95¢. 4 printings.

A 26.3.a
*Third edition, first printing:* [London]: Four Square, [1966].

Not seen. "Open market" edition sold in Australia and Canada.

A 26.3.b
*Third edition, second printing:* [London]: Four Square, [1967].

In printed paper box. #1816. $1.75. On copyright page: 'Special Four Square Edition
for limited distribution only November 1966 | THIS FIRST FOUR SQUARE EDITION
MAY 1967'.

A 27 MY TURN

A 27.1
*First edition, only printing (1966)*

# MY TURN

## JOHN O'HARA

RANDOM HOUSE · NEW YORK

A 27.1: 5⁵/₈″ × 8³/₈″

[i–vi] vii–viii [ix–x] [1–2] 3–214

[1–7]¹⁶

*Contents:*   p. i: half title; p. ii: 'BOOKS BY JOHN O'HARA'; p. iii: title; p. iv: copyright; p. v: '*To* | JIM FORRESTAL'; p. vi: blank; pp. vii–ix: 'FOREWORD'; p. x: blank; p. 1: half title; p. 2: blank; pp. 3–214: text, headed '*October 3, 1964*'. Columns from *Newsday;* see E 5.

*Typography and paper:*   Primer, 11 point on 15. 6″ (6³/₄″) × 3¹³/₁₆″; 29 lines per page. Running heads: rectos, dates; versos, 'MY TURN'. Wove paper.

*Binding:*   Dark blue (#183) V cloth (smooth). Front goldstamped with facsimile of O'Hara's signature. Spine goldstamped: '[5 rules] | MY | TURN | [ 2 rules] | John | O'Hara | [2 rules] | [Random House device] | RANDOM | HOUSE'. Top and bottom edges trimmed; fore edge rough trimmed. Top edge stained red. Grayish red (#19) endpapers.

*Dust jacket:*   Front and spine lettered on black background. Front: '[outlined in white] MY | TURN | [orange] *fifty-three pieces* | *by* | [yellow] | *John* | *O'Hara* | [gray] *A Random House Book*'. Spine: '[vertically] [orange] MY | TURN [yellow] *John O'Hara* | [horizontally, white] [Random House device] | *Random* | *House*'. Back has photo of O'Hara. Front flap has blurb for *MT*. Back flap: '*Books by John O'Hara*'.

*Publication:*   8,432 copies of the first printing. Published 15 April 1966. $4.95. Copyright #A832020.

*Printing:*   Manufactured by H. Wolff, New York.

*Locations:*   LC (APR 27 1966), Lilly (dj), MJB (dj), PSt.

*Note:*   Galley proofs are at PSt.

A 27.2
*Second edition:* [New York]: Signet, [1967].

#T 3196. 75¢.

Timidity of opinion will get you nowhere, and writing for anyone's approval but your own will get you there fast. So I shall make no effort to present my opinions in equivocal style. You will always know which side I'm on... What I intend to offer in these messages are comments on the human race in my time, as seen by my prejudiced eye."

With this statement of intention, John O'Hara launched his weekly column, "My Turn," on October 3, 1964, and for fifty-three consecutive weeks his unbridled typewriter gave abundant evidence that he means what he had announced. Ranging over an astonishingly wide variety of topics and personalities, his "prejudiced eye" takes a hard look at politics and politicians (domestic and foreign), education, morality, journalism, writers and writing, movies and television (and their personnel), and a great deal more of the passing show. His commentary, witty and astringent, sometimes slashing, will delight some readers as much as it enrages others. One thing is certain: there will be no monotonous uniformity of opinion about the contents of this book.

Featured and syndicated by Newsday, the Nassau County, New York, weekly, "My Turn" appeared in about forty-five newspapers throughout the country. What happened in this chapter of the history of journalism, which ended with the publication of the fifty-third column on October 2, 1965, is fully covered in Mr. O'Hara's foreword to this volume.

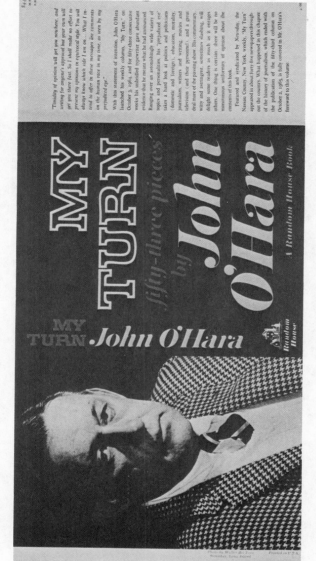

MY TURN

fifty-three pieces

by John O'Hara

A Random House Book

MY TURN · John O'Hara

Random House

Photo by Walter de Tore
Newsday, Long Island

Printed in U.S.A.

**Books by John O'Hara**

Appointment in Samarra
The Doctor's Son and Other Stories
Butterfield 8
Hope of Heaven
Files on Parade
Pal Joey
Pipe Night
Hellbox

A Rage to Live
The Farmers Hotel
Sweet and Sour
Ten North Frederick
A Family Party
Selected Short Stories
From the Terrace
Ourselves to Know
Sermons and Soda-Water: A Trilogy
Five Plays
Assembly
The Big Laugh
The Cape Cod Lighter
Elizabeth Appleton
49 Stories
The Hat on the Bed
The Horse Knows the Way
The Lockwood Concern
My Turn

Dust jacket for A27.1

A 28 WAITING FOR WINTER

A 28.1.a
*First edition, trade printing (1966)*

# JOHN O'HARA

# WAITING FOR WINTER

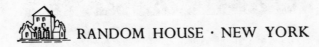 RANDOM HOUSE · NEW YORK

A 28.1.a: 5⅝″ × 8⅜″

---

*First Printing*

© *Copyright, 1964, 1965, 1966, by John O'Hara*

*All rights reserved under International and Pan-American Copyright Conventions. Published in New York by Random House, Inc., and simultaneously in Toronto, Canada, by Random House of Canada Limited.*

*Library of Congress Catalog Card Number: 66-21459*

*Manufactured in the United States of America by H. Wolff, New York*

*Of the twenty-one stories in this book, six first appeared in* The New Yorker, *three first appeared in* The Saturday Evening Post, *and one appeared in* Sports Illustrated. *The remaining stories are herein published for the first time.*

---

[A–D] [i–v] vi [vii–viii] [1–3] 4–466 [467–468]; first page of each story unnumbered [1–15]¹⁶

*Contents:* pp. A–C: blank; p. D: 'BOOKS BY JOHN O'HARA'; p. i: half title; p. ii: blank; p. iii: title; p. iv: copyright; pp. v–vi: 'AUTHOR'S NOTE'; p. vii: 'CONTENTS'; p. viii: blank; p. 1: half title; p. 2: blank; pp. 3–466: text, headed 'AFTERNOON WALTZ'; pp. 467–468: blank.

*21 stories:* "Afternoon Waltz," "Andrea,"* "The Assistant," "Fatimas and Kisses," "Flight,"* "The Gambler," "The General,"* "A Good Location," "The Jama," "James Francis and the Star,"* "Late, Late Show,"* "Leonard," "Natica Jackson,"* "The Neighborhood," "The Pomeranian,"* "The Portly Gentleman,"* "The Skeletons,"* "The Tackle," "The Way to Majorca,"* "The Weakling,"* "Yostie." Asterisks follow previously unpublished stories.

*Typography and paper:* Times Roman, 10 point on 12. 6⁹/₁₆″ (6⁷/₈) × 4¹/₈″; 41 lines per page. Running heads: rectos, story titles; versos, 'WAITING FOR WINTER'. Wove paper.

*Binding:* Dark red (#16) V cloth (smooth). Front goldstamped: 'JOHN O'HARA'. Spine goldstamped on 3 very dark red panels: '[top panel] *John O'Hara* | [middle panel] WAITING | FOR | WINTER | [bottom panel] *Random* | *House* | [Random House device below panels]'. Top and bottom edges trimmed; fore edge rough trimmed. Top edge stained red. Red and yellow bands at top and bottom. Brownish orange (#54) endpapers.

*Dust jacket:* Front and spine lettered on red. Front: '[white] WAITING | FOR | WINTER | [black] A | COLLECTION | OF 21 NEW | STORIES BY | [white] JOHN | O'HARA | [black] A RANDOM HOUSE BOOK'. Spine: '[white] WAITING | FOR | WINTER | JOHN | O'HARA | [black Random House device] | [white] RANDOM HOUSE'. Back lists books by O'Hara. Front flap has blurb for *WFW*. Back flap lists books by O'Hara published in Modern Library and Vintage Books.

*Publication:* 47,095 copies of the first printing. Published 24 November 1966. $5.95. Copyright #A894173.

*Printing:* Manufactured by H. Wolff, New York.

*Locations:* LC (FEB 27 1967), Lilly (dj), MJB (dj), PSt.

*Note:* Galley proofs are at MJB and PSt.

*Review copy:* Spiral-bound proof with blue paper covers. 'ADVANCE PROOFS | Uncorrected | [rule] | WAITING FOR WINTER | by | John O'Hara | [rule] | PRICE: | PUBLICATION | DATE: | [rule] | RANDOM HOUSE, INC. | 457 Madison Avenue, New York 22, N.Y. | [Random House device]'. Location: MJB.

$5.95

JOHN O'HARA

WAITING
FOR
WINTER

This collection of twenty-one new stories—including four of novella length—is John O'Hara's fifth volume of stories since, in 1960, he began to write them again after an eleven-year abstention.

In every year from 1961 to the present (except 1963, when his novel *The Lockwood Concern* appeared), he has delivered to his publishers for fall publication the manuscript of an outstanding volume of new stories. Thus, in six years (a period in which he also published three novels, a volume of five plays, and a book of essays) Mr. O'Hara has written the 122 stories, long and short, that make up the five collections.

Even if the stories had been only moderately good, this abundance would be astonishing; but since he has maintained throughout such a high level of excellence, variety, and significance in his production, he now has only himself to surpass.

WAITING
FOR
WINTER

JOHN
O'HARA

RANDOM HOUSE

BOOKS BY
JOHN
O'HARA

Appointment in Samarra
The Doctor's Son and Other Stories
Butterfield 8
Hope of Heaven
Files on Parade
Pal Joey
Pipe Night
Hellbox
A Rage to Live
The Farmers Hotel
Sweet and Sour
Ten North Frederick
A Family Party
Selected Short Stories
From the Terrace
Ourselves to Know
Sermons and Soda-Water: A Trilogy
Five Plays
Assembly
The Big Laugh
The Cape Cod Lighter
Elizabeth Appleton
49 Stories
The Hat on the Bed
The Horse Knows the Way
The Lockwood Concern
My Turn
Waiting for Winter

BOOKS BY
JOHN
O'HARA

AVAILABLE IN

THE MODERN LIBRARY

Appointment in Samarra, ML. 42
Butterfield 8, ML. 323
Selected Short Stories, ML. 211
49 Stories, G 55

AVAILABLE IN

VINTAGE BOOKS

Butterfield 8, v 49

Jacket design by Leon Karl

Random House, Inc.
457 Madison Avenue, New York, New York 10022
Publisher of The Random House Dictionary of the
English Language, The American College Dictionary
and The Modern Library

PRINTED IN U.S.A.

Dust jacket for A 28.1.a

A 28.1.b
*Limited printing*

*Statement of limitation:* 'Of the first edition of | WAITING FOR WINTER | *three hundred copies have been printed on* | *special paper and specially bound.* | *Each copy is signed by the author and numbered.* | [signature] | [number] | [rule]'.

[A–F] [i–v] vi [vii–viii] [1–3] 4–466 [467–468]; first page of each story unnumbered

[1]¹⁶ (1+1₁) [2–15]¹⁶

*Contents:* Same as trade printing, but with extra leaf tipped in before first gathering; p. A: certificate of limitation; p. B: blank.

*Paper:* Laid, with horizontal chains.

*Binding:* Deep red (#13) natural finish buckram. Front goldstamped with facsimile of O'Hara's signature. Spine goldstamped: '[following 6 lines on blindstamped oval panel] WAITING | FOR | WINTER | [thick rule] | JOHN | O'HARA | [below panel] [Random House device] | [thick rule] | *Random House*'. Top and bottom edges trimmed; fore edge rough trimmed. Top edge stained black. Reddish brown (#43) endpapers.

*Dust jacket and box:* Unprinted cellophane jacket. Unprinted gray box.

*Publication:* Published simultaneously with trade printing. $12.50. Priority of printing undetermined.

*Locations:* Lilly, MJB, PSt.

A 28.1.c
*First edition, first English printing (1967)*

# WAITING FOR WINTER

BY

## JOHN O'HARA

### HODDER AND STOUGHTON

A 28.1.c: 5$^7$/$_{16}$″ × 8$^1$/$_2$″

*Copyright page:* 'First printed in Great Britain 1967 | © Copyright, 1964, 1965, 1966 by John O'Hara | Reproduced from the U.S. edition by arrangement with Random House, New York | Printed in Great Britain for Hodder and Stoughton Limited, St. Paul's House, | Warwick Lane, London, E.C.4, by Fletcher & Son Ltd, Norwich'.

[A–B] [i–v] vi [vii–viii] [1–3] 4–466 [467–470]; first page of each story unnumbered [1–15]¹⁶

*Contents:*   pp. A–B: blank; p. i: half title; p. ii: 'BOOKS BY JOHN O'HARA'; p. iii: title; p. iv: copyright; pp. v–vi: 'AUTHOR'S NOTE'; p. vii: 'CONTENTS'; p. viii: blank; p. 1: half title; p. 2: blank; pp. 3–466: text; pp. 467–470: blank.

Contains 21 stories.

*Paper:*   Wove paper.

*Binding:*   Olive green (#126) paper-covered boards, with V grain. Spine gold-stamped vertically: 'Waiting For Winter John O'Hara | [horizontally] [Hodder & Stoughton device]'. All edges trimmed. Top edge stained gray. White wove calendered endpapers.

*Dust jacket:*   Front and spine have illustration of baseball glove with pack of Camels, dice, coins, matches, toy car, and picture of nude. Front: '[red] WAITING | FOR | WINTER | [black] JOHN O'HARA'. Spine: '[vertically] [red] Waiting For Winter [white] John O'Hara | [horizontally] [Hodder & Stoughton device]'. Back has blurb for *The Lockwood Concern*. Front flap has blurb for *WFW*. Back flap: 'Books by JOHN O'HARA'.

*Publication:*   8,200 copies of the first printing. Published March 1967. 35s.

*Locations:*   BL (6 MAR 67), Bod (16 MAR 1967), Lilly (dj), MJB (dj), PSt.

A 28.2.a
*Second edition, Bantam printings:* New York: Bantam, [1967].

#N3537. 95¢. 8 printings: November 1967 (3 printings), December 1967, January 1968, March 1968, October 1969, November 1970.

A 28.2.b
*Second edition, Popular printings:* New York: Popular Library, [1973].

#445-03009-150. $1.50. Reprinted.

A 28.3
*Third edition:* [London]: New English Library, [1968].

#2121. 7s. 6d.

A 29 THE INSTRUMENT

A 29.1.a
*First edition, trade printing (1967)*

# THE
# INSTRUMENT

A NOVEL BY

# JOHN O'HARA

RANDOM HOUSE

NEW YORK

A 29.1.a: 5⅝″ × 8⁵⁄₁₆″

[i–vi] [1–2] 3–138 [139–140] 141–221 [222–224] 225–297 [298]

[1–8]$^{16}$ [9]$^{8}$ 10$^{16}$

*Contents:*  p. i: blank; p. ii: 'BOOKS BY JOHN O'HARA'; p. iii: half title; p. iv: blank; p. v: title; p. vi: copyright; p. 1: '[type decoration] I [type decoration]; p. 2: blank; pp. 3–297: text; p. 298: blank.

*Typography and paper:*  Caledonia, 12 point on 16. 6$^{1}/_{8}$" (6$^{3}/_{4}$") × 4"; 27 or 28 lines per page. Running heads: rectos, 'THE INSTRUMENT'; versos, 'JOHN O'HARA'. Wove paper.

*Binding:*  Pale green (#149) V cloth (smooth). Front goldstamped with facsimile of O'Hara's signature. Spine goldstamped on 2 olive green panels: '[top panel] [Random House device] | [thick and thin rules] | THE | INSTRUMENT | John O'Hara | [thick and thin rules] | [lower panel] RANDOM HOUSE'. Top and bottom edges trimmed; fore edge rough trimmed. Top edge stained blue. Yellow (#87) wove endpapers.

*Dust jacket:*  Front and spine lettered on blue background. Front: '[green] JOHN | O'HARA | [black] *a novel* | [white] The | Instrument'. Spine lettered vertically: '[white] JOHN | O'HARA [green] The Instrument | [horizontally, black] [Random House device] | *Random* | *House*'. Back: 'BOOKS BY JOHN O'HARA'. Front flap has blurb for *Instrument*. Back flap: 'BOOKS BY | JOHN O'HARA'.

*Publication:*  49,880 copies of the first printing. Published 23 NOVEMBER 1967. $5.95. Copyright #A953738.

*Printing:*  Manufactured by The Book Press, Brattleboro, Vt.

*Locations:*  LC (NOV 24 1967), Lilly (dj), MJB (dj), PSt.

*Note:*  Galley proofs are at PSt.

*Review copy:*  Unbound galley proofs. White paper label printed in red on first galley: '[all the following within single-rule frame] ADVANCE PROOFS | [bracket] *UNCORRECTED* [bracket] | TITLE: [typed] THE INSTRUMENT | [printed] AUTHOR: [typed] John O'Hara | [printed] PRICE: [typed] $5.95 | Limited 12.50 | [printed] PUBLICATION DATE: [typed] 11/23/57 | [printed] *All information is tentative. Please check for | final details.* | RANDOM HOUSE, INC. | 457 MADISON AVE. | NEW YORK 22, N.Y. | [Random House device]'. Location: MJB.

A 29.1.b
*Limited printing*

*Certificate of limitation:*  'Of the first edition of | THE INSTRUMENT | three hundred copies have been printed on | special paper and specially bound. | Each copy is signed by the author and numbered. | [signature] | [rule] | [number]'.

JOHN O'HARA

The Instrument

JOHN O'HARA  The Instrument

BOOKS BY
JOHN O'HARA

AVAILABLE IN
THE MODERN LIBRARY
APPOINTMENT IN SAMARRA ML 42
BUTTERFIELD 8 ML 323
SELECTED SHORT STORIES ML 211
49 STORIES G 88

AVAILABLE IN
VINTAGE BOOKS
BUTTERFIELD 8 V 49

Jacket design by Muriel Nasser

Random House, Inc.
457 Madison Avenue, New York, New York 10022

Dust jacket for A 29.1.a

[i–viii] [1–2] 3–138 [139–140] 141–221 [222–224] 225–297 [298]

[1]¹⁶ (1+1₁) [2–8]¹⁶ [9]⁸ [10]¹⁶

*Contents:*  Same as trade printing, but with extra leaf tipped in before first gathering; p. i: certificate of limitation; p. ii: blank.

*Paper:*  Laid paper, vertical chain lines.

*Binding:*  Red brown (#47) natural finish buckram. Front goldstamped with facsimile of O'Hara's signature. Spine goldstamped: '[the following within blindstamped oval panel] THE | INSTRUMENT | [thick rule] | JOHN | O'HARA | [below panel] [Random House device] | [thick rule] | *Random House*'. Top edge stained brown. Red and yellow bands at top and bottom. Dark yellow (#88) wove endpapers.

*Dust jacket and box:*  Unprinted glassine jacket. Unprinted gray box.

*Publication:*  Published simultaneously with trade printing, 23 November 1967. $12.50. Priority of printing undetermined.

*Locations:*  Lilly, MJB, PSt.

A 29.1.c
*Third printing:* New York: Random House, [1967].

Literary Guild printing.

A 29.1.d
*Fourth printing:* New York: Random House, [1968].

On copyright page: '*Second Printing*'.

A 29.1.e
*First edition, first English printing (1968)*

# THE
# INSTRUMENT

A NOVEL BY

# JOHN O'HARA

HODDER AND STOUGHTON

A 29.1.e: $5^{1}/_{2}'' \times 8^{7}/_{16}''$

*Copyright page:* '© Copyright, 1967 by John O'Hara | First printed in Great Britain, 1968 | SBN 340 02958 7 | [2 lines] | Printed in Great Britain for Hodder and Stoughton Limited | St. Paul's House, Warwick Lane, London, E.C.4 | by Compton Printing Limited, | London and Aylesbury'.

Same pagination as first Random House printing.

[1–19]$^8$

*Contents:* Same as first Random House printing.

*Typography and paper:* Same as first Random House printing.

*Binding:* Strong red (#12) V cloth (smooth). Spine goldstamped vertically: 'John O'Hara [slash] THE INSTRUMENT | [horizontally] [Hodder & Stoughton device]'. All edges trimmed. Top edge stained bluish gray. White wove calendered endpapers.

*Dust jacket:* Photo on front, spine, and back in shades of blue of woman and man kissing, with man's hand holding cigarette. Front: '[black] John O'Hara | [red] The Instrument'. Spine: '[vertically] John O'Hara The Instrument | [horizontally] [Hodder & Stoughton device]'. Front flap has blurb for *Instrument*. Back flap has excerpts from reviews of O'Hara's books.

*Publication:* 16,400 copies of first English printing. Published 28 March 1968. 30s.

*Locations:* BL (22 MAR 68), Bod (25 APR 1968), Lilly (dj), MJB (dj), PSt.

### A 29.1.f
*Fifth printing:* New York: Random House, [1968].

On copyright page: *'Third Printing'*.

### A 29.1.g
*Sixth printing:* New York: Random House, 1968.

Not seen.

### A 29.1.h
*Unidentified printing:* New York: Random House, [1968].

Dollar Book Club printing.

### A 29.2.a
*Second edition, first printing:* London: New English Library, 1968.

Not seen. "Open Market" edition sold in Australia and Canada.

### A 29.2.b
*Second printing:* [London]: New English Library, [1969].

On copyright page: 'SPECIAL NEL EDITION FOR SALE IN OPEN MARKET TERRITORIES | ONLY SEPTEMBER 1968 | THIS NEL EDITION MARCH 1969'.

Four Square #2376. 7s. 6d.

### A 29.3
*Third edition:* New York: Bantam, [1969].

#Q 4565. $1.25. 9 printings: January 1969 (4 printings), February 1969, March 1969, April 1969, September 1969, November 1970.

A 30.1.a
*First edition, trade printing (1968)*

# JOHN O'HARA

# AND

# OTHER

# STORIES

RANDOM HOUSE · NEW YORK

A 30.1.a: 5⁹/₁₆″ × 8¹/₄″

*First Printing*
*Copyright ©, 1966, 1967, 1968, by John O'Hara*
*All rights reserved under International and Pan-American Copyright*
*Conventions. Published in the United States by Random House, Inc., New*
*York, and simultaneously in Canada by Random House of Canada Limited,*
*Toronto*
*Library of Congress Catalog Card Number: 68–28527*
*Manufactured in the United States of America*

*Of the twelve stories in this book, four first appeared in* The Saturday Evening
Post, *and one appeared in* The New Yorker. *The remaining stories are herein*
*published for the first time.*

[A–B] [i–vii] viii–ix [x–xii] [1–3] 4–336 [337–338]; first page of each story unnumbered.

[1–11]¹⁶

*Contents:* p. A: blank; p. B: 'BOOKS BY JOHN O'HARA'; p. i: half title; p. ii: blank; p. iii: title; p. iv: copyright; p. v: *'To* BENNETT CERF, *an amiable man';* p. vi: blank; pp. vii–ix: 'FOREWORD'; p. x: blank; p. xi: 'CONTENTS'; p. xii: blank; p. 1: half title; p. 2: blank; pp. 3–336: text, headed 'Barred'; pp. 337–338: blank.

*12 stories:* "Barred," "The Broken Giraffe,"* "The Farmer,"* "A Few Trips and Some Poetry,"* "The Gangster," "The Gunboat and Madge," "How Old, How Young," "A Man on a Porch,"* "Papa Gibralter,"* "The Private People," "The Strong Man,"* "We'll Have Fun."* Asterisks follow previously unpublished stories.

*Typography and paper:* Caslon, 11 point on 15. 6⁵/₁₆″ (6⁵/₈″) × 4″; 35 lines per page. Running heads: rectos, story titles; versos, 'AND OTHER STORIES'. Wove paper.

*Binding:* Medium green (#145) V cloth (smooth). Front goldstamped: 'JOHN O'HARA'. Spine goldstamped on 3 dark green panels: '[top panel] *John O'Hara* | [middle panel] AND | OTHER | STORIES | [bottom panel] *Random* | *House* | [Random House device below panels]'. Top and bottom edges trimmed. Fore edge rough trimmed. Top edge stained green. Green and white bands top and bottom. Dark greenish gray (#156) endpapers.

*Dust jacket:* Front and spine lettered on grayish olive background. Front: '[white] AND | OTHER | STORIES | [yellowish green] A | COLLECTION | OF 12 NEW | STORIES BY | [white] JOHN | O'HARA | [yellowish green] A RANDOM HOUSE BOOK'. Spine: '[white] AND | OTHER | STORIES | [yellowish green] JOHN | O'HARA | [white] [Random House device] | RANDOM | HOUSE'. Back has *New York Times* photo of O'Hara. Front flap has blurb for *AOS*. Back flap: 'BOOKS BY JOHN O'HARA'.

*Publication:* 49,941 copies of the first printing. Published 28 November 1968. $5.95. Copyright #A49413.

*Printing:* Manufactured by The Book Press, Brattleboro, Vt.

*Locations:* LC (FEB 20 1969), Lilly (dj), MJB (dj), PSt.

*Note:* Galley proofs and page proofs are at PSt.

*Review copies:* (A) Spiral-bound proof with blue paper covers. White label on front printed in red: '[within single-rule frame] [printed] ADVANCE PROOFS | [bracket] UNCORRECTED [bracket] | TITLE: [typed] AND OTHER STORIES | [printed] AUTHOR: [typed] John O'Hara | [printed] PRICE: [typed] $5.95; $12.50 Limited signed edition | [printed] PUBLICATION DATE: [typed] 11-28-68 | [printed] *All information is*

AND OTHER STORIES

This volume contains twelve brilliant new stories, all written in the two years following the completion of *Waiting for Winter* (1966). One of them, "A Few Trips and Some Poetry," is a novel of medium length.

Mr. O'Hara says in his foreword: "I am writing a strange play, and I am well along with a long novel. But the writing of short stories is becoming an expensive luxury at my age ... in energy and time they have become costly because the energy and time come out of resources that I must budget for the long novel." It is possible, therefore, that a few years may have to go by before another book of O'Hara stories is ready for publication.

"The quality of *And Other Stories*—which contains some of the author's finest work—shows what a great amount of his energy and time has gone into it. But since in the first eight years of the 1960s he has already produced more and better work than most writers manage in a lifetime, it is clear that Mr. O'Hara's 'budget' will not be too restrictive. As he said in an earlier foreword: 'I have work to do, and I am afraid not to do it.'"

Jacket design by Muriel Nasser

AND OTHER STORIES

A COLLECTION OF 12 NEW STORIES BY JOHN O'HARA

A RANDOM HOUSE BOOK

RANDOM HOUSE

AND OTHER STORIES

JOHN O'HARA

BOOKS BY JOHN O'HARA

APPOINTMENT IN SAMARRA  THE DOCTORS
SON AND OTHER STORIES  BUTTERFIELD 8
HOPE OF HEAVEN  FILES ON PARADE  PAL
JOEY  PIPE NIGHT  HELLBOX  A RAGE TO
LIVE  THE FARMERS HOTEL  SWEET AND
SOUR  TEN NORTH FREDERICK  A FAMILY
PARTY  SELECTED SHORT STORIES  FROM
THE TERRACE  OURSELVES TO KNOW
SERMONS AND SODA-WATER: A TRILOGY
FIVE PLAYS  ASSEMBLY  THE BIG LAUGH
THE CAPE COD LIGHTER  ELIZABETH
APPLETON  49 STORIES  THE HAT ON THE
BED  THE HORSE KNOWS THE WAY  THE
LOCKWOOD CONCERN  MY TURN  WAITING
FOR WINTER  THE INSTRUMENT  AND
OTHER STORIES

Available in THE MODERN LIBRARY
APPOINTMENT IN SAMARRA  ML 42
BUTTERFIELD 8  ML 323
SELECTED SHORT STORIES  ML 211
49 STORIES  G 48

Available in VINTAGE BOOKS
BUTTERFIELD 8  V 49

RANDOM HOUSE, INC., New York, New York 10022
Publishers of *The Random House Dictionary of the English Language: the Unabridged* and *College Editions* · The Modern Library and Vintage Books.
Printed in U.S.A.

Dust jacket for A 30.1.a

tentative. Please check for | final details. | RANDOM HOUSE, INC. | 457 MADISON AVE. | NEW YORK 22, N.Y. | [Random House device]'. Location: MJB.

(B) Spiral-bound proof with blue paper covers printed in black. Front: 'ADVANCE PROOFS | Uncorrected | [rule] | AND OTHER STORIES | by | John O'Hara | [rule] | PRICE: [written in ink] $5.95 | [printed] PUBLICATION | DATE: | [written in ink] Nov. 28, 1968 | [printed] [rule] RANDOM HOUSE, INC. | 457 Madison Avenue, New York 22, N.Y.' Location: MJB.

A 30.1.b.
*Limited printing*

*Certificate of limitation:* 'Of the first edition of | AND OTHER STORIES | *three hundred copies have been printed on* | *special paper and specially bound.* | *Each copy is signed by the author and numbered.* | *[number]* | *[rule]* | *[signature]*'.

[A–D] [i–vii] viii–ix [x–xii] [1–3] 4–336 [337–338]; first page of each story unnumbered

[1]$^{16}$ (1$_1$+1) [2–11]$^{16}$

*Contents:* Same as trade printing, but with extra leaf tipped in after first leaf; p. C: certificate of limitation; p. D: blank.

*Paper:* Laid, with vertical chains.

*Binding:* Dark green (#146) natural-finish buckram. Front goldstamped with facsimile of O'Hara's signature. Spine goldstamped: '[on blindstamped oval panel] AND | OTHER | STORIES | [thick rule] | JOHN | O'HARA | [below panel] [Random House device] [thick rule] | Random House'. Top and bottom edges trimmed; fore edge rough trimmed. Top edge stained green. Green and white bands top and bottom. Dark green (#146) endpapers.

*Box:* Unprinted green box.

*Publication:* Published simultaneously with trade printing, 28 November 1968. $12.50. Priority of printing undetermined.

*Locations:* Lilly, MJB, PSt.

A 30.1.c
*Third printing:* New York: Random House, [1969].

On copyright page: '*Second Printing*'.

A 30.1.d
*Pirated printing*

Offset reprint of first edition, probably printed in Taiwan, ca. 1969.

*Location:* P. B. Eppard.

A 30.1.e
*First edition, first English printing (1968)*

# JOHN O'HARA

# AND
# OTHER
# STORIES

**HODDER AND STOUGHTON**

A 30.1.e: 5³/₈″ × 8⁷/₁₆″

*Copyright page:* 'Copyright © 1966, 1967, 1968, *by John O'Hara* | *First Printed in Great Britain* 1969 | *SBN* 340 04275 3 | [6 lines of italic] | *Printed in Great Britain for* HODDER AND STOUGHTON LIMITED, | *St. Paul's House, Warwick Lane, London, E.C.4.* | *by* COMPTON PRINTING LIMITED, *London and Aylesbury.*'

Same pagination as American edition.

Same collation as American edition.

*Contents:* Same as American edition.

*Paper:* Wove.

*Binding:* Black paper-covered boards with V grain. Spine goldstamped: '[on green panel] AND | OTHER | STORIES | John | O'Hara | [below panel] [Hodder & Stoughton device on gold square]'. All edges trimmed. Top edge stained light green. Pale green (#148) wove calendered endpapers.

*Dust jacket:* Front spine lettered on black background. Front: '[white] JOHN | O'HARA | [green] AND OTHER | STORIES'. Spine lettered vertically: '[white] JOHN O'HARA | [green] AND OTHER STORIES | [horizontally] [Hodder & Stoughton device on white]'. Back has photo of O'Hara by Ann Zane Shanks. Front flap has blurb for AOS. Back flap has blurbs for *Instrument* and *Waiting for Winter*.

*Publication:* 8,500 copies. Published May 1969. 35s.

*Locations:* BL (25 APR 69), MJB (dj), PSt.

A 30.2
*Second edition:* New York: Bantam, [1970].

#Q4816. $1.25.

A 30.3
*Third edition:* [London]: New English Library, [1970].

#2638. 6s.

A 31 LOVEY CHILDS: A PHILADELPHIAN'S STORY

A 31.1.a
*First edition, trade printing (1969)*

# LOVEY CHILDS

## *A Philadelphian's Story*

A NOVEL BY

# John O'Hara

RANDOM HOUSE
NEW YORK

A 31.1.a: 5$^{1}$/$_{2}$″ × 8$^{1}$/$_{4}$″

FIRST PRINTING

9 8 7 6 5 4 3 2

Copyright © 1969 by John O'Hara

All rights reserved under International
and Pan-American Copyright Conventions.

Published in the United States by Random House, Inc., New York,
and simultaneously in Canada
by Random House of Canada Limited, Toronto.

Library of Congress Catalog Card Number: 73-85571

Manufactured in the United States of America
by The Book Press, Brattleboro, Vt.

Typography & binding design
by Mary M. Ahern

[i–vi] [1–2] 3–249 [250]

[1–8]$^{16}$

*Contents:*   p. i: half title; p. ii: 'BOOKS BY JOHN O'HARA'; p. iii: title; p. iv: copyright; p. v: '*To* ALBERT ERSKINE'; p. vi: blank; p. 1: half title; p. 2: blank; pp. 3–249: text; p. 250: blank.

*Typography and paper:*   Caledonia, 11 point on 17. 5$^7/_8$" (7") × 3$^7/_8$"; 24 or 25 lines per page. Running heads: rectos, 'LOVEY CHILDS'; versos, 'JOHN O'HARA'. Wove paper.

*Binding:*   Dark orange yellow (#72) or yellowish white (#92) V cloth (smooth). Front goldstamped with O'Hara's signature. Spine goldstamped on two blue panels: '[upper panel] [Random House device] | [thick and thin rules] | Lovey | Childs: | A PHILA- | DELPHIAN'S | STORY | John | O'Hara | [thin and thick rules] | [lower panel] Random | House'. Top and bottom edges trimmed. Fore edge rough trimmed. Top edge stained yellow. Olive green (#125) endpapers.

*Dust jacket:*   Front and spine lettered on purple background. Front: '[green] JOHN | O'HARA | [white] Lovey | Childs: | [dark orange yellow] A | PHILADELPHIAN'S | STORY'. Spine: '[vertically] [green] JOHN [white] Lovey Childs: | [green] O'HARA [white] A PHILADELPHIAN'S STORY | [horizontally, at bottom] [dark orange yellow] [Random House device] | [gold] RANDOM | HOUSE'. Back: 'BOOKS BY JOHN O'HARA'. Front and back flaps have blurb for *LC*.

*Publication:*   47,807 copies of the first printing. Published 27 November 1969. $5.95. Copyright #A162315.

*Printing:*   Manufactured by The Book Press, Brattleboro, Vt.

*Locations:*   LC (orange yellow; JUN 18 1970), Lilly (orange yellow; dj), MJB (orange yellow and yellowish white; both in dj), PSt (orange yellow; dj).

*Note:*   Galley proofs and page proofs are at PSt.

*Textual note:*   Two typos appear at 8.17: 'a hunting' *should read* 'a-hunting'; 'said' *should read* 'and'.

*Review copies:*   (A) Unbound galley proofs. White label printed in red on first galley: '[all the following within single-rule frame] ADVANCE PROOFS | [bracket] *UNCOR-RECTED* [bracket] | TITLE: [typed] LOVEY CHILDS: A Philadelphian's | Story |

This is the story of Lovey Childs, of Philadelphia. In a certain world it would not be necessary to say 'of Philadelphia'; the inhabitants of that world needed no more than her nickname, and that had always been hers from the time she was a little girl and not yet Lovey Childs. In shops, on trains, she would fix her gaze on a stranger who interested her, and say, 'I'm Lovey.'

...Other children have often said, 'I'm Mary' and 'I'm Helen,' but when a sapphire-eyed child says 'I'm Lovey,' it can be taken as a self-appraisal, an invitation, or a statement of fact. In her childhood, where Lovey introduced herself to grownups, they would at least smile, and she grew up in the belief that the grownup world was a friendly place. She could hardly wait to become a member of that world and she did all she could to hasten her entrance into it.

Lovey Childs's efforts to join the adult world were aided by matters she could not foresee. Her control—her father's financial ineptitude, his early death, her mother's aberrations. At seventeen she completed the process by her impetuous marriage to Sky Childs, all-American (football) wealthy and worthless. "...the union of two prominent families. If they were not made for each other, they were made for the biblical press."

(continued on back flap)

---

# JOHN O'HARA
# Lovey Childs:
## A PHILADELPHIAN'S STORY

JOHN O'HARA · Lovey Childs: A PHILADELPHIAN'S STORY · RANDOM HOUSE

---

BOOKS BY JOHN O'HARA

APPOINTMENT IN SAMARRA · THE DOCTOR'S SON AND OTHER STORIES · BUTTERFIELD 8 · HOPE OF HEAVEN · FILES ON PARADE · PAL JOEY · PIPE NIGHT · HELLBOX · A RACE TO LIVE · THE FARMERS HOTEL · SWEET AND SOUR · TEN NORTH FREDERICK · A FAMILY PARTY · SELECTED SHORT STORIES · FROM THE TERRACE · OURSELVES TO KNOW · SERMONS AND SODA-WATER: A TRILOGY · FIVE PLAYS · ASSEMBLY · THE BIG LAUGH · THE CAPE COD LIGHTER · ELIZABETH APPLETON · THE HAT ON THE BED · THE HORSE KNOWS THE WAY · THE LOCKWOOD CONCERN · MY TURN · WAITING FOR WINTER · THE INSTRUMENT AND OTHER STORIES · THE O'HARA GENERATION · LOVEY CHILDS: A PHILADELPHIAN'S STORY

---

(continued from front flap)

The main events of the story take place in the second half, the downhill side of the hectic 1920's, a period about which the author has frequently written before with equal authority and conviction. This is one of John O'Hara's shortest novels—practically a miniature in comparison to From the Terrace or Ten North Frederick—but its brevity is a matter of method rather than of content. It is a long full-bodied story deliberately foreshortened, presented primarily through key scenes, with the connecting links sketched in briefly or suggested to the imagination. The characters are seldom described; it is through what they do and say that the reader comes to know them, and also, in some cases with reluctance, to believe them.

Jacket design by Muriel Nasser

Random House, Inc., New York, N.Y. 10022. Publishers of THE RANDOM HOUSE DICTIONARY OF THE ENGLISH LANGUAGE, the Unabridged and College Editions, The Modern Library and Vintage Books

Printed in U.S.A.

11/69

Dust jacket for A31.1.a

[printed] AUTHOR: [ typed] John O'Hara [printed] PRICE: [typed] $5.95 | [printed] PUBLICATION DATE: [typed] Nov. 27, 1969 | [printed] *All information is tentative. Please check for* | final details. | RANDOM HOUSE, INC. | 201 EAST FIFTIETH STREET | NEW YORK, N.Y. 10022 | [Random House device]'. Location: MJB.

(B) Spiral-bound proof in pink paper covers. Front: '[slanting up] UNCORRECTED PROOF | [horizontally] LOVEY CHILDS | *A Philadelphian's Story* | A NOVEL BY | John O'Hara | [Random House device] | RANDOM HOUSE | NEW YORK.' Produced by Crane Duplicating Service. Location: MJB.

A 31.1.b
*Limited printing*

*Certification of limitation:* 'Of the first edition of | LOVEY CHILDS: | A PHILADEL-PHIAN'S STORY | *two hundred copies have been printed on* | *special paper and specially bound.* | *Each copy is signed by the author and numbered.* | [number] | [rule] | [signature].'

[i–viii] [1–2] 3–249 [250]

[1]$^{16}$ (1 + 1$_1$) [2–8]$^{16}$

*Contents:* Same as trade printing, but with extra leaf tipped in before first gathering; p. i: certificate of limitation; p. ii: blank.

*Paper:* Laid, with vertical chains.

*Binding:* Pale yellow (#89) natural finish buckram. Front goldstamped with facsimile of O'Hara's signature. Spine goldstamped: '[the following 8 lines on blindstamped panel] LOVEY | CHILDS | A PHILA- | DELPHIAN'S | STORY | [thick rule] | JOHN | O'HARA | [Random House device] | [thick rule] | Random | House'. Top and bottom edges trimmed. Fore edge rough trimmed. Top edge stained green. Blue and white bands at top and bottom. Deep yellow (#85) endpapers.

*Dust jacket and box:* Unprinted glassine jacket. Unprinted light olive brown box.

*Publication:* Published simultaneously with trade printing, 27 November 1969. $15. Priority of printing undetermined.

*Locations:* Lilly, MJB, PSt.

A 31.1.c
*First edition, first English printing (1970)*

# LOVEY CHILDS

## *A Philadelphian's Story*

A NOVEL BY

# John O'Hara

HODDER AND STOUGHTON

A 31.1.c: 5³/₈″ × 8¹/₂″

*Copyright page:* '[2 lines] | Copyright © 1969 by John O'Hara | First Printed in Great Britain 1970 | SBN 340 12891 7 | [7 lines] | Printed in Great Britain for Hodder and Stoughton Limited, | St. Paul's House, Warwick Lane, London, E.C.4, by | Compton Printing Ltd., London and Aylesbury'.

Same pagination as first American printing.

[1–16]$^8$

*Contents:*   Same as first American printing.

*Typography and paper:*   24 or 25 lines per page. Wove paper.

*Binding:*   Medium olive green (#125) paper-covered boards with V grain. Front goldstamped with facsimile of O'Hara's signature. Spine goldstamped on purple panel: '[thick and thin rules] | Lovey | Childs | A PHILA- | DELPHIAN'S | STORY | John | O'Hara | [thin and thick rules] | [Hodder & Stoughton device stamped in purple at bottom]'. All edges trimmed. Top edge stained green. Brownish orange (#54) endpapers.

*Dust jacket:*   Same as Random House first printing, with substitution of green Hodder & Stoughton device for Random House device on spine and editorial changes on flap copy; last 3 lines on front are green.

*Publication:*   13,000 copies of first printing. Published June 1970. 31s.

*Locations:*   BL (10 JUN 70), Bod (16 JUL 1970), Lilly (dj), MJB (dj), PSt.

A 31.2
*Second edition:* New York: Bantam, [1970].

#Q5688. $1.25.

A 31.3
*Third edition:* [London]: New English Library, [1972].

#2801. 35p.

A 32   FACSIMILE OF ACADEMY ADDRESS

A 32.1
*Only printing (1970)*

---

## JOHN O'HARA

1905 - 1970

A Keepsake for a Memorial Exhibit
The Pennsylvania State University Libraries
Tuesday, July 7 - Friday, August 14, 1970

In recognition of John O'Hara's services to literature,
and in token of his gifts to The Pennsylvania State
University, we hereby print a facsimile of an address
delivered by Mr. O'Hara on February 29, 1964, on the
occasion of his being awarded the Merit Medal for the
Novel of the American Academy of Arts and Letters.

---

A 32.1: cover; 8¹/₂″ × 11″

[1–6]; printed on rectos only.

3 leaves stapled in paper covers.

*Contents:*   pp. 1, 3, 5: facsimile of O'Hara's corrected typescript.

*Binding:*   Stiff pale yellow (#89) covers.

*Paper:*   Yellow wove paper, watermarked: 'TA-NON-KA | BPM | MIMEO BOND'.

*Publication:*   Unknown number of copies distributed by the Pennsylvania State University Libraries, commencing 7 July 1970. Not for sale. See A 37 and B 29.

*Locations:*   MJB, PSt.

A 33 THE EWINGS

A 33.1.a
*First edition, first printing (1972)*

*The*

# EWINGS

*by JOHN O'HARA*

*Random House* 🏠 *New York*

A 33.1.a: 5⁷/₁₆″ × 8³/₁₆″

[i–x] [1–2] 3–310 [311–314]

Perfect binding.

*Contents:* pp. i–iii: blank; p. iv: 'BOOKS BY JOHN O'HARA'; p. v: half title; p. vi: blank; p. vii: title; p. viii: copyright; p. ix: *'To Graham Watson';* p. x: blank; p. 1: half title; p. 2: blank; pp. 3–311: text; p. 312: 'About the Author'; pp. 313–314: blank.

*Typography and paper:* Caledonia, 11 point on 13. 6¹/₈″ (6¹³/₁₆″) × 4″; 33 or 34 lines per page. Running heads: rectos, 'THE EWINGS'; versos, 'JOHN O'HARA'. Wove paper.

*Binding:* Orange yellow (#66) V cloth (smooth). Front goldstamped with facsimile of O'Hara's signature. Spine goldstamped on 2 gray panels: '[top panel] [Random House device] | [thick and thin rules] | THE | EWINGS | John | O'Hara | [thin and thick rules] | [lower panel] Random | House'. All edges trimmed. Top edge stained light green. Green and yellow bands at top and bottom. Olive green (#127) endpapers.

*Dust jacket:* Front and spine lettered on black background. Front: '[white] John | O'Hara | [orange yellow] The | Ewings | A NOVEL'. Spine: '[vertically] [white] John O'Hara | [yellow] The Ewings | [horizontally] [Random House device] | Random | House'. Back: has photo of O'Hara. Front flap has blurb for *Ewings.* Back flap has biographical sketch of O'Hara.

*Publication:* 30,149 copies of the first printing. Published 28 February 1972. $6.95. Copyright #A354712.

*Printing:* Manufactured by The Book Press, Brattleboro, Vt.

*Locations:* LC (JUL 5 1972), Lilly (dj), MJB (dj), PSt.

*Note:* Galley proofs are at MJB.

*Textual note:* The first printing reads at 231.16–17: 'NOTE: GET WORDING OF TELEGRAM ANNOUNCING BOB HOTCHKISS'S DEATH AT CHATEAU-THIERRY'; corrected in second printing to: ' " . . . GAVE HIS LIFE IN THE FIRST GREAT AMERICAN ADVANCE BEFORE CHATEAU THIERRY . . . " '.

John O'Hara

The Ewings

A NOVEL

John O'Hara
The Ewings

Random House

Dust jacket for A 33.1.a

*Review copy:*　Proof bound in red wrappers. Front: 'UNCORRECTED PROOF | *The* | EWINGS | *by JOHN O'HARA* | *Random House* [device] *New York*'. Produced by Crane Duplicating Service. Location: PSt.

A 33.1.b
*Second printing:*　New York: Random House, [1972].

A 33.1.c
*First edition, first English printing (1972)*

# *The*

# EWINGS

## *by JOHN O'HARA*

**HODDER AND STOUGHTON**
**LONDON  SYDNEY  AUCKLAND  TORONTO**

A 33.1.c: 5³/₈″ × 8⁷/₁₆″

*Copyright page:* 'Copyright © 1972 by United States Trust Company of New York, as Executor of the Will of John O'Hara. First printed in Great Britain 1972. ISBN 0 340 12576 4.... Printed in Great Britain for Hodder and Stoughton Limited, St. Paul's House, Warwick Lane, London EC4P 4AH by Compton Printing Ltd., London and Aylesbury.'

[i–viii] [1–2] 3–310 [311–312]

[1–10]¹⁶

*Contents:* p. i: blank; p. ii: 'BOOKS BY JOHN O'HARA'; p. iii: half title; p. iv: blank; p. v: title; p. vi: copyright; p. vii: *'To Graham Watson'*; p. viii: blank; p. 1: half title; p. 2: blank; pp. 3–311: text; p. 312: 'About the Author'.

*Typography and paper:* 33 or 34 lines per page. Wove paper.

*Binding:* Medium green (#145) paper-covered boards with V grain (smooth). Spine goldstamped: '[against dark yellow panel] [thick and thin rules] | THE | EWINGS | [diamond] | John | O'Hara | [thin and thick rules] | [below panel] [Hodder & Stoughton device]'. All edges trimmed. Top edge stained light bluish green. Light brown (#79) laid endpapers.

*Dust jacket:* Lettered on white background. Front: '[green] JOHN | O'HARA | [black] *The Ewings* | [house, car, figures]'. Spine: '[vertically] [green] JOHN O'HARA [black] *The* | *Ewings* | [horizontally] [Hodder & Stoughton device]'. Back lists books by O'Hara. Front flap has blurb for *Ewings* and note on O'Hara. Back flap has excerpts from reviews.

*Publication and printing:* 10,000 copies of the first printing. Published July 1972. £2.25.

*Locations:* BL (4 AUG 72), Bod (24 AUG 1972), Lilly (dj), MLB (dj), PSt.

A 33.1.d
*Fourth printing:* London: Coronet, [1973].

#17423 4. 50p.

A 33.2
*Second edition:* New York: Popular Library, [1972].

#445-00136-125. $1.25. Reprinted.

A 34 THE TIME ELEMENT AND OTHER STORIES

A 34.1.a
*First edition, first printing (1972)*

# JOHN O'HARA
# THE
# TIME
# ELEMENT

### AND OTHER STORIES

RANDOM HOUSE · NEW YORK

A 34.1.a: 5$^1$/$_2$″ × 8$^3$/$_{16}$″

A–B [i–vii] viii–ix [x–xi] xii [1–3] 4–7 [8] 9–10 [11] 12–21 [22] 23–26 [27] 28–32 [33] 34–38 [39] 40–42 [43] 44–47 [48] 49–55 [56] 57–58 [59] 60–66 [67] 68–71 [72] 73–79 [80] 81–86 [87] 88–92 [93] 94–98 [99] 100–104 [105] 106–109 [110] 111–118 [119] 120–128 [129] 130–133 [134] 135–142 [143] 144–150 [151] 152–156 [157] 158–168 [169] 170–173 [174] 175–183 [184] 185–189 [190] 191–196 [197] 198–206 [207] 208–218 [219] 220–227 [228] 229–234 [235] 236–244 [245–250]

Perfect binding.

*Contents:*   pp. A–B: blank; p. i: blank; p. ii: 'BOOKS BY JOHN O'HARA'; p. iii: half title; p. iv: blank; p. v: title; p. vi: copyright; pp. vii–ix: 'FOREWORD' by Albert Erskine; p. x: blank; pp. xi–xii: 'CONTENTS'; p. 1: half title; p. 2: blank; pp. 3–244: text, headed 'ENCOUNTER: 1943'; p. 245: 'About the Author'; pp. 246–250: blank.

*34 stories:* "Encounter: 1943,"* "Conversation at Lunch," "Pilgrimage," "One for the Road," "The Skipper,"* "Not Always," "No Justice,"* "The Lady Takes an Interest," "Interior with Figures," "At the Cothurnos Club," "The Last of Haley," "Memorial Fund,"* "The Heart of Lee W. Lee," "The Brothers,"* "He Thinks He Owns Me,"* "The Dry Murders," "Eileen," "The War,"* "Nil Nisi," "The Time Element,"* "Family Evening,"* "Requiescat," "The Frozen Face," "Last Respects,"* "The Industry and the Professor," "The Busybody,"* "This Time,"* "Grief," "The Kids," "The Big Gleaming Coach,"* "For Help and Pity,"* "All I've Tried to Be," "The Favor," "That First Husband." All previously uncollected. Asterisks indicate previously unpublished stories.

*Typography and paper:*   Caledonia, 11 point on 13. 6⅜" (6¹¹/₁₆") × 4"; 34 or 35 lines per page. Running heads: rectos, story titles; versos, 'THE TIME ELEMENT AND OTHER STORIES'. Wove paper.

*Binding:*   Yellow green (#120) V cloth (smooth). Front goldstamped: 'JOHN O'HARA'. Spine goldstamped on 3 dark green panels: '[top panel] *John | O'Hara* | [middle panel] THE | TIME | ELEMENT | AND | OTHER | STORIES | [bottom panel] *Random | House* | [below panels] [Random House device]'. All edges trimmed. Top edge stained yellowish green. Greenish yellow (#102) wove endpapers.

*Dust jacket:*   Lettered on black background. Front: '[photo of O'Hara at upper right] [white] John | O'Hara | [light green] The Time | Element [dark green] & | Other

The thirty-four stories in this volume have never before been published in book form, and fourteen of them have not previously been printed. They all appear to have been written in the 1960's and therefore to belong—in quality as well as in period—with the collection *Pipe Night* (1945) and *Hellbox* (1947).

Of the twenty stories that have appeared in magazines, fifteen were published in *The New Yorker* in the last three years of the forties (November 9, 1946 to November 26, 1949), one each in *Good Housekeeping* (1944), *The Princeton Tiger* (1952), *The Saturday Evening Post* (1950), and two in *Collier's* (1947). Most of them were written after *Hellbox* was prepared for publication, and they would surely have been collected by the author for another volume in the early fifties had he not ceased writing short stories altogether in 1949, not to resume until 1960. In the sixties his output was so prodigious that he did not need, and perhaps did not even remember, earlier uncollected work for the long-since undiscriminating publishers who could not lose money with his name. Whatever the reason, it is fortunate, since these stories from the earlier time belong together and can now be so presented.

John O'Hara
**The Time Element** &
**Other Stories**
34 previously uncollected stories

John O'Hara
**The Time Element** & Other Stories

Random House

394-48211-5

## Books By John O'Hara

APPOINTMENT IN SAMARRA
THE DOCTOR'S SON AND OTHER STORIES
BUTTERFIELD 8
HOPE OF HEAVEN
FILES ON PARADE
PAL JOEY
PIPE NIGHT
HELLBOX
A RAGE TO LIVE
THE FARMERS HOTEL
SWEET AND SOUR
TEN NORTH FREDERICK
A FAMILY PARTY
SELECTED SHORT STORIES
FROM THE TERRACE
OURSELVES TO KNOW
SERMONS AND SODA-WATER: A TRILOGY
FIVE PLAYS
ASSEMBLY
THE BIG LAUGH
THE CAPE COD LIGHTER
ELIZABETH APPLETON
THE HAT ON THE BED
THE HORSE KNOWS THE WAY
THE LOCKWOOD CONCERN
MY TURN
WAITING FOR WINTER
THE INSTRUMENT
AND OTHER STORIES
THE O'HARA GENERATION
LOVEY CHILDS: A PHILADELPHIAN'S STORY
THE EWINGS
THE TIME ELEMENT AND OTHER STORIES

Son of a doctor and the eldest of eight children, John O'Hara was born in Pottsville, Pennsylvania, January 31, 1905; he died at his home in Princeton, New Jersey, on April 11, 1970.

After graduation from Niagara Prep School, he worked at a great variety of jobs. His career as a reporter was also varied. He worked first for two Pennsylvania papers and then for three in New York, where he covered everything from sports to religion. He also was on the staff of *Newsweek* and *Time*, and over the years, wrote columns for *Collier's*, the *Trenton Times-Advertiser*, *Newsday* and *Holiday*.

His first novel was *Appointment in Samarra*, published in 1934, and with its appearance he became, and continued to be throughout his life, a major figure on the American literary scene. He published seventeen novels and eleven volumes of short stories, in addition to plays, essays, sketches and stories, many of which he never got around to collecting for books.

His novel *Ten North Frederick* (1955) received the National Book Award for 1956, and in 1964 the American Academy of Arts and Letters presented to him the Gold Medal of Merit.

Jacket design by Muriel Nasser
Random House, Inc., New York, N.Y. 10022
Publishers of THE RANDOM HOUSE DICTIONARY OF THE ENGLISH LANGUAGE, The Unabridged and College Editions · The Modern Library and Vintage Books
Printed in U.S.A.
11/72

Dust jacket for A 34.1.a

Stories | [blue] 34 previously | uncollected | stories'. Spine: '[vertically] [white] John O'Hara | [light green] The Time Element [dark green] & Other Stories | [horizontally] [blue Random House device] | [white] Random House'. Back: '[white] Books By John O'Hara | [33 titles in light green, dark green, and blue] | 394-48211-5'. Front flap has blurb for *TE*. Back flap has biographical sketch of O'Hara.

*Publication:* 20,252 copies of first printing. Published 23 November 1972. $6.95. Copyright #A406360.

*Printing:* Manufactured by The Book Press, Brattleboro, Vt.

*Locations:* Lilly (dj), MJB (dj), PSt.

*Note:* Galley proofs are at MJB.

A 34.1.b
*First edition, first English printing (1973)*

# JOHN O'HARA

# THE

# TIME

# ELEMENT

## AND OTHER STORIES

**HODDER AND STOUGHTON**
LONDON · SYDNEY · AUCKLAND · TORONTO

A 34.1.b: 5³/₈″ × 8³/₈″

*Copyright page:* '*Copyright 1944, 1946, 1947, 1948, 1949, 1952, 1959 and 1972 by United States Trust Company of New York, as executor of and trustee under the will of John O'Hara. Copyright renewed 1972 by Katharine B. O'Hara and Wylie O. Holahan. First printed in Great Britain 1973. ISBN 0 340 17749 7. . . . Printed in Great Britain for Hodder and Stoughton Limited, St. Paul's House, Warwick Lane, London EC4P 4AH by Compton Printing Limited, London and Aylesbury.*'

[iii–vii] viii–ix [x–xi] xii [1–3] 4–244 [245–246]; first page of each new story not numbered

[1–16]⁸

*Contents:* p. iii: half title; p. iv: 'BOOKS BY JOHN O'HARA'; p. v: title; p. vi: copyright; pp. vii–ix: 'FOREWORD' by Albert Erskine; p. x: blank; pp. xi–xii: 'CONTENTS'; pp. 1–2: blank; pp. 3–244: text, headed 'ENCOUNTER: 1943'; p. 245: 'About the Author'; p. 246: blank.

Contains 34 stories.

*Typography and paper:* 34 or 35 lines per page. Wove paper.

*Binding:* Black paper-covered boards with V grain (smooth). Spine goldstamped: 'John | O'Hara | The | TIME | ELEMENT | and other | stories | [Hodder & Stoughton device]'. All edges trimmed. Top edge stained rust. White wove endpapers of heavier stock than text paper.

*Dust jacket:* Lettered on black background. Front: '[white] John | O'Hara | [orange] The | TIME ELEMENT | [yellowish green] and other | stories | [brownish orange] 34 | previously | uncollected stories'. Spine: '[white] John | O'Hara | [orange] The | TIME | ELEMENT | [yellowish green] and other | stories | [brownish orange Hodder & Stoughton device]'. Back lists books by O'Hara. Front flap has blurb for *TE*. Back flap has biographical sketch of O'Hara.

*Publication:* 5,000 copies of first English printing. Published August 1973. £2.50.

*Locations:* Lilly (dj), MJB (dj), PSt (dj).

A 34.2
*Second edition:* New York: Popular Library, [1973].

#445-00164-125. $1.25. Reprinted.

A 35 A CUB TELLS HIS STORY

A 35.1
*Only printing (1974)*

---

**A CUB TELLS HIS STORY**

John O'Hara

The Windhover Press, Iowa City
and Bruccoli Clark, 1974

---

A 35.1: title line in vivid reddish orange (#34); $4^7/_8''$ × $8^1/_4''$

[1–16]

[1]⁸

*Contents:*  pp. 1–2: blank; p. 3: half title and epigraph; p. 4: blank; p. 5: title; p. 6: 'Copyright © 1974 by Katherine B. O'Hara | and Wylie O'Hara Holahan.'; p. 7: 'Preface'; p. 8: blank; pp. 9–13: text; p. 14: blank; p. 15: 'One hundred and fifty copies have been printed on a Washington | press from handset Bembo type. The paper was specially made for | The Windhover Press by the Wookey Hole Mill in England. | The Preface is by Matthew J. Bruccoli.'; p. 16: blank.

See D1 for original publication of "A Cub Tells His Story."

*Typography and paper:*  See "Contents." $5^1/4'' \times 3^5/16''$; 32 lines per page. No running heads. White wove paper.

*Binding:*  Light brownish pink (#33) stiff paper wrappers. Front: " 'the thing was to write, for I have always loved it.' "

*Publication:*  See "Contents." 150 copies. $3. Published March 1974.

*Locations:*  MJB, PSt.

A 36 GOOD SAMARITAN AND OTHER STORIES

A 36.1.a
*First edition, first printing (1974)*

# JOHN O'HARA

# GOOD

# SAMARITAN

## AND OTHER STORIES

RANDOM HOUSE · NEW YORK

A 36.1.a: 5$^1$/$_2$″ × 8$^1$/$_8$″

[i–vii] viii–ix [x–xii] [1–3] 4–24 [25] 26–49 [50] 51–81 [82] 83–98 [99] 100–126 [127] 128–142 [143] 144–174 [175] 176–182 [183] 184–209 [210] 211–221 [222] 223–253 [254] 255–268 [269] 270–281 [282] 283–296 [297–300]

Perfect binding.

*Contents:* p. i: blank; p. ii: 'BOOKS BY JOHN O'HARA'; p. iii: half title; p. iv: blank; p. v: title; p. vi: copyright; pp. vii–ix: 'FOREWORD' by Albert Erskine; p. x: blank; p. xi: 'CONTENTS'; p. xii: blank; p. 1: half title; p. 2: blank; pp. 3–296: text, headed 'THE GENTRY'; p. 297: 'ABOUT THE AUTHOR'; pp. 298–300: blank.

*14 stories:* "The Gentry,"* "The Sun Room," "Sound View,"* "Good Samaritan," "A Man to Be Trusted,"* "Malibu from the Sky,"* "Harrington and Whitehill,"* "Noblesse Oblige,"* "Heather Hill,"* "Tuesday's as Good as Any,"* "George Munson,"* "The Journey to Mount Clemens," "The Mechanical Man," "Christmas Poem." Asterisks follow previously unpublished stories.

*Typography and paper:* Caledonia, 12 point on 15. 6¼" (6½") × 4"; 33 or 34 lines per page. Running heads: rectos, story titles; versos, 'GOOD SAMARITAN'. Wove paper.

*Binding:* Vivid dark red (#17) V cloth (smooth). Front goldstamped: 'JOHN O'HARA'. Spine goldstamped on 3 red panels: '[top panel] *John | O'Hara* | [middle panel] GOOD | SAMARITAN | AND | OTHER | STORIES | [bottom panel] Random | House | [below panels] [Random House device]'. All edges trimmed. Top edge stained red. Red and yellow bands at top and bottom. Light brownish gray (#63) endpapers with ripple grain.

*Dust jacket:* All lettering on black background. Front: '[photo of O'Hara in upper right] [white] John | O'Hara | [yellowish] Good | Samaritan [yellowish orange] & | Other Stories | [orange] 14 previously | uncollected | stories'. Spine printed vertically: '[white] John O'Hara | [orange] Good Samaritan [yellowish orange] & Other Stories | [horizontally at bottom] [orange Random House device] | [white] RANDOM | HOUSE'. Back: 34 O'Hara titles in yellow and orange and serial number '394-49070-3'. Front flap: blurb for *GS*. Back flap: biographical note on O'Hara.

$7.95

John O'Hara
Good Samaritan & Other Stories
14 previously uncollected stories

John O'Hara
Good Samaritan & Other Stories

RANDOM HOUSE

APPOINTMENT IN SAMARRA
THE DOCTOR'S SON AND OTHER STORIES
BUTTERFIELD 8
HOPE OF HEAVEN
FILES ON PARADE
PAL JOEY
PIPE NIGHT
HELLBOX
A RAGE TO LIVE
THE FARMERS HOTEL
TEN NORTH FREDERICK
A FAMILY PARTY
SWEET AND SOUR
SELECTED SHORT STORIES
FROM THE TERRACE
OURSELVES TO KNOW
SERMONS AND SODA-WATER: A TRILOGY
FIVE PLAYS
ASSEMBLY
THE BIG LAUGH
THE CAPE COD LIGHTER
ELIZABETH APPLETON
THE HAT ON THE BED
THE HORSE KNOWS THE WAY
THE LOCKWOOD CONCERN
MY TURN
WAITING FOR WINTER
THE INSTRUMENT
AND OTHER STORIES
THE O'HARA GENERATION
LOVEY CHILDS: A PHILADELPHIAN'S STORY
THE EWINGS
THE TIME ELEMENT AND OTHER STORIES
GOOD SAMARITAN AND OTHER STORIES

Son of a doctor and the eldest of eight children, John O'Hara, was born in Pottsville, Pennsylvania, January 31, 1905; he died at his home in Princeton, New Jersey, on April 11, 1970.

After graduation from Niagara Prep School, he worked at a great variety of jobs. His career as a reporter was also varied. He worked first for two Pennsylvania papers and then for three in New York, where he covered everything from sports to religion. He also was on the staff of Newsweek and Time, and over the years, wrote columns for Collier's, the Trenton Times-Advertiser, Newsday and Holiday.

His first novel was Appointment in Samarra, published in 1934, and with its appearance he became, and continued to be throughout his life, a major figure on the American literary scene. He published seventeen novels and eleven volumes of short stories, in addition to plays, essays, sketches and stories, many of which he never got around to collecting for books.

His novel Ten North Frederick (1955) received the National Book Award for 1956, and in 1964 the American Academy of Arts and Letters presented to him the Gold Medal Award of Merit.

Photograph of John O'Hara
by Ann Zane Shanks

Random House, Inc., New York, N.Y. 10022
Publishers of THE RANDOM HOUSE DICTIONARY OF THE ENGLISH LANGUAGE the Unabridged and College Editions, The Modern Library and Vintage Books
Printed in U.S.A.
6/74

These stories have never before appeared in a book. The title story, the last to be printed in a magazine during O'Hara's lifetime, was published by The Saturday Evening Post on November 30, 1968, too late for inclusion in the last volume he himself collected. "Christmas Poem" came out in The New Yorker (December 19, 1964) and "The Journey to Mount Clemens" in The Saturday Evening Post (August 1974).

All of this group, which contains some of the best he produced, were apparently written during the nineteen sixties, the decade during which O'Hara completed six big collections. They are on average much longer than those of the thirties and forties, when, as he put it, "time was cheap and everlasting" and one could say it all in 2,000 words. These fourteen stories produce, therefore, a larger book than the thirty-four that comprise The Time Element and Other Stories (1972).

The publication date of Appointment in Samarra was August 16, 1934; Good Samaritan and Other Stories that comes on the fortieth anniversary of that date.

Dust jacket for A 36.1.a

*Publication:*   Unknown number of copies of the first printing. Published 16 August 1974. $7.95. Copyright #A574585.

*Printing:*   Manufactured by The Book Press, Brattleborg, Vt.

*Locations:*   LC (OCT 11 1974), MJB (dj), PSt.

*Note:*   Galley proofs are at MJB.

*Review copy:*   Proof bound in red wrappers. Front: 'Uncorrected First Proof | JOHN O'HARA | GOOD | SAMARITAN | AND OTHER STORIES | [Random House device] | RANDOM HOUSE • NEW YORK'. Produced by the Crane Duplicating Service. Location: MJB.

A 36.1.b
*Second printing:*   New York: Random House, [1974].

A 36.1.c
*First edition, first English printing (1976)*

# JOHN O'HARA

# GOOD

# SAMARITAN

## AND OTHER STORIES

**HODDER AND STOUGHTON**

LONDON · SYDNEY · AUCKLAND · TORONTO

A 36.1.c: $8^7/_{16}'' \times 5^3/_8''$

*Copyright page:* 'Copyright © 1964, 1968 and 1974 by United States Trust Company of New York, as executor of and trustee under the will of John O'Hara. First printed in Great Britain 1976. ISBN 0 340 19436 7. . . . Printed in Great Britain for Hodder and Stoughton Limited, St. Paul's House, Warwick Lane, London EC4P 4AH, by Lowe & Brydone (Printers) Ltd., Thetford, Norfolk.'

[i–vii] viii–ix [x] [1–3] 4–296 [297–302]; first page of each new story not numbered

[1–8]$^{16}$ [9]$^{12}$ [10]$^{16}$

*Contents:*   p. i: half title; p. ii: 'BOOKS BY JOHN O'HARA'; p. iii: title; p. iv: copyright; p. v: 'CONTENTS'; p. vi: blank; pp. vii–ix: 'FOREWORD' by Albert Erskine; p. x: blank; p. 1: half title; p. 2: blank; pp. 3–296: text; p. 297: 'ABOUT THE AUTHOR'; pp. 298–302: blank.

*Paper:*   Wove.

*Binding:*   Black paper-covered boards, with B grain (linen). Spine goldstamped: 'John | O'Hara | GOOD | SAMARITAN | and other | stories | [Hodder & Stoughton device]'. All edges trimmed. White wove endpapers.

*Dust jacket:*   Front, spine, and back lettered on navy blue. Front: '[white] John | O'Hara | [within turquoise frame] [yellow] GOOD | SAMARITAN | [white] and other stories | [yellow] 14 | previously | uncollected stories'. Spine: '[vertically] [white] John O'Hara [yellow] GOOD SAMARITAN | [white] and other stories | [horizontally] [Hodder & Stoughton device]'. Back has photo of O'Hara and biographical sketch. Front flap has blurb for *GS*. Back flap quotes reviews for *Lovey Childs* and *The Ewings*.

*Publications:*   3,250 copies. Published March 1976. £3.95.

*Locations:*   BL (4 JUNE 1976), MJB (dj).

A 37 "AN ARTIST IS HIS OWN FAULT"

A 37.1
*First edition, only printing (1977)*

# "An Artist Is His Own Fault"

## John O'Hara

*on Writers and Writing*

*Edited with an Introduction by*
**Matthew J. Bruccoli**
*Jefferies Professor of English*
*University of South Carolina*

**Southern Illinois University Press**
*Carbondale and Edwardsville*

**Feffer & Simons, Inc.**
*London and Amsterdam*

A 37.1: 7$^{15}$/$_{16}$" × 4$^{7}$/$_{8}$"

Library of Congress Cataloging in Publication Data

O'Hara, John, 1905-1970.
    "An artist is his own fault."

    1. O'Hara, John, 1905-1970—Technique—Addresses,
essays, lectures.  2.  Fiction—Technique—
Addresses, essays, lectures.  I.  Bruccoli, Matthew
Joseph, 1931-    II.  Title.
PS3529.H29Z78  1977        813'.5'2        76-43279
ISBN 0-8093-0796-0

[i–vi] vii–xv [xvi] [1–2] 3–52 [53–54] 55–118 [119–120] 121–131 [132–134] 135–154 [155–156] 157–173 [174–176] 177–226 [227–232]

[1–3]¹⁶ [4–5]¹⁴ [6–8]¹⁶

*Contents:* p. i: SIU Press device; p. ii: blank; p. iii: title; p. iv: copyright; p. v: 'To Peter Shepherd of | Harold Ober Associates'; p. vi: blank; pp. vii–viii: 'Contents'; pp. ix–xv: 'Introduction | by Matthew J. Bruccoli'; p. xvi: blank; p. 1: 'The Rider College Lectures'; p. 2: O'Hara's 'Foreword'; pp. 3–226: text; pp. 227–232: blank.

*The Rider College Lectures:* "Dialog, Detail, and Type,"* "Logistics of the Novel,"* "Method and Technique of the Novel."* *Speeches:* "Writing—What's in It for Me?"* "What Makes a Writer?"* "The Prize Is a Good One,"* "Remarks on the Novel," "We All Know How Good We Are," "Every Great Writer of Fiction Was a Great Social Historian." *Unpublished Essays and Forewords:* "These Stories Were Part of Me,"* "I Was Determined to Make Plain What I Had Seen,"* "Characters in Search,"* "My Favorite Room."* *On F. Scott Fitzgerald:* "In Memory of Scott Fitzgerald: Certain Aspects," "Scott Fitzgerald—Odds and Ends," "An Artist Is His Own Fault." *Book Reviews and Reading Lists:* "Good Reading," "Dorothy Parker, Hip Pocket Size," "That Benny Greenspan," "The Novels Novelists Read," "The Author's Name Is Hemingway," "My Ten Favorite Plays." *Interviews and Public Statements:* "John O'Hara, Who Talks Like His Stories," "The Only Good Thing I Ever Got Out of Booze," "Talk With John O'Hara," "How Do I Write?" "Talk With John O'Hara," "John O'Hara From Pottsville, Pa.," "As *From the Terrace* Goes to Press," "Mr. O'Hara," "Appt. With O'Hara," "Talk With the Author," "Reply to Questionnaire," "Good Writers Get Published," "If You're Going to Write, Nothing Will Stop You," "A Writer's Look at His Town, Career, and Future," "Don't Say It Never Happened," "I Have Recently Been Putting Action Back Into My Stories," "The World, I Think, Is Better Off . . . ,'" "Two Blows He Had to Beat," "O'Hara, in Rare Interview, Calls the Literary Landscape Fairly Bleak." Asterisks follow previously unpublished material.

*Typography and paper:* Palatino, 10 point on 12. 5¹⁵/₁₆″ (6¹/₄″) × 3¹/₂″; 36 lines per page. Running heads: rectos, section titles; versos, 'John O'Hara on Writers and Writing'. Wove paper.

*Binding:* Three-piece binding. Black V-cloth (smooth) sides; grayish brown (#61) V-cloth shelfback. Front blindstamped: '*John O'Hara*'. Spine goldstamped: '[vertically]

*O'Hara* [leaf] "An Artist Is His Own Fault" | [horizontally] Southern | Illinois | University | Press.' All edges trimmed. Maroon and yellow bands at top and bottom. Medium yellow (#87) endpapers.

*Dust jacket:* Printed on white background. Front: '[dark yellowish brown] John O'Hara | [black] on Writers and Writing | [dark red] *"An Artist Is His | Own Fault"* | [black] Edited with an Introduction by | Matthew J. Bruccoli | [sketch of O'Hara in brown tweed suit]'. Spine: '[vertically] [black] John O'Hara [dark red] "An Artist Is His Own Fault" [horizontally] [brown SIU Press device]'. Back: photo of O'Hara. Front flap: blurb. Back flap: continuation of blurb and note on Bruccoli.

*Publication:* 3,075 copies of the first printing. Published 31 January 1977. $8.95.

*Printing:* Composition by Heritage Printers, Charlotte, N.C.; printed and bound by Colonial Press, Clinton, Mass.

*Locations:* MJB (dj), PSt (dj).

*Review copy:* Spiral-bound proof in yellow paper covers. Printed white label on front: ' "An Artist Is His Own Fault" | John O'Hara | *on Writers and Writing* | Southern Illinois University Press | *Carbondale and Edwardsville* | Feffer & Simons, Inc. | *London and Amsterdam'*. Location: MJB.

John O'Hara
on Writers and Writing

"An Artist Is His
Own Fault"

Edited with an Introduction by
Matthew J. Bruccoli

John O'Hara    "An Artist Is His Own Fault"

$8.95

This important gathering of previously uncollected and unpublished material enlarges the assessment of John O'Hara as a craftsman and a conscious literary artist.

In 1959 O'Hara was invited to be the first novelist to participate in the new Liberal Arts program at Rider College in Trenton, N.J. He was then at the peak of his writing career, and it followed that his first two lectures and the subsequent third (1961) were on the American Novel. These lectures comprise the core of O'Hara's major critical statement. The lectures are techniques of fiction writing. The first lecture dealt with "Duke, Detail, and Type," the second with "Logistics of the Novel," and the last with "Style and Technique of the Novel." Throughout the Rider lectures O'Hara's main concern was with character creation—with the problem of making characters believable, and with the greater problem of creating a character who would carry a novel. Also, the lectures are of particular value because they were developed with close reference to his own work and reveal the lessons he learned and the rules he formulated while practicing his profession.

In addition, the editor of this important collection has assembled thirty-eight other pieces which, brought together, provide a fresh perspective on this author whose outspokenness antagonized literary critics and prize-givers, revealing him as a sensitive man, deeply loyal to his friends and the native muse, held in high esteem, such as Steinbeck, Faulkner, Hemingway, Fitzgerald and Thornton Wilder. Among O'Hara's speeches we have his acceptance of the National Book Award for Ten North Frederick, "Ten Years as a Cad," and of the Merit Medal for the Novel awarded by the Academy of Arts and Letters, "We All Know How Good We Are." In his London talk, given at the Foyles bookstore luncheon marking the English paperback publication of The

Continued on back flap

Continued from front flap

Lockwood Concern, he speaks of his thirty-year love affair with England and comments on his reputation as a "social historian."

Among the rest of the pieces in this volume, two previously unpublished ones of particular value to the understanding of O'Hara's work, the foreword to The Selected Stories of John O'Hara ("These Stories Were Part of Me") and "Characters in Search." There are also three useful pieces on F. Scott Fitzgerald, and O'Hara's reviews and interviews, and public statements present six with sums of his strongest comments on writers and writing.

The material contained in "An Artist Is His Own Fault" reveals the scope and level of O'Hara's thinking about his craft, and will stimulate the reader to read O'Hara's novels as Appointment in Samarra, Rage to Live, Ten North Frederick, and From the Terrace.

Matthew J. Bruccoli, Jefferies Professor of English at the University of South Carolina and editor of the Southern Illinois University Press's Lost American Fiction series, has prepared a valuable Introduction for this volume. He is the author of The O'Hara Concern, a biography of John O'Hara.

Crayon Union photograph by George V. Bigelow, courtesy the Pennsylvania State University Library O'Hara Collection

Printed in the United States of America

ISBN 0-8093-0796-0

Dust jacket for A37.1

A 38 THE SECOND EWINGS

A 38.1
*Only printing (1977)*

## The Second Ewings

*Bloomfield Hills, Michigan*
BRUCCOLI CLARK, 1977
*Columbia, South Carolina*

A 38.1: 10$^7/_8$″ × 8$^3/_8$″

[A–B] [i–iii] [1] 2–74; pp. i–74 printed on rectos only

78 unbound leaves.

*Contents:*　p. A: title page; p. B: certificate of limitation and copyright; p. i: 'Foreword' signed 'M.J.B.'; p. ii: 'THE SECOND EWINGS'; p. iii: plot-sheet; pp. 1–74: text, headed 'John O'Hara | 13 Feb 1970'.

*Typography and paper:*　Facsimile of typescript. $10^7/_8''$ × $8^3/_8''$. Yellow wove paper.

*Binding:*　Box covered with brown orange (#54) paper. Printed white label on front with reduced title page.

*Publication:*　500 numbered copies published 15 June 1977. $30.

*Printing:*　Printed by Vogue Press, Columbia, S.C. Box manufactured by Imperial Paper Box Corp., Brooklyn, N.Y.

*Locations:*　Lilly, MJB, PSt.

*Review copies:*　25 unnumbered stapled sets for review.

　　　　A 39 SELECTED LETTERS
　　　　　*Forthcoming (1978)*

*Selected Letters of John O'Hara,* ed. Matthew J. Bruccoli. New York: Random House, 1978.

# AA. Supplement

## Collections of O'Hara's Work

Arranged chronologically.

### AA 1

Here's | O'Hara | THREE NOVELS | AND | TWENTY SHORT STORIES | BY | JOHN O'HARA | DUELL, SLOAN AND PEARCE | NEW YORK

1946. $3.

*On copyright page:* 'first edition'.

*Contents:* "Foreword" by O'Hara; *Butterfield 8; Hope of Heaven* (lacks final chapter); *Pal Joey;* "Where's the Game?" "Patriotism," "The King of the Desert," "Radio," "Can You Carry Me?" "The Magical Numbers," "The Doctor's Son," "Trouble in 1949," "Price's Always Open," "Days," "Are We Leaving Tomorrow?" "Lunch Tuesday," "Sidesaddle," Saffercisco," "Ice Cream," "The Gentleman in the Tan Suit," "I Could Have Had a Yacht," "Invite," "Most Gorgeous Thing," "Do You Like It Here?" No first book material except previously unpublished "Foreword."

*Second printing:* Cleveland & New York: World, [1946].

See A 4, A 5, and A 7.

### AA 2

[line of type decorations] | All The Girls | He Wanted | *& Other Stories* | By John O'Hara | [circular device] | No. 50 | AVON NOVELS INC. | 119 W. 57th St. New York 19, N.Y. | [line of type decorations]

1949. Modern Short Story Monthly #50. 35¢.

*32 stories:* "All the Girls He Wanted," "Never a Dull Moment," "The Gentleman in the Tan Suit," "I Could Have Had a Yacht," "Peggy," "Days," "Are We Leaving Tomorrow?" "Portisan on the Portis," "Lunch Tuesday," "Shave," "Price's Always Open," "Mary," "I Never Seen Anything Like It," "Frankie," "Sportsmanship," "Good-By, Herman," "New Day," "It Wouldn't Break Your Arm," "Pleasure," "Saffercisco," "Ice Cream," "Screen Test," "Sidesaddle," "Most Gorgeous Thing," "A Day Like Today," "Brother," "Hotel Kid," "Except in My Memory," "My Girls," "The Ideal Man," "On His Hands," "Of Thee I Sing, Baby." No first book material.

*Second edition:* New York: Avon, [1951]. #368.

### AA 3

Selected | Short Stories | of | John O'Hara | WITH AN INTRODUCTION BY | Lionel Trilling | [torchbearer] | THE MODERN LIBRARY *New York*

215

1956. #211. $1.95.

*On copyright page:*   'First Modern Library Edition, 1956'.

*32 stories:*   "The Decision," "Everything Satisfactory," "The Moccasins," "Doctor and Mrs. Parsons," "Pardner," "A Phase of Life," "Walter T. Carriman," "Now We Know," "Too Young," "Summer's Day," "The King of the Desert," "Bread Alone," "Graven Image," "The Next-to-Last Dance of the Season," "Where's the Game?" "Mrs. Whitman," "Price's Always Open," "The Cold House," "Are We Leaving Tomorrow?" "No Mistakes," "The Ideal Man," "Do You Like It Here?" "The Doctor's Son," "Hotel Kid," "The Public Career of Mr. Seymour Harrisburg," "In the Morning Sun," "War Aims," "Secret Meeting," "Other Women's Households," "Over the River and Through the Wood," "I Could Have Had a Yacht," "A Respectable Place." No first book material.

7 printings.


AA 4

the | great | short | stories | of | JOHN | O'HARA | *stories from* | THE DOCTOR'S SON AND OTHER STORIES | *and* | FILES ON PARADE | [left] [Bantam device] [right] BANTAM BOOKS | NEW YORK

1956. #A 1484. 35¢.

*On copyright page:*   'Bantam edition published July 1956'.

*70 stories:*   Includes *The Doctor's Son* and *Files on Parade.* No first book material.

5 printings, 1956–1965.

*Second edition:*   New York: Popular Library, [1973]. #445-00148-125. $1.25.

See A 3 and A 6.


AA 5

[first 2 lines within decorated single-rule frame] 49 | STORIES | *by* | JOHN O'HARA | [torchbearer] | [rule] *The Modern Library* • *New York* | [rule]

1963. Modern Library Giant #G-88. $3.95.

*Contents:*   "Introduction" by John K. Hutchens, *Assembly,* and *The Cape Cod Lighter.* No first book material.

2 printings. See A 20, A 22.


AA 6

John O'Hara | Appointment | in Samarra | BUtterfield 8 | Hope of Heaven | RANDOM HOUSE New York

1968.

Distributed by the Literary Guild and associated book clubs in 1968; distributed by the Doubleday Bargain Book Club in 1973.

No first book material.

See A 2, A 4, A 5.

AA 7

[Random House device] | THE O'HARA GENERATION | JOHN O'HARA | RANDOM HOUSE [slash] NEW YORK

1969. $6.95.

*On copyright page:* 'First Printing.'

*Contents:* Introduction by Albert Erskine; 22 stories: "The Doctor's Son," "Over the River and Through the Wood," "Do You Like It Here?" "Summer's Day," "The Decision," "Drawing Room B," "Mrs. Stratton of Oak Knoll," "Mary and Norma," "You Can Always Tell Newark," "Pat Collins," "The First Day," "Your Fah Neefah Neeface," "The Friends of Miss Julia," "The Manager," "The Madeline Wherry Case," "The Bonfire," "The Hardware Man," "Andrea,' "Flight," "The General," "Afternoon Waltz," "Fatimas and Kisses." No first book material.

*Second printing:* New York: Popular Library, [1975]. #445-08375-175. $1.75.

*Second edition:* New York: Bantam, [1970]. #Q5546. $1.25.

# B. First-Appearance Contributions to Books and Pamphlets

Titles in which material by O'Hara appears for the first time in a book or pamphlet, arranged chronologically. Previously unpublished items are so identified. The first printings only of these titles are described, but English editions are also noted. Locations are provided for scarce items.

B 1 NEW YORKER SCRAPBOOK
*1931*

THE NEW YORKER | SCRAPBOOK | [DD device] | DOUBLEDAY, DORAN & COM-
PANY, INC. | GARDEN CITY, NEW YORK, 1931

*On copyright page:* 'FIRST EDITION'.

"Ten Eyck or Pershing? Pershing or Ten Eyck?" pp. 94–98; "The New Office," pp.
321–324. See C 46, C 49.


B 2 BEST SHORT SHORTS
*1932*

THE BEST | SHORT SHORTS | OF 1932 | *Edited by* | PAUL ERNEST ANDERSON |
*and* | LIONEL WHITE | [GPP emblem] | G. P. PUTNAM'S SONS | NEW YORK:
LONDON | 1932

"Early Afternoon," pp. 200–205. See C 79.


B 3 THESE OUR MODERNS
*1933*

[within shaded single-rule frame] [swash T, O, M] *These Our Moderns* | Edited by |
ROBERT E. GALBRAITH | PENNSYLVANIA STATE COLLEGE | 1933 | THOMAS NELSON
& SONS • NEW YORK

"Portrait of a Referee," pp. 121–124; briefly quotes O'Hara, p. 396. See C 57.


B 4 O. HENRY MEMORIAL AWARD
*1937*

O. HENRY | MEMORIAL AWARD | [swash P, S, f] *Prize Stories of 1937* | SELECTED
AND EDITED BY | HARRY HANSEN | *Literary Editor* | of the New York World-Tele-
gram | [DD anchor device] | DOUBLEDAY, DORAN & COMPANY, INC. | GARDEN
CITY, NEW YORK | 1937

*On copyright page:* 'FIRST EDITION'.

"My Girls," pp. 165–168. See C 131.

221

### B 5 SHORT STORIES FROM THE NEW YORKER
*1940*

SHORT STORIES | FROM | THE | NEW YORKER | 19[Eustace Tilly in circle]40 | SIMON AND SCHUSTER • NEW YORK

"Are We Leaving Tomorrow?" pp, 426–430. See C 135.

London: Gollancz, 1951.

### B 6 RINGLING BROS. PROGRAM
*[1941]*

[red] RINGLING BROS AND BARNUM & BAILEY 15¢ | [red, yellow, and blue] CIRCUS | [black] MAGAZINE AND DAILY REVIEW | [color photo of tiger] | FEATURE ARTICLES AND ILLUSTRATIONS BY OUTSTANDING CONTRIBUTORS

1941. Cover title.

"From Winter Quarters, N.Y.," pp. 8, 60. Previously unpublished. Also autobiographical note, p. 8.

*Location:* MJB.

### B 7 REVUE SKETCHES
*1943*

VOLUME VII | (COMEDY SKETCH BOOK NO. 1) | REVUE SKETCHES | VAUDEVILLE COMEDY ACTS | *Prepared by the* | COMMITTEE ON SCRIPTS | FOR SOLDIER AND SAILOR SHOWS | *of the* | WRITERS' WAR BOARD | [shield with comic and tragic masks; stars; SOLDIER SHOWS] | *For use exclusively in* | MILITARY AND NAVAL ESTABLISHMENTS | *By personnel of the* | ARMED FORCES OF THE UNITED STATES | 1943 | THE INFANTRY JOURNAL, INC. | WASHINGTON, D.C.

Cover title.

"Is This the Army, Mr. Jones?" pp. 71–76. Previously unpublished.

*Location:* PSt.

### B 8 HALF-A-HUNDRED TALES
*[1945]*

Half-A-Hundred | [man with book leaning on large T] TALES BY GREAT | AMERICAN WRITERS | EDITED, WITH AN INTRODUCTION | BY CHARLES GRAYSON | THE BLAKISTON COMPANY—PHILADELPHIA

1945.

"The Lieutenant," pp. 329–333. See C 178. This story is included in *Pipe Night* (1945)—priority undetermined.

### B 9 PORTABLE F. SCOTT FITZGERALD
*1945*

[within double-rules frame, decorated at sides] *The Portable* | F. SCOTT | FITZGERALD | [decoration] | *Selected by Dorothy Parker* | [decoration] | *Introduction by John O'Hara* | NEW YORK | THE VIKING PRESS | 1945

*On copyright page:* 'Published by The Viking Press in September 1945'.

"Introduction," pp. vii–xix. Previously unpublished. Also published as *The Indispensable F. Scott Fitzgerald* (New York: The Book Society, 1949). See A 37.

#### B 10 HERE'S O'HARA
[*1946*]

Here's | O'Hara | THREE NOVELS | AND | TWENTY SHORT STORIES | BY | JOHN O'HARA | DUELL, SLOAN AND PEARCE | NEW YORK

1946.

*On copyright page:* 'first edition'.

"Foreword" by O'Hara, pp. vii–viii. Previously unpublished. See AA 1.

#### B 11 WRITERS AND WRITING
*1946*

[within shaded single-rule frame] WRITERS AND WRITING | by Robert Van Gelder | [below frame] Charles Scribner's Sons     New York 1946

*On copyright page:* Scribner Press seal.

"John O'Hara, Who Talks Like His Stories," pp. 59–61; interview. See A 37 and D 174.

#### B 12 MIXTURE FOR MEN
*1946*

[2-page title] *A COLLECTION OF FACT AND HUMOR BY SOME OF THE BEST WRITERS OF SHORT PIECES IN OUR TIME* | Edited by FRED FELDKAMP | [diagonally] Mixture for Men | [right page: cartoon of gentleman and butler] | [following 5 lines on left page] *With illustrations by* | PAUL GALDONE • *LEO HERSHFIELD* • *JOHN* | MACKEY • *CHARLES D. PEARSON* • *GEORGE* | PRICE • | *BARBARA SHERMUND* • SAUL | STEINBERG • JAMES THURBER | Doubleday & Company, Inc. Garden City, New York, 1946.

*On copyright page:* 'FIRST EDITION'.

"The English—They Are a Funny Race," pp. 170–176. See D 166.

*Second edition:* New York: Editions for the Armed Forces. [1946]. #1253.

#### B 13 BEST SHORT SHORT STORIES FROM COLLIER'S
[*1948*]

THE BEST | *Short Short Stories* | FROM *Collier's* | SELECTED, WITH AN INTRODUCTION AND NOTES, BY | Barthold Fles | [Forum device] | CLEVELAND AND NEW YORK | THE WORLD PUBLISHING COMPANY

1948.

*On copyright page:* 'FIRST PRINTING APRIL 1948'.

"On Time," pp. 220–223. See C 180.

#### B 14 RINGLING BROS. PROGRAM
*1948*

[yellow] RINGLING BROS [white] and | [green] BARNUM & BAILEY | [painting of clown] | [green] PHOTOS [red] FEATURES | [white] STORIES | [white] COMICS | [black] CIRCUS MAGAZINE & PROGRAM [red] 1948 Edition 25¢

Cover title.

"A Visit to 'Quarters," pp. 34, 50. Previously unpublished.

*Location:*   MJB.


#### B 15 HEYWOOD BROUN
*1949*

Heywood Broun | A BIOGRAPHICAL PORTRAIT | *by* DALE KRAMER | [sketch of man at desk] | NEW YORK • 1949 | CURRENT BOOKS, INC. | A. A. WYN, PUBLISHER

O'Hara quoted, p. 203. Previously unpublished.


#### B 16 IRON GATE OF "21"
*1950*

[swash T] The | IRON GATE | of | [script] Jack + Charlie's | "21" | Thru which is presented a vivid portrayal of a | unique institution--by a distinguished group of | authors, artists and celebrities. | *Issued on the twenty-fifth anniversary of the founding of "21,"* | *in memory of John Carl Kriendler for the benefit of the* | *New York Heart Association.* | Published by the Jack Kriendler Memorial Foundation, Inc. | New York | MCML | © 1950.

" '21' Is My Club," p. 209. Previously unpublished.


#### B 17 MONSTER RALLY
*[1950]*

[on 4 banners between poles] MONSTER RALLY | [signature] Chas Addams | SIMON AND SCHUSTER | NEW YORK

1950.

"Foreword," pp. v–vii. Previously unpublished.

London: Hamish Hamilton, [1951].


#### B 18 PAL JOEY RECORDING
*[1952]*

Sleeve for Columbia recording (#ML 4364) of *Pal Joey.*

1952.

Letter to Richard Rodgers. See D 178. Also in Rodgers's *Musical Stages* (New York: Random House, 1975).

B 19 APPOINTMENT IN SAMARRA
[1953]

APPOINTMENT | IN SAMARRA | BY JOHN O'HARA | WITH A NEW FOREWORD BY THE AUTHOR | [torchbearer] | [rule] | THE MODERN LIBRARY • NEW YORK | [rule] 1953.

On copyright page: 'First Modern Library Edition, 1953'.

"Foreword," vii–xi. Previously unpublished. See A 2.1.j.


B 20 HARVARD CLASS OF 1929 REPORT
1954

HARVARD CLASS | OF 1929 | Twenty-fifth Anniversary Report | [Harvard seal] | CAMBRIDGE | Printed for the Class | 1954

"Joseph Willetts Outerbridge," pp. 895–898. Previously unpublished.


B 21 THE WRITER OBSERVED
[1956]

HARVEY BREIT | The Writer Observed | [World device] | THE WORLD PUBLISHING COMPANY | CLEVELAND AND NEW YORK

1956.

On copyright page: 'FIRST EDITION'.

Interview with O'Hara, pp. 81–83. See A 37 and D 199.

London: Alvin Redman, [1957].


B 22 ACLU STATEMENT
[1957]

Head title: AMERICAN CIVIL LIBERTIES UNION | STATEMENT ON CENSORSHIP ACTIVITY BY PRIVATE ORGANIZATIONS | AND THE NATIONAL ORGANIZATION FOR DECENT LITERATURE

Printed statement, issued 5 May 1957. O'Hara was among the more than 150 signatories.


B 23 THREE VIEWS OF THE NOVEL
1957

Three Views of | the Novel | by | Irving Stone, John O'Hara and MacKinlay Kantor | Lectures Presented Under the | Auspices of the Gertrude Clarke Whittall | Poetry and Literature Fund | [LC seal] | REFERENCE DEPARTMENT | THE LIBRARY OF CONGRESS | WASHINGTON: 1957

"Remarks on the Novel," pp. 17–29. Previously unpublished.

Printed paper wrappers. See A 37.

*Literary Lectures Presented at the Library of Congress.* Washington: Library of Congress, 1973.

*Note:* A cassette recording of John O'Hara delivering this lecture was distributed by Bruccoli Clark Publishers in 1977.

### B 24 GERSHWIN SONG BOOK
*[1960]*

[following 3 lines on music paper] [script] The George and Ira | [roman] GERSHWIN | SONG BOOK | [horizontal cigar] | [vertical pencil] | Foreword by Ira Gershwin [slash] Illustrations by Milton Glaser [slash] Arrangements by Dr. Albert Sirmay | [script] Simon and Schuster

1960.

*On copyright page:* 'FIRST PRINTING'.

O'Hara telegram, p. x. Previously unpublished.

### B 25 SATURDAY EVENING POST STORIES
*1960*

THE SATURDAY EVENING | Post | STORIES 1959 | DOUBLEDAY & COMPANY, INC., GARDEN CITY, NEW YORK, 1960

"That First Husband," pp. 27–36. See C 235.

### B 26 SINCLAIR LEWIS
*[1961]*

[two-page title; left] [drawing of Lewis] | *McGraw-Hill Book Company Inc.* | [right] Sinclair | Lewis | AN AMERICAN LIFE | BY [shaded] Mark | Schorer | [black] *New York, Toronto, London*

1961.

*On copyright page:* 'FIRST EDITION'.

Previously unpublished. Letter to Schorer (17 February 1959), p. 351.

London: Heinemann, [1963].

### B 27 62 QUOGUE QUIPS
*[1962]*

[against background of horizontal lines with asterisks and globe] 62 | [letters of next two lines suspended from '62' with strings] QUOGUE | QUIPS | [signature] Adele Greeff

1962.

"Long May They—," p. 1. Previously unpublished.

*Location:* PSt.

B 28 FACES OF FIVE DECADES
[*1964*]

THE FACES OF | FIVE DECADES | SELECTIONS FROM FIFTY YEARS OF | *The New Republic* | 1914–1964 | EDITED BY *Robert B. Luce* | COMMENTARY BY | *Arthur M. Schlesinger, Jr.* | [device] | SIMON AND SCHUSTER • NEW YORK

1964.

*On copyright page:*  'First Printing'.

"In Memory of Scott Fitzgerald," pp. 275–276. See A 37 and D 183.

*Fifty Years of The New Republic.* London: Allen & Unwin, [1965].


B 29 PROCEEDINGS OF THE AMERICAN ACADEMY
*1965*

[red] PROCEEDINGS | OF THE | [black] AMERICAN ACADEMY | OF ARTS AND LETTERS | [red] AND THE | [black] NATIONAL INSTITUTE | OF ARTS AND LETTERS | [red & white Academy seal and black & white Institute seal] | *SECOND SERIES* • *NUMBER FIFTEEN* [tapered red rule] | NEW YORK • 1965

"Acceptance by Mr. O'Hara," pp. 428–430. Previously unpublished. See A 32 and A 37.


B 30 MEMORIAL SERVICE
*1970*

JOHN | O'HARA | [leaf decoration] | January 31, 1905 | April 11, 1970

Memorial service at Random House, 13 May 1970. Privately printed for Katharine Barnes O'Hara.

1970.

Previously unpublished letter to Wylie O'Hara Holahan, [January 1962], pp. [15–16].

Unknown number of copies in printed paper wrappers; also copies bound in full leather.


B 31 FILM AS FILM
*1971*

FILM AS FILM: | Critical Responses to Film Art | JOY COULD BOYUM | *New York University* | ADRIENNE SCOTT | *Fordham University* | Allyn & Bacon, Inc. Boston

1971.

Review of *Citizen Kane,* pp. 138–140. See E 2 (17 March 1941).

*Note: Film as Film* precedes *Focus on Citizen Kane,* ed. Ronald Gottesman (Englewood Cliffs, N.J.: Prentice-Hall, [1971]).

B 32 FEET FIRST
[*1971*]

FEET FIRST | by BEN FINNEY | Foreword by John O'Hara | *with five decades of personal photos* | crown publishers, inc.   new york

1971.

"Foreword," p. ix. Previously unpublished.


B 33 HAMILTON AUCTION
*1972*

Cover title: [2 lines in gothic to right of owl] Charles | Hamilton | AUCTION | Number 56 | THE | WALDORF | ASTORIA | *Park Avenue at fiftieth* | MARCH 9, 1972

Quotes from previously unpublished letters to Charles Poore, item #226.


B 34 JOHN O'HARA: A CHECKLIST
[*1972*]

[two-page title; left] [double rules separated by angle brackets running across both pages] | *Compiled by* | MATTHEW J. BRUCCOLI | *With a previously unpublished speech by* | JOHN O'HARA | *Random House* [Random House device] *New York* | [right] *John O'Hara: | A Checklist*

1972.

*On copyright page:*  'FIRST PRINTING'.

Foyles speech (3 May 1967), pp. ix–xxi. Previously unpublished. Also reproduces inscriptions and typescript page from *The Lockwood Concern.*


B 35 CHICAGO
[*1973*]

CHICAGO | A PERSONAL HISTORY | OF AMERICA'S MOST AMERICAN CITY | *FINIS FARR* | ARLINGTON HOUSE     *New Rochelle, N. Y.*

1973.

O'Hara briefly quoted, p. 369.


B 36 O'HARA: A BIOGRAPHY
[*1973*]

O'HARA | [photo] | A BIOGRAPHY | BY FINIS FARR | LITTLE, BROWN AND COM-PANY-BOSTON-TORONTO

1973.

*On copyright page:*  'FIRST EDITION'.

Excerpts from previously unpublished letters.

London & New York: Allen, 1974.

        B 37 THE WORLD AND THE 20's
            [*1973*]

[two-page title; left] [rule] | The Golden Years | of New York's | Legendary News-
paper | [rule] | edited by James Boylan | [rule] | [publisher's device] THE DIAL
PRESS 1973 | [rule] | [right] [rule] | THE | [rule] | WORLD | [rule] | AND THE | [rule]
| [*World* logo] 20'S | [rule]

*On copyright page:* 'FIRST PRINTING 1973'.

"George F. Gabbitry Settles Once and for All the Democratic Situation—If Any," pp.
279–281. From "The Conning Tower." See D 15.

        B 38 THE ROMANTIC EGOISTS
            [*1974*]

THE | ROMANTIC | EGOISTS | *EDITED BY* | MATTHEW J. BRUCCOLI | SCOTTIE
FITZGERALD SMITH | *AND* | JOAN P. KERR | *ART EDITOR* | MARGARETA A.
LYONS | [decoration] | *CHARLES SCRIBNER'S SONS* [slash] *NEW YORK*

1974.

*On copyright page:* '1 . . . MD/C . . . 2'.

Facsimile of previously unpublished letter to F. Scott Fitzgerald, p. 200.

Also 500 numbered copies, signed by Scottie Fitzgerald Smith. Boxed.

        B 39 THE ELEVENTH HOUSE
            [*1975*]

HUDSON STRODE | The | Eleventh | House | [rule] | MEMOIRS | [device] | New
York and London | HARCOURT BRACE JOVANOVICH

1975.

*On copyright page:* 'First edition'.

Previously unpublished letter to Strode, pp. 159–160.

        B 40 STRANGER AT THE PARTY
            [*1975*]

STRANGER | AT THE | PARTY | [rule] | *A* | *Memoir* | [rule] | Helen | Lawrenson |
[device] | *Random House* | *New York*

1975.

*On copyright page:* 'First Edition'.

Excerpts from previously unpublished letters to Lawrenson, pp. 83–84.

        B 41 THE O'HARA CONCERN
            [*1975*]

THE | O'HARA | CONCERN | [rule] | *A Biography of John O'Hara* | [rule] | BY |
MATTHEW J. BRUCCOLI | [Random House Device] | *Random House* | *New York*

1975.

*On copyright page:* 'First Edition'.

Previously unpublished letters; "Famous Author Writes of His Early Days on Journal," pp. 34–37 (see D 218); "A Speech by George F. Gabbitry at a Christmas Party . . . ," pp. 46–47 (see D 9); facsimiles of inscriptions; excerpts from other previously unpublished material.

            B 42 STEINBECK: A LIFE IN LETTERS
                 [*1975*]

[2-page title; left] Edited by | ELAINE STEINBECK | and | ROBERT WALLSTEN | [swash A] *A Life* | [right] [in shades of gray against black panel] STEINBECK | STEINBECK | STEINBECK | [to left of panel] *in* | [within panel] LETTERS | [below panel] THE VIKING PRESS NEW YORK | [rule]

1975. Limited and trade printings.

Passages from previously unpublished letters to Steinbeck, pp. 123, 745. Quotes O'Hara conversation, p. 242. Letters to O'Hara, pp. 359–361, 432, 435, 587–589, 745, 770–771.

London: Heinemann, [1976].

# C. Short Stories

The first publication of all O'Hara short stories in periodicals or books, arranged chronologically.

C 1

"The Alumnae Bulletin," *The New Yorker,* IV (5 May 1928), 101.[1]

C 2

"Overheard in a Telephone Booth," *The New Yorker,* IV (19 May 1928), 77–78.

C 3

"Tennis," *The New Yorker,* IV (9 June 1928), 85.

C 4

"The Follow-up," *The New Yorker,* IV (7 July 1928), 37.

C 5

"Do You Know ———?" *The New Yorker,* IV (14 July 1928), 41.

C 6

"Spring 3100," *The New Yorker,* IV (8 September 1928), 56.

C 7

"A Safe and Sane Fourth," *The New Yorker,* IV (15 September 1928), 79–82.

Delphian.[2]

C 8

"The Hallowe'en Party," *The New Yorker,* IV (22 September 1928), 84–85.

Delphian.

C 9

"Taking Up Sport," *The New Yorker,* IV (13 October 1928), 58–63.

Delphian.

C 10

"The Coal Fields," *The New Yorker,* IV (20 October 1928), 85–88.

Delphian.

C 11

"The Boss' Present," *The New Yorker,* IV (1 December 1928), 56, 58, 62.

Hagedorn & Brownmiller.[3]

---

1. The paginations and occasionally the contents may differ in the metropolitan and out-of-town editions of *The New Yorker.*

2. The first of a series of 15 stories about the Orange County Afternoon Delphian Society.

3. The first of a series of 14 stories about the Hagedorn & Brownmiller Paint and Varnish Co.

C 12
"The Yule in Retrospect," *The New Yorker,* IV (29 December 1928), 40–41.

Delphian.

C 13
"Theatre," *The New Yorker,* IV (5 January 1929), 70.

C 14
"Fifty-Cent Meal," *The New Yorker,* IV (12 January 1929), 63–64.

C 15
"The House Organ," *The New Yorker,* V (23 March 1929), 113–114.

Hagedorn & Brownmiller.

C 16
"Fifteen-Minutes-for-Efficiency," *The New Yorker,* V (30 March 1929), 47–50.

Hagedorn & Brownmiller.

C 17
"A New Apparatus," *The New Yorker,* V (6 April 1929), 61–64.

Delphian.

C 18
"Appreciation," *The New Yorker,* V (13 April 1929), 97–98.

Hagedorn & Brownmiller.

C 19
"Mr. Bonner," *The New Yorker,* V (25 May 1929), 74–75.

C 20
"Fun for the Kiddies," *The New Yorker,* V (1 June 1929), 76–78.

Delphian.

C 21
"The Tournament," *The New Yorker,* V (8 June 1929), 81–83.

Hagedorn & Brownmiller.

C 22
"Convention," *The New Yorker,* V (15 June 1929), 80–82.

Hagedorn & Brownmiller.

C 23
"Holes in Stockings," *The New Yorker,* V (22 June 1929), 52.

C 24
"Conditions at the Pool," *The New Yorker,* V (6 July 1929), 45–47.

Delphian.

C 25
"Mr. Rosenthal," *The New Yorker*, V (20 July 1929), 24–25.

Hagedorn & Brownmiller.

C 26
"The Boss Talks," *The New Yorker*, V (3 August 1929), 43–45.

Hagedorn & Brownmiller.

C 27
"Unconditioned Reflexes," *The New Yorker*, V (31 August 1929), 58–61.

C 28
"Staff Picture," *The New Yorker*, V (7 September 1929), 84–85.

Hagedorn & Brownmiller.

C 29
"Mauve Starts Early Grid Drill," *The New Yorker*, V (21 September 1929), 101–102.

C 30
"Out of the West," *The New Yorker*, V (28 September 1929), 51–52.

C 31
"Between the Halves," *The New Yorker*, V (12 October 1929), 85–89.

C 32
"The Cannons Are a Disgrace," *The New Yorker*, V (19 October 1929), 105–106.

Delphian.

C 33
"Halloween Party," *The New Yorker*, V (26 October 1929), 36.

Hagedorn & Brownmiller.

C 34
"Getting Ready for 1930," *The New Yorker*, V (9 November 1929), 77–78.

Hagedorn & Brownmiller.

C 35
"Americanization," *The New Yorker*, V (23 November 1929), 81–82.

Delphian.

C 36
"Merrie, Merrie, Merrie," *The New Yorker*, V (7 December 1929), 98–100.

Delphian.

C 37
"Memo and Another Memo," *The New Yorker*, V (14 December 1929), 89.

C 38
"Beaux Arts," *The New Yorker,* V (25 January 1930), 30.

C 39
"Suits Pressed," *The New Yorker,* V (8 February 1930), 28.

C 40
"Mr. Cleary Misses a Party," *The New Yorker,* VI (22 February 1930), 90–91.

Hagedorn & Brownmiller.

C 41
"Delphian Hits Girls' Cage-Game Foes," *The New Yorker,* VI (8 March 1930), 84–86.

Delphian.

C 42
"The Elevator Starter," *The New Yorker,* VI (15 March 1930), 72.

C 43
"On His Hands," *The New Yorker,* VI (22 March 1930), 54–56.

*The Doctor's Son.*

C 44
"Conversation with a Russian," *The New Yorker,* VI (29 March 1930), 93.

C 45
"Little Remembrances," *The New Yorker,* VI (12 April 1930), 96–97.

C 46
"Ten Eyck or Pershing? Pershing or Ten Eyck?" *The New Yorker,* VI (19 April 1930), 81–83.

Delphian. *The Doctor's Son.* See B 1.

C 47
"A Convert to Equitation," *The New Yorker,* VI (3 May 1930), 97.

C 48
"Don't Let It Get You," *The New Yorker,* VI (10 May 1930), 51–52.

C 49
"The New Office," *The New Yorker,* VI (17 May 1930), 98–99.

Hagedorn & Brownmiller. See B 1.

C 50
"The Girl Who Had Been Presented," *The New Yorker,* VI (31 May 1930), 63–64.

*The Doctor's Son.*

C 51
"Most Likely to Succeed," *The New Yorker,* VI (7 June 1930), 38–40.

C 52

"Paper Drinking Cups?" *The New Yorker*, VI (26 July 1930), 47–49.

Hagedorn & Brownmiller.

C 53

"New Day," *The New Yorker*, VI (23 August 1930), 38–39.

*The Doctor's Son.*

C 54

"The Man Who Had to Talk to Somebody," *The New Yorker*, VI (11 October 1930), 77–78.

*The Doctor's Son.*

C 55

"Old Boy," *The New Yorker*, VI (18 October 1930), 28.

C 56

"Varsity Manager," *The New Yorker*, VI (25 October 1930), 87–88.

C 57

"Portrait of a Referee," *The New Yorker*, VI (15 November 1930), 80–82.

See B 3.

C 58

"John," *The New Yorker*, VI (27 December 1930), 28.

C 59

"Getting a Drink," *The New Yorker*, VI (10 January 1931), 60–61.

C 60

"One Reason for Betsy's Diffidence," *The New Yorker*, VII (28 February 1931), 65.

C 61

"Divorce," *The New Yorker*, VII (11 April 1931), 69–71.

C 62

"The Office Switchboard," *The New Yorker*, VII (25 April 1931), 71–72.

C 63

"Mary," *The New Yorker*, VII (2 May 1931), 72.

*The Doctor's Son.*

C 64

"Revolt Among the Women," *The New Yorker*, VII (9 May 1931), 73.

Idlewood.[4]

C 65

"Papa and Smoking," *The New Yorker*, VII (16 May 1931), 68–69.

---

4. The first of a series of 4 stories about the Idlewood Country Club.

C 66
"Ninety Cents for a Sardine," *The New Yorker,* VII (23 May 1931), 75.
Idlewood.

C 67
"Help the Younger Element," *The New Yorker,* VII (6 June 1931), 75.
Idlewood.

C 68
"Holiday Plans," *The New Yorker,* VII (27 June 1931), 46–48.
·Idlewood.

C 69
"Mort and Mary," *The New Yorker,* VII (19 September 1931), 38–40.
*The Doctor's Son.*

C 70
"Nancy and Mr. Zinzindorf," *The New Yorker,* VII (26 September 1931), 65.

C 71
"Paolo and Francesca," *The New Yorker,* VII (24 October 1931), 56–57.
Delphian.

C 72
"Let Us Hang on to It," *The New Yorker,* VII (7 November 1931), 56–57.
Delphian.

C 73
". . . His Partner, Henry T. Collins," *The New Yorker,* VII (28 November 1931), 76–78.

C 74
"Alone," *Scribner's Magazine,* XC (December 1931), 647–648.
*The Doctor's Son.*

C 75
"Coffee Pot," *The New Yorker,* VII (12 December 1931), 54, 56–57.
*The Doctor's Son.*

C 76
"Ella and the Chinee," *The New Yorker,* VII (23 January 1932), 57–59.
*The Doctor's Son.*

C 77
"Good Evening, Ladies and Gentlemen . . . ," *The New Yorker,* VIII (30 April 1932), 19–20.

C 78
"Mr. Cass and the Ten Thousand Dollars," *The New Yorker,* VIII (25 June 1932), 53–55.
*The Doctor's Son.*

C 79
"Early Afternoon," *Scribner's Magazine*, XCII (July 1932), 25–26.

*The Doctor's Son.* See B 2.

C 80
"It Is Easy Enough to Blame Russia," *The New Yorker*, VIII (13 August 1932), 34–36.

C 81
"I Never Seen Anything Like It," *The New Yorker*, VIII (3 September 1932), 35–36.

*The Doctor's Son.*

C 82
"Lombard's Kick," *The New Yorker*, VIII (24 September 1932), 40–43.

*The Doctor's Son.*

C 83
"Frankie," *The New Yorker*, VIII (8 October 1932), 16–17.

*The Doctor's Son.*

C 84
"Profiles: Of Thee I Sing, Baby," *The New Yorker*, VIII (15 October 1932), 23–25.

Originally published as a profile, but collected by O'Hara as a story. *The Doctor's Son.*

C 85
"Screen Test," *The New Yorker*, VIII (3 December 1932), 44–48.

*The Doctor's Son.*

C 86
"Mr. Sidney Gainsborough: Quality Pictures," *The New Yorker*, VIII (17 December 1932), 36–40.

*The Doctor's Son.*

C 87
"You Need a Rest," *The New Yorker*, VIII (14 January 1933), 57–58.

C 88
"Mrs. Galt and Edwin," *The New Yorker*, IX (18 February 1933), 58–61.

*The Doctor's Son.*

C 89
"Mr. Cowley and the Young," *The New Yorker*, IX (24 June 1933), 31–34.

*The Doctor's Son.*

C 90
"Never a Dull Moment," *The New Yorker*, IX (8 July 1933), 28–30.

*The Doctor's Son.*

C 91
"Hotel Kid," *Vanity Fair,* XLI (September 1933), 4b, 4e.

*The Doctor's Son.*

C 92
"If I Was Brought up a Holy Roller," *The New Yorker,* IX (16 September 1933), 54–55.

C 93
"My Friend in Washington," *The New Yorker,* IX (23 September 1933), 20.

C 94
"The Tenacity of Mr. Crenshaw," *The New Yorker,* IX (30 September 1933), 67–68.

C 95
"Dynamite Is Like a Mill Pond," *The New Yorker,* IX (14 October 1933), 44–47.

C 96
"The Public Career of Mr. Seymour Harrisburg," *Brooklyn Daily Eagle,* (5 November 1933), magazine section.

*The Doctor's Son.*

C 97
"Mrs. McMorrow," *The New Yorker,* IX (18 November 1933), 48–55.

C 98
"Master of Ceremonies," *The New Yorker,* IX (25 November 1933), 40–43.

*The Doctor's Son.*

C 99
"Straight Pool," *The New Yorker,* IX (16 December 1933), 38–42.

*The Doctor's Son.*

C 100
"Pleasure," *The New Yorker,* X (10 March 1934), 70–73.

*The Doctor's Son.*

C 101
"The Deke Flag," *The New Yorker,* X (24 March 1934), 81–82.

C 102
"It Must Have Been Spring," *The New Yorker,* X (21 April 1934), 101–104.

*The Doctor's Son.*

C 103
"Sportsmanship," *The New Yorker,* X (12 May 1934), 95–99.

*The Doctor's Son.*

C 104
"In the Morning Sun," *The New Yorker,* X (14 July 1934), 15–17.

*The Doctor's Son.*

C 105
"Dr. Wyeth's Son," *The New Yorker,* X (28 July 1934), 25–26.

*The Doctor's Son.*

C 106
"Salute a Thoroughbred," *The New Yorker,* X (1 September 1934), 17–18.

*The Doctor's Son.*

C 107
"Teddy and Ann," *The New Yorker,* X (15 September 1934), 80–81.

C 108
"All the Girls He Wanted," *Harper's Bazaar,* no. 2664 (October 1934), 175–176, 179.

*The Doctor's Son* and *Files on Parade.*

C 109
"Back in New Haven," *The New Yorker,* X (6 October 1934), 23–24.

*The Doctor's Son.*

C 110
"Except in My Memory," *Harper's Bazaar,* no. 2665 (November 1934), 149, 152.

*The Doctor's Son.*

C 111
"Over the River and Through the Wood," *The New Yorker,* X (15 December 1934), 23–25.

*The Doctor's Son.*

C 112
"It Wouldn't Break Your Arm," *Harper's Bazaar,* no. 2667 (January 1935), 138, 140.

*The Doctor's Son* and *Files on Parade.*

C 113
"You Know How to Live," *The New Yorker,* X (2 February 1935), 20–21.

C 114
"I Could Have Had a Yacht," *The New Yorker,* XI (6 April 1935), 19.

*Files on Parade.*

C 115
"Ice Cream," *The New Yorker,* XI (20 July 1935), 39–41.

*Files on Parade.*

C 116
"Olive," *The New Yorker,* XI (17 August 1935), 13–15.

*Files on Parade.*

C 117
"The Gentleman in the Tan Suit," *The New Yorker,* XI (7 September 1935), 21–22.

*Files on Parade.*

C 118
"Portisan on the Portis," *The New Yorker,* XI (23 November 1935), 17–18.

*Files on Parade.*

C 119
"Stand-Up," *Collier's,* XCVI (30 November 1935), 17.

C 120
"The Doctor's Son," *The Doctor's Son* (1935).

C 121
"Most Gorgeous Thing," *The New Yorker,* XII (7 March 1936), 23–24.

*Files on Parade.*

C 122
"Saffercisco," *The New Yorker,* XII (11 April 1936), 14.

*Files on Parade.*

C 123
"Brother," *The New Yorker,* XII (18 July 1936), 23–24.

*Files on Parade.*

C 124
"Pretty Little Mrs. Harper," *Scribner's Magazine,* C (August 1936), 92–93.

C 125
"Little 'Chita," *Esquire,* VI (August 1936), 41, 168.

C 126
"Give and Take," *The New Yorker,* XII (13 February 1937), 17–18.

*Files on Parade.*

C 127
"By Way of Yonkers," *The New Yorker,* XIII (27 February 1937), 28–30.

*Files on Parade.*

C 128
"Shave," *The New Yorker,* XIII (20 March 1937), 22–23.

*Files on Parade.*

C 129
"Lunch Tuesday," *The New Yorker,* XIII (3 April 1937), 18–20.

*Files on Parade.*

C 130

"Peggy," *The New Yorker,* XIII (17 April 1937), 24.

*Files on Parade.*

C 131

"My Girls," *The New Yorker,* XIII (29 May 1937), 17–18.

*Files on Parade.* See B 4.

C 132

"No Sooner Said," *The New Yorker,* XIII (31 July 1937), 13–14.

*Files on Parade.*

C 133

"Price's Always Open," *The New Yorker,* XIII (14 August 1937), 15–17.

*Files on Parade.*

C 134

"Good-by, Herman," *The New Yorker,* XIII (4 September 1937), 17–18.

*Files on Parade.*

C 135

"Are We Leaving Tomorrow?" *The New Yorker,* XIV (19 March 1938), 17–18.

*Files on Parade.* See B 5.

C 136

"The Cold House," *The New Yorker,* XIV (2 April 1938), 15–16.

*Files on Parade.*

C 137

"Days," *The New Yorker,* XIV (30 April 1938), 21.

*Files on Parade.*

C 138

"And You Want a Mountain," *The New Yorker,* XIV (11 June 1938), 22–23.

*Files on Parade.*

C 139

"A Day Like Today," *The New Yorker,* XIV (6 August 1938), 14–15.

*Files on Parade.*

C 140

"Richard Wagner: Public Domain?" *The New Yorker,* XIV (3 September 1938), 14.

*Files on Parade.*

C 141

"No Mistakes," *The New Yorker,* XIV (17 September 1938), 18–20.

*Files on Parade.*

C 142
"Pal Joey," *The New Yorker*, XIV (22 October 1938), 23–24.

*Files on Parade* and *Pal Joey*.[5]

C 143
"Trouble in 1949," *Harper's Bazaar*, no. 2716 (November 1938), 110–111, 130, 132.

*Files on Parade*.

C 144
"Sidesaddle," *The New Yorker*, XIV (5 November 1938), 21–22.

*Files on Parade*.

C 145
"Ex-Pal," *The New Yorker*, XIV (26 November 1938), 20–21.

*Files on Parade* and *Pal Joey*.

C 146
"Invite," *The New Yorker*, XIV (10 December 1938), 27–28.

*Files on Parade*.

C 147
"Do You Like It Here?" *The New Yorker*, XV (18 February 1939), 17–18.

*Files on Parade*.

C 148
"How I Am Now in Chi," *The New Yorker*, XV (1 April 1939), 19–21.

*Files on Parade* and *Pal Joey*.

C 149
"The Ideal Man," *The New Yorker*, XV (29 April 1939), 21–22.

*Files on Parade*.

C 150
"Bow Wow," *The New Yorker*, XV (13 May 1939), 21–23.

*Files on Parade* and *Pal Joey*.

C 151
"Can You Carry Me?" *The New Yorker*, XV (3 June 1939), 17–18.

*Pipe Night*.

C 152
"Reunion Over Lightly," *The New Yorker*, XV (29 July 1939), 25–26.

*Pipe Night*.

---

5. The first of a series of 14 stories about Pal Joey.

C 153
"Too Young," *The New Yorker*, XV (9 September 1939), 15–16.
*Pipe Night.*

C 154
"Bread Alone," *The New Yorker*, XV (23 September 1939), 17–18.
*Pipe Night.*

C 155
"Avast and Belay," *The New Yorker*, XV (7 October 1939), 22–23.
*Pal Joey.*

C 156
"Joey on Herta," *The New Yorker*, XV (25 November 1939), 19–22.
*Pal Joey.*

C 157
"Joey on the Cake Line," *The New Yorker*, XV (23 December 1939), 19–20.
*Pal Joey.*

C 158
"The Erloff," *The New Yorker*, XV (3 February 1940), 22–23.
*Pal Joey* and *Pipe Night.*

C 159
"Even the Greeks," *The New Yorker*, XVI (2 March 1940), 18–19.
*Pal Joey.*

C 160
"Joey and the Calcutta Club," *The New Yorker*, XVI (30 March 1940), 30–31.
*Pal Joey* and *Pipe Night.*

C 161
"Joey and Mavis," *The New Yorker*, XVI (4 May 1940), 21–22.
*Pal Joey.*

C 162
"A New Career," *The New Yorker*, XVI (13 July 1940), 17–18.
*Pal Joey.*

C 163
"A Respectable Place," *The New Yorker*, XVI (19 October 1940), 26–27.
*Pipe Night.*

C 164
"The King of the Desert," *The New Yorker*, XVI (30 November 1940), 16–17.
*Pipe Night.*

C 165
"A Bit of a Shock," *Pal Joey* (1940).

C 166
"Reminiss?" *Pal Joey* (1940).

C 167
"The Magical Numbers," *The New Yorker,* XVI (18 January 1941), 18–19.

*Pipe Night.*

C 168
"Nothing Missing," *The New Yorker,* XVII (14 June 1941), 21–23.

*Pipe Night.*

C 169
"Adventure on the Set," *The New Yorker,* XVII (15 November 1941), 26–27.

*Pipe Night.*

C 170
"Summer's Day," *The New Yorker,* XVIII (29 August 1942), 15–16.

*Pipe Night.*

C 171
"Graven Image," *The New Yorker,* XIX (13 March 1943), 17–18.

*Pipe Night.*

C 172
"Radio," *The New Yorker,* XIX (22 May 1943), 20–21.

*Pipe Night.*

C 173
"Now We Know," *The New Yorker,* XIX (5 June 1943), 19–20.

*Pipe Night.*

C 174
"The Next-to-Last Dance of the Season," *The New Yorker,* XIX (18 September 1943), 22–24.

*Pipe Night.*

C 175
"Revenge," *Collier's,* CXII (25 September 1943), 21.

*Pipe Night.*

C 176
"Walter T. Carriman," *The New Yorker,* XIX (16 October 1943), 23–27.

*Pipe Night.*

C 177
"Memo to a Kind Stranger," *Collier's,* CXII (6 November 1943), 19.

*Pipe Night.*

C 178
"The Lieutenant," *The New Yorker,* XIX (13 November 1943), 22–23.

*Pipe Night.* See B 8.

C 179
"Civilized," *The New Yorker,* XIX (4 December 1943), 32–33.

*Pipe Night.*

C 180
"On Time," *Collier's,* CXIII (8 April 1944), 72.

*Pipe Night.* See B 13.

C 181
"Conversation at Lunch," *Good Housekeeping,* CXIX (July 1944), 28.

*The Time Element.*

C 182
"Name in the Book," *Good Housekeeping,* CXIX (December 1944), 38, 172–173.

C 183
"Leave," *Collier's,* CXIV (2 December 1944), 13.

*Pipe Night.*

C 184
"Mrs. Whitman," *The New Yorker,* XX (27 January 1945), 20–22.

*Pipe Night.*

C 185
"The Pretty Daughters," *The New Yorker,* XXI (3 March 1945), 24–26.

*Hellbox.*

C 186
"War Aims," *The New Yorker,* XXI (17 March 1945), 27–28.

*Hellbox.*

C 187
"Wise Guy," *The New Yorker,* XXI (26 May 1945), 20–21.

*Hellbox.*

C 188
"Horizon," *The New Yorker,* XXI (23 June 1945), 18.

*Hellbox.*

C 189
"Life Among These Unforgettable Characters," *The New Yorker,* XXI (25 August 1945),
19–20.

*Hellbox.*

C 190
"Fire!" *Pipe Night* (1945).

C 191
"Free," *Pipe Night* (1945).

C 192
"The Handler," *Pipe Night* (1945).

C 193
"Patriotism," *Pipe Night* (1945).

C 194
"Platform," *Pipe Night* (1945).

C 195
"A Purchase of Some Golf Clubs," *Pipe Night* (1945).

C 196
"Where's the Game," *Pipe Night* (1945).

C 197
"Conversation in the Atomic Age," *The New Yorker,* XXI (12 January 1946), 22–23.

*Hellbox.*

C 198
"Common Sense Should Tell You," *The New Yorker,* XXI (9 February 1946), 20–22.

*Hellbox.*

C 199
"Doctor and Mrs. Parsons," *The New Yorker,* XXII (23 February 1946), 29–31.

*Hellbox.*

C 200
"Everything Satisfactory," *The New Yorker,* XXII (23 March 1946), 25–26.

*Hellbox.*

C 201
"Like Old Times," *The New Yorker,* XXII (13 April 1946), 29–30.

*Hellbox.*

C 202
"Clara," *The New Yorker,* XXII (27 April 1946), 21–23.

*Hellbox.*

C 203
"The Decision," *The New Yorker*, XXII (18 May 1946), 23–25.

*Hellbox.*

C 204
"Secret Meeting," *The New Yorker*, XXII (6 July 1946), 18–19.

*Hellbox.*

C 205
"The Three Musketeers," *The New Yorker*, XXII (28 September 1946), 25–26.

*Hellbox.*

C 206
"Ellie," *The New Yorker*, XXII (19 October 1946), 29–30.

*Hellbox.*

C 207
"Pilgrimage," *The New Yorker*, XXII (9 November 1946), 29–32.

*The Time Element.*

C 208
"One for the Road," *The New Yorker*, XXII (30 November 1946), 37–38.

C 209
"Not Always," *The New Yorker*, XXII (11 January 1947), 23–24.

*The Time Element.*

C 210
"The Moccasins," *The New Yorker*, XXII (25 January 1947), 20–22.

*Hellbox.*

C 211
"Pardner," *The New Yorker*, XXIII (22 February 1947), 24–26.

*Hellbox.*

C 212
"Someone to Trust," *The New Yorker*, XXIII (22 March 1947), 31–33.

*Hellbox.*

C 213
"Drawing Room B," *The New Yorker*, XXIII (19 April 1947), 25–28.

*Hellbox.*

C 214
"Miss W.," *The New Yorker*, XXIII (3 May 1947), 29–30.

*Hellbox.*

C 215
"Other Women's Households," *The New Yorker*, XXIII (24 May 1947), 32–34.
*Hellbox.*

C 216
"The Lady Takes an Interest," *The New Yorker*, XXIII (28 June 1947), 22–23.
*The Time Element.*

C 217
"Interior with Figures," *The New Yorker*, XXIII (19 July 1947), 22–24.
*The Time Element.*

C 218
"The Last of Haley," *The New Yorker*, XXIII (30 August 1947), 21–23.
*The Time Element.*

C 219
"The Heart of Lee W. Lee," *The New Yorker*, XXIII (13 September 1947), 29–31.
*The Time Element.*

C 220
"The Dry Murders," *The New Yorker*, XXIII (18 October 1947), 33–34.
*The Time Element.*

C 221
"Eileen," *The New Yorker*, XXIII (20 December 1947), 25–26.
*The Time Element.*

C 222
"The Chink in the Armor," *Hellbox* (1947).

C 223
"A Phase of Life," *Hellbox* (1947).

C 224
"Somebody Can Help Somebody," *Hellbox* (1947).

C 225
"Time to Go," *Hellbox* (1947).

C 226
"Transaction," *Hellbox* (1947).

C 227
"Nil Nisi," *The New Yorker*, XXIII (10 January 1948), 23–25.
*The Time Element.*

C 228
"Requiescat," *The New Yorker*, XXIV (3 April 1948), 27–30.
*The Time Element.*

C 229

"The Frozen Face," *The New Yorker*, XXV (23 April 1949), 22–24.

*The Time Element.*

C 230

"The Industry and the Professor," *The New Yorker*, XXV (16 July 1949), 16–20.

*The Time Element.*

C 231

"Grief," *The New Yorker*, XXV (22 October 1949), 28–29.

*The Time Element.*

C 232

"The Kids," *The New Yorker*, XXV (26 November 1949), 32–34.

*The Time Element.*

C 233

"The Favor," *The Princeton Tiger*, LXIII (March–April 1952), 8–10.

*The Time Element.*

C 234

"A Family Party," *Collier's*, CXXXVII (2 March 1956), 34–36, 38, 40–41, 44, 46.

See A 15.

C 235

"That First Husband," *The Saturday Evening Post*, CCXXXII (21 November 1959), 23–24, 52.

*The Time Element.* See B 25.

C 236

"Imagine Kissing Pete," *The New Yorker*, XXXVI (17 September 1960), 43–134.

*Sermons and Soda-Water.* See A 18.

C 237

"It's Mental Work," *The New Yorker*, XXXVI (26 November 1960), 50–56.

*Assembly.*

C 238

"Exactly Eight Thousand Dollars Exactly," *The New Yorker*, XXXVI (31 December 1960), 24–26.

*Assembly.*

C 239

*The Girl on the Baggage Truck, Sermons and Soda-Water* (1960).

C 240

*We're Friends Again, Sermons and Soda-Water* (1960).

C 241
"The Cellar Domain," *The New Yorker*, XXXVI (11 February 1961), 28–34.

*Assembly*.

C 242
"Sterling Silver," *The New Yorker*, XXXVII (11 March 1961), 38–42.

*Assembly*.

C 243
"The Man with the Broken Arm," *The New Yorker*, XXXVII (22 April 1961), 42–47.

*Assembly*.

C 244
"The Girl from California," *The New Yorker*, XXXVII (27 May 1961), 34–42.

*Assembly*.

C 245
"The Weakness," *The New Yorker*, XXXVII (8 July 1961), 23–29.

*Assembly*.

C 246
"Mary and Norma," *The New Yorker*, XXXVII (5 August 1961), 22–26.

*Assembly*.

C 247
"The Trip," *The New Yorker*, XXXVII (23 September 1961), 39–42.

*Assembly*.

C 248
"Call Me, Call Me," *The New Yorker*, XXXVII (7 October 1961), 56–58.

*Assembly*.

C 249
"The Father," *The New Yorker*, XXXVII (28 October 1961), 48–49.

*The Cape Cod Lighter*.

C 250
"Two Turtledoves," *The New Yorker*, XXXVII (23 December 1961), 22–23.

*The Cape Cod Lighter*.

C 251
"A Case History," *Assembly* (1961).

C 252
"A Cold Calculating Thing," *Assembly (1961)*.

C 253
"The Compliment," *Assembly* (1961).

C 254
"First Day in Town," *Assembly* (1961).

C 255
"The Free," *Assembly* (1961).

C 256
"The High Point," *Assembly* (1961).

C 257
"In a Grove," *Assembly* (1961).

C 258
In the Silence," *Assembly* (1961).

C 259
"The Lighter When Needed," *Assembly* (1961).

C 260
"Mrs. Stratton of Oak Knoll," *Assembly* (1961).

C 261
"The Old Folks," *Assembly* (1961).

C 262
"The Pioneer Hep-Cat," *Assembly* (1961).

C 263
"The Properties of Love," *Assembly* (1961).

C 264
"Reassurance," *Assembly* (1961).

C 265
"The Sharks," *Assembly* (1961).

C 266
"You Can Always Tell Newark," *Assembly* (1961).

C 267
"Sunday Morning," *The New Yorker*, XXXVII (13 January 1962), 24–26.

*The Cape Cod Lighter*.

C 268
"The Women of Madison Avenue," *The New Yorker*, XXXVII (10 February 1962), 32–33.

*The Cape Cod Lighter*.

C 269
"A Short Walk from the Station," *The New Yorker*, XXXVIII (24 February 1962), 32–34.

*The Cape Cod Lighter*.

C 270
"Money," *The New Yorker,* XXXVIII (24 March 1962), 38–46.

*The Cape Cod Lighter.*

C 271
"The Bucket of Blood," *The New Yorker,* XXXVIII (25 August 1962), 31–62.

*The Cape Cod Lighter.*

C 272
"Winter Dance," *The New Yorker,* XXXVIII (22 September 1962), 34–36.

*The Cape Cod Lighter.*

C 273
"How Can I Tell You?" *The New Yorker,* XXXVIII (1 December 1962), 57–59.

*The Hat on the Bed.*

C 274
"The Public Dorothy," *The New Yorker,* XXXVIII (15 December 1962), 36–37.

*The Hat on the Bed.*

C 275
"Appearances," *The Cape Cod Lighter* (1962).

C 276
"The Butterfly," *The Cape Cod Lighter* (1962).

C 277
"Claude Emerson, Reporter," *The Cape Cod Lighter* (1962).

C 278
"Jurge Dulrumple," *The Cape Cod Lighter* (1962).

C 279
"The Engineer," *The Cape Cod Lighter* (1962).

C 280
"The First Day," *The Cape Cod Lighter* (1962).

C 281
"Justice," *The Cape Cod Lighter* (1962).

C 282
"The Lesson," *The Cape Cod Lighter* (1962).

C 283
"The Nothing Machine," *The Cape Cod Lighter* (1962).

C 284
"Pat Collins," *The Cape Cod Lighter* (1962).

C 285
"The Professors," *The Cape Cod Lighter* (1962).

C 286
"The Sun-Dodgers," *The Cape Cod Lighter* (1962).

C 287
"Things You Really Want," *The Cape Cod Lighter* (1962).

C 288
"You Don't Remember Me," *The Cape Cod Lighter* (1962).

C 289
"Your Fah Neefah Neeface," *The Cape Cod Lighter* (1962).

C 290
"Saturday Lunch," *The New Yorker,* XXXVIII (12 January 1963), 27–30.

*The Hat on the Bed.*

C 291
"Agatha," *The New Yorker,* XXXIX (23 February 1963), 33–39.

*The Hat on the Bed.*

C 292
"The Glendale People," *The Saturday Evening Post,* CCXXXVI (2 March 1963), 34–41.

*The Hat on the Bed.*

C 293
"John Barton Rosedale, Actors' Actor," *The New Yorker,* XXXIX (16 March 1963), 46–53.

*The Hat on the Bed.*

C 294
"Aunt Anna," *The Saturday Evening Post,* CCXXXVI (23 March 1963), 50–56.

*The Hat on the Bed.*

C 295
"Yucca Knolls," *Show Magazine,* III (April 1963), 85–100.

*The Hat on the Bed.*

C 296
"The Ride from Mauch Chunk," *The Saturday Evening Post,* CCXXXVI (13 April 1963), 38–41.

*The Hat on the Bed.*

C 297
"The Manager," *The New Yorker,* XXXIX (4 May 1963), 42–48.

*The Hat on the Bed.*

C 298
"Exterior: with Figure," *The Saturday Evening Post,* CCXXXVI (1 June 1963), 54–61.

*The Hat on the Bed.*

C 299
"The Flatted Saxophone," *The New Yorker,* XXXIX (1 June 1963), 28–29.

*The Hat on the Bed.*

C 300
"The Man on the Tractor," *The New Yorker,* XXXIX (22 June 1963), 25–30.

*The Hat on the Bed.*

C 301
"The Locomobile," *The New Yorker,* XXXIX (20 July 1963), 22–27.

*The Hat on the Bed.*

C 302
"Our Friend the Sea," *The Saturday Evening Post,* CCXXXVI (24–31 August 1963), 60–65.

*The Hat on the Bed.*

C 303
"The Lawbreaker," *The Saturday Evening Post,* CCXXXVI (16 November 1963), 52–54, 58, 62, 64, 68–69, 70, 72–77.

*The Horse Knows the Way.*

C 304
"Zero," *The New Yorker,* XXXIX (28 December 1963), 28–32.

*The Horse Knows the Way.*

C 305
"Eminent Domain," *The Hat on the Bed* (1963).

C 306
"The Friends of Miss Julia," *The Hat on the Bed* (1963).

C 307
"The Golden," *The Hat on the Bed* (1963).

C 308
"I Know That, Roy," *The Hat on the Bed* (1963).

C 309
"The Mayor," *The Hat on the Bed* (1963).

C 310
"Ninety Minutes Away," *The Hat on the Bed* (1963).

C 311
"Teddy and the Special Friends," *The Hat on the Bed* (1963).

C 312
"The Twinkle in His Eye," *The Hat on the Bed* (1963).

C 313
"The Windowpane Check," *The Hat on the Bed* (1963).

C 314
"The Whole Cherry Pie," *The Saturday Evening Post*, CCXXXVII (8 February 1964), 32–33.

*The Horse Knows the Way.*

C 315
"At the Window," *The New Yorker*, XL (22 February 1964), 28–32.

*The Horse Knows the Way.*

C 316
"The Hardware Man," *The Saturday Evening Post*, CCXXXVII (29 February 1964), 46–53.

*The Horse Knows the Way.*

C 317
"The Victim," *The Saturday Evening Post*, CCXXXVII (14 March 1964), 46–51.

*The Horse Knows the Way.*

C 318
"Arnold Stone," *The Saturday Evening Post*, CCXXXVII (28 March 1964), 52–59.

*The Horse Knows the Way.*

C 319
"The Answer Depends," *The Saturday Evening Post*, CCXXXVII (18 April 1964), 46–51.

*The Horse Knows the Way.*

C 320
"Can I Stay Here?" *The Saturday Evening Post*, CCXXXVII (16 May 1964), 44–45, 48.

*The Horse Knows the Way.*

C 321
"I Spend My Days in Longing," *The New Yorker*, XL (23 May 1964), 40–46.

*The Horse Knows the Way.*

C 322
"His Excellency," *The Saturday Evening Post*, CCXXXVII (11 July 1964), 56–60.

*The Horse Knows the Way.*

C 323
"The House on the Corner," *The Saturday Evening Post,* CCXXXVII (22 August 1964), 64–66.

*The Horse Knows the Way.*

C 324
"Aunt Fran," *The Saturday Evening Post,* CCXXXVII (19 September 1964), 56–57.

*The Horse Knows the Way.*

C 325
"The Tackle," *Sports Illustrated,* XXI (21 September 1964), 108–113.

*Waiting for Winter.*

C 326
"School," *The Saturday Evening Post,* CCXXXVII (26 September 1964), 56–61.

*The Horse Knows the Way.*

C 327
"All Tied Up," *The New Yorker,* XL (3 October 1964), 48–55.

*The Horse Knows the Way.*

C 328
"The Bonfire," *The Saturday Evening Post,* CCXXXVII (10 October 1964), 46–53.

*The Horse Knows the Way.*

C 329
"The Madeline Wherry Case," *The Horse Knows the Way* (1964).

C 330
"Mrs. Allanson," *The Horse Knows the Way* (1964).

C 331
"The Pig," *The Horse Knows the Way* (1964).

C 332
"The Staring Game," *The Horse Knows the Way* (1964).

C 333
"What's the Good of Knowing?" *The Horse Knows the Way* (1964).

C 334
"The Gambler," *The New Yorker,* XLI (1 May 1965), 40–42.

*Waiting for Winter.*

C 335
"The Neighborhood," *The New Yorker,* XLI (15 May 1965), 49–53.

*Waiting for Winter.*

C 336
"The Assistant," *The New Yorker,* XLI (3 July 1965), 22–28.
*Waiting for Winter.*

C 337
"The Clear Track," *The Saturday Evening Post,* CCXXXVII (24 October 1964), 58–62.
*The Horse Knows the Way.*

C 338
"Christmas Poem," *The New Yorker,* XL (19 December 1964), 34–39.
*Good Samaritan.*

C 339
"The Brain," *The Horse Knows the Way* (1964).

C 340
"Clayton Bunter," *The Horse Knows the Way* (1964).

C 341
"The Gun," *The Horse Knows the Way* (1964).

C 342
"I Can't Thank You Enough," *The Horse Knows the Way* (1964).

C 343
"In the Mist," *The Horse Knows the Way* (1964).

C 344
"The Jet Set," *The Horse Knows the Way* (1964).

C 345
"A Good Location," *The New Yorker,* XLI (4 September 1965), 29–31.
*Waiting for Winter.*

C 346
"Leonard," *The New Yorker,* XLII (26 February 1966), 33–37.
*Waiting for Winter.*

C 347
"Afternoon Waltz," *The Saturday Evening Post,* CCXXXIX (23 April 1966), 56–74.
*Waiting for Winter.*

C 348
"Fatimas and Kisses," *The New Yorker,* XLII (21 May 1966), 44–53.
*Waiting for Winter.*

C 349
"Yostie," *The Saturday Evening Post,* CCXXXIX (4 June 1966), 46–62.
*Waiting for Winter.*

C 350
"The Jama," *The Saturday Evening Post*, CCXXXIX (22 October 1966).

*Waiting for Winter.*

C 351
"The Private People," *The Saturday Evening Post*, CCXXXIX (17 December 1966), 56–72.

*And Other Stories.*

C 352
"Andrea," *Waiting for Winter* (1966).

C 353
"Flight," *Waiting for Winter* (1966).

C 354
"The General," *Waiting for Winter* (1966).

C 355
"James Francis and the Star," *Waiting for Winter* (1966).

C 356
"Late, Late Show," *Waiting for Winter* (1966).

C 357
"Natica Jackson," *Waiting for Winter* (1966).

C 358
"The Pomeranian," *Waiting for Winter* (1966).

C 359
"The Portly Gentleman," *Waiting for Winter* (1966).

C 360
"The Skeletons," *Waiting for Winter* (1966).

C 361
"The Way to Majorca," *Waiting for Winter* (1966).

C 362
"The Weakling," *Waiting for Winter* (1966).

C 363
"The Gunboat and Madge," *The Saturday Evening Post*, CCXL (25 February 1967), 64–77.

*And Other Stories.*

C 364
"How Old, How Young," *The New Yorker*, XLIII (1 July 1967), 28–32.

*And Other Stories.*

C 365
"Barred," *The Saturday Evening Post,* CCXL (7 October 1967), 60–62.

*And Other Stories.*

C 366
"The Gangster," *The Saturday Evening Post,* CCXL (18 November 1967), 56–66.

*And Other Stories.*

C 367
"Good Samaritan," *The Saturday Evening Post,* CCXLI (30 November 1968), 62–64, 66, 68–70.

*Good Samaritan.*

C 368
"The Sun Room," *The Saturday Evening Post,* CCXLII (8 February 1969), 40–42, 44, 46, 48.

*Good Samaritan.*

C 369
"The Broken Giraffe," *And Other Stories* (1968).

C 370
"The Farmer," *And Other Stories* (1968).

C 371
"A Few Trips and Some Poetry," *And Other Stories* (1968).

C 372
"A Man on a Porch," *And Other Stories* (1968).

C 373
"Papa Gibraltar," *And Other Stories* (1968).

C 374
"The Strong Man," *And Other Stories* (1968).

C 375
"We'll Have Fun," *And Other Stories* (1968).

C 376
"At the Cothurnos Club," *Esquire,* LXXVIII (July 1972), 114–115.

*The Time Element.* This story and "All I've Tried to Be" appear under *Esquire's* general title, "The Little Mysteries of Pomp and Circumstance."

C 377
"All I've Tried to Be," *Esquire,* LXXVIII (July 1972), 115–116, 162–164.

*The Time Element.* See preceding entry.

C 378
"Encounter: 1943," *The Time Element* (1972).

C 379
"The Skipper," *The Time Element* (1972).

C 380
"No Justice," *The Time Element* (1972).

C 381
"Memorial Fund," *The Time Element* (1972).

C 382
"The Brothers," *The Time Element* (1972).

C 383
"He Thinks He Owns Me," *The Time Element* (1972).

C 384
"The War," *The Time Element* (1972).

C 385
"The Time Element," *The Time Element* (1972).

C 386
"Family Evening," *The Time Element* (1972).

C 387
"Last Respects," *The Time Element* (1972).

C 388
"The Busybody," *The Time Element* (1972).

C 389
"This Time," *The Time Element* (1972).

C 390
"The Big Gleaming Coach," *The Time Element* (1972).

C 391
"For Help and Pity," *The Time Element* (1972).

C 392
"The Gentry," *Good Samaritan* (1974).

C 393
"Sound View," *Good Samaritan* (1974).

C 394
"A Man to Be Trusted," *Good Samaritan* (1974).

C 395
"Malibu from the Sky," *Good Samaritan* (1974).

C 396
"Harrington and Whitehill," *Good Samaritan* (1974).

C 397
"Noblesse Oblige," *Good Samaritan* (1974).

C 398
"Heather Hill," *Good Samaritan* (1974).

C 399
"Tuesday's as Good as Any," *Good Samaritan* (1974).

C 400
"George Munson," *Good Samaritan* (1974).

C 401
"The Journey to Mount Clemens," *The Saturday Evening Post,* CCXLVI (August/September 1974), 62–64, 92–94.

*Good Samaritan.*

C 402
"The Mechanical Man," *Good Samaritan* (1974).

# D. Articles, Letters, Reviews, Verse, Statements, and Interviews

First publication in magazines or newspapers, arranged chronologically.

**D 1**

"A Cub Tells His Story," *Pottsville Journal* (2 May 1925), 17.[1]

Article. See A 35.

**D 2**

O'Hara quoted, "The Conning Tower," *New York World* (17 March 1927), 13.

**D 3**

Letter to the Editor, *Time,* IX (9 May 1927), 6.

**D 4**

"From the Tower's Attention-Caller," "The Conning Tower," *New York World* (16 June 1927), 13.

Letter.

**D 5**

"The Literary Quest," "The Conning Tower," *New York World* (15 July 1927), 13.

Couplet.

**D 6**

"The Weather and the Public," "The Conning Tower," *New York World* (15 September 1927), 15.

Letter.

**D 7**

"The City Hall Plaza Talkers," "The Conning Tower," *New York World* (1 December 1927), 13.

Sketch.

**D 8**

"The Veteran Reporter Goes Just Slightly Insane," "The Conning Tower," *New York World* (2 December 1927), 13.

Sketch.

**D 9**

"A Speech by George F. Gabbitry at a Christmas Party, Delivered at, Let Us Say, Scott

---

1. This is the only O'Hara appearance in the *Pottsville Journal* during his 1924–1926 reportorial stint that has been found.

High, Toledo, Before the Entire School," "The Conning Tower," *New York World* (13 December 1927), 11.

Parody. See B 40.

D 10
"The Private Branch Exchange Talker," "The Conning Tower," *New York World* (16 December 1927), 15.

Sketch.

D 11
"Famed Folk Plan Big Feast," "The Conning Tower," *New York World* (11 January 1928), 19.

Letter.

D 12
"George F. Gabbitry Stops a Little Early for the Wife at Her Literary Club Meeting," "The Conning Tower," *New York World* (12 January 1928), 15.

Parody.

D 13
Letter to the Editor, *Time,* XI (23 January 1928), 1.

D 14
"The Man Who Knew Sinclair Lewis," "The Conning Tower," *New York World* (27 January 1928), 13.

Parody.

D 15
"George F. Gabbitry Settles Once and for All the Democratic Situation—If Any," "The Conning Tower," *New York World* (13 March 1928), 13.

Parody. See B 36.

D 16
"Why Dr. Bdrplf, Who Spoke for Eighty-Five Minutes, Was Listed Among the 'Other Speakers,' Who Totalled Half an Hour," "The Conning Tower," *New York World* (16 April 1928), 13.

Sketch.

D 17
"Famed Convivial Hurt, Flags Tower," "The Conning Tower," *New York World* (19 April 1928), 13.

Sketch.

D 18
"Old Fashioned," "The Conning Tower," *New York World* (28 May 1928), 13.

Sketch.

D 19
"Laboratory Stuff," "The Conning Tower," *New York World* (29 May 1928), 11.

Letter, signed 'J. H. O'H'.

D 20

"A Boy Who Made Good," "The Conning Tower," *New York World* (13 September 1928), 15.

Sketch.

D 21

"Christmas Is for the Kiddies," "The Conning Tower," *New York World* (24 December 1928), 11.

Sketch.

D 22

Review of *Polly, Time,* XIII (21 January 1929), 36.

Unsigned, but claimed by O'Hara.

D 23

"A Style Sheet Goes to a Copyreader's Head," "The Conning Tower," *New York World* (13 February 1929), 13.

Sketch.

D 24

"Saxophonic Fever," *New York Herald Tribune* (17 February 1929), II, 7.

One-shot column.

D 25

"Aged Muser Sighs for Old Days," "The Conning Tower," *New York World* (21 June 1929), 15.

Sketch.

D 26

"Conning Tower, I Love You." "The Conning Tower," *New York World* (26 June 1929), 15.

Verse.

D 27

"J. R. Clarke Admits Guilt, Faces Life," *New York Daily Mirror* (24 July 1929), 2, 6.

By-lined 'John F. O'Hara'.

D 28

Jeanne Atherton, "Girl Invades Yale Club Bar, Only for Men," *New York Daily Mirror* (29 July 1929), 4

Ghosted by O'Hara. See D 268.

D 29

"The Pennsylvania Irish," *New York Herald Tribune* (9 March 1930), II, 7.

One-shot column.

D 30
Untitled piece on the Manhattan skyline, "The Talk of the Town," *The New Yorker,* VI (22 March 1930), 9.

Unsigned, but credited to O'Hara by *The New Yorker* records.

D 31
"Buffalo Wins Belasco Cup," *Morning Telegraph* (13 May 1930), 2.

Play review.

D 32
"Short Turns on Dial," *Morning Telegraph* (13 May 1930), 4.

Radio feature.

D 33
" 'Wooden Idol' in Cup Trials," *Morning Telegraph* (14 May 1930), 2.

Play review.

D 34
"Ad Club's Ad on Air," *Morning Telegraph* (14 May 1930), 3.

Radio feature.

D 35
"In Praise of Ballew," *Morning Telegraph* (15 May 1930), 4.

Radio feature.

D 36
" 'New Freedom' Tourney Hit," *Morning Telegraph* (16 May 1930), 3.

Play review.

D 37
"Chic Sale Takes Air," *Morning Telegraph* (16 May 1930), 3.

Radio feature.

D 38
"Derby on Air Today," *Morning Telegraph* (17 May 1930), 3.

Radio feature.

D 39
"New Freedom Wins Prize," *Morning Telegraph* (18 May 1930), 3.

Play review.

D 40
"Radio Tube News," *Morning Telegraph* (19 May 1930), 3.

Radio feature.

D 41
"Radio and Press Pals," *Morning Telegraph* (20 May 1930), 4.

Radio feature.

D 42
"Sure—It's a Horse—On the O'Haras!" *Morning Telegraph* (21 May 1930), 1, 3.
Article.

D 43
"What! No Politics?" *Morning Telegraph* (21 May 1930), 3.
Radio feature.

D 44
"Yes, with Noodles," *Morning Telegraph* (23 May 1930), 3.
Radio feature.

D 45
"Not Enough Salt on Bar Pretzels," *Morning Telegraph* (26 May 1930), 1–2.
Article.

D 46
"Race Rehearsal," *Morning Telegraph* (26 May 1930), 2.
Radio feature.

D 47
"Radios and Gas," *Morning Telegraph* (28 May 1930), 6.
Radio feature.

D 48
"Lucky Strike Music," *Morning Telegraph* (29 May 1930), 6.
Radio feature.

D 49
"Radio Gossip in Air," *Morning Telegraph* (30 May 1930), 4.
Radio feature.

D 50
"Radio Door to Stage," *Morning Telegraph* (31 May 1930), 3.
Radio feature.

D 51
"Radio Aids Lingo," *Morning Telegraph* (1 June 1930), 3.
Radio feature.

D 52
"Tennis Racket Skips Pun," *Morning Telegraph* (2 June 1930), 1, 3.
Article.

D 53
"Radio Recollections," *Morning Telegraph* (2 June 1930), 2.
Radio feature.

D 54

"Mauve Decade Yarn," *Morning Telegraph* (3 June 1930), 2.

Movie review.

D 55

"Derby on Air Early," *Morning Telegraph* (4 June 1930), 3.

Radio feature.

D 56

"Fans Hear Aviatrix," *Morning Telegraph* (5 June 1930), 2.

Radio feature.

D 57

"Corinne Griffith Achieves Accurate Characterization in 'Back Pay,'" *Morning Telegraph* (5 June 1930), 3.

Movie review.

D 58

"Hill-Billy Songs," *Morning Telegraph* (6 June 1930), 3.

Radio feature.

D 59

"O'Hara Gets the Air," *Morning Telegraph* (7 June 1930), 2.

Radio feature.

D 60

"William Powell Wades Through Pain and Prison at Paramounts," *Morning Telegraph* (7 June 1930), 3.

Movie review.

D 61

"Novarro Film at Capitol," *Morning Telegraph* (8 June 1930), 2.

Movie review.

D 62

"O'Hara's Ordeal," *Morning Telegraph* (9 June 1930), 2.

Radio feature.

D 63

"Edmund Lowe's War in Trenches and Night Clubs Shown in Roxy Film," *Morning Telegraph* (9 June 1930), 3.

Movie review.

D 64

"New Star Dawns: Bernice Claire Steals the Lead in 'Numbered Men,'" *Morning Telegraph* (10 June 1930), 2.

Movie review.

D 65

"Cuban Band Novel," *Morning Telegraph* (11 June 1930), 2.

Radio feature.

D 66

"Lois Moran Gets Her Englishman in 'Not Damaged' at the Globe," *Morning Telegraph* (11 June 1930), 3.

Movie review.

D 67

"Russian Cameramen Repeat Triumphs in 'Cain and Artem' at Cameo," *Morning Telegraph* (12 June 1930), 3.

Movie review.

D 68

"Bout on Air Tonight," *Morning Telegraph* (12 June 1930), 4.

Radio feature.

D 69

"Press Agents Slip," *Morning Telegraph* (13 June 1930), 2.

Radio feature.

D 70

"Milestone's Genius Makes Spectators See 'All Quiet' Via German Eyes," *Morning Telegraph* (13 June 1930), 3.

D 71

"Oar Race June 20," *Morning Telegraph* (14 June 1930), 2.

Radio feature.

D 72

"Edmund Lowe Wisecracks, Dolores Del Rio 'Figures' in 'The Bad One,'" *Morning Telegraph* (14 June 1930), 3.

Movie review.

D 73

"Capitol Picture Sophisticated," *Morning Telegraph* (15 June 1930), 2.

Movie review.

D 74

"M'Namee Version," *Morning Telegraph* (16 June 1930), 2.

Radio feature.

D 75

"Silent Film Die Hards Exhorted to Lend Their Talents to Talkies," *Morning Telegraph* (16 June 1930), 3.

Article.

D 76
"Pepper Passes," *Morning Telegraph* (17 June 1930), 2.

Radio feature.

D 77
"Clara Bow Fan Sea-Sick," *Morning Telegraph* (17 June 1930), 3.

Article.

D 78
"Radio Wags Liberal," *Morning Telegraph* (18 June 1930), 2.

Radio feature. Probably by O'Hara.

D 79
"Secrets Barred in 'All Quiet,' " *Morning Telegraph* (19 June 1930), 2.

Article.

D 80
Franey Delaney, "Air Pocket Spotted," *Morning Telegraph* (19 June 1930), 2.

Radio feature.[2]

D 81
"Films' Diaper Days," *Morning Telegraph* (20 June 1930), 2.

Article.

D 82
Franey Delaney, "Mike to Pace Crews," *Morning Telegraph* (20 June 1930), 3.

Radio feature.

D 83
"Terrifying Whales, Comic Penguins Caught by Cameras in Byrd Record," *Morning Telegraph* (21 June 1930), 2.

Movie review.

D 84
Franey Delaney, "Pillow Fight on Air," *Morning Telegraph* (21 June 1930), 3.

Radio feature.

D 85
"Critics Disagree," *Morning Telegraph* (22 June 1930), 5.

Article.

D 86
Franey Delaney, "How to Get on Stage," *Morning Telegraph* (23 June 1930), 2.

Radio feature.

---

2. Beginning 19 June, O'Hara wrote radio articles under the by-line "Franey Delaney."

D 87

"Marie Dressler 'Funny as Ever' Amidst Woes of Wall Street Crash," *Morning Telegraph* (23 June 1930), 3.

Movie review.

D 88

Franey Delaney, "Song Helps Organ," *Morning Telegraph* (24 June 1930), 2.

Radio feature.

D 89

" 'She's My Weakness' Proves Mildly Amusing Fare at Globe Theatre," *Morning Telegraph* (24 June 1930), 3.

Movie review.

D 90

Franey Delaney, "Comic Strip Stumped," *Morning Telegraph* (25 June 1930), 2.

Radio feature.

D 91

" 'Women Everywhere' Has Exciting Beginning but Lets Interest Die Out," *Morning Telegraph* (25 June 1930), 3.

Movie review.

D 92

" 'The Big House' Brings Thrilling Prison Riot to Astor Screen," *Morning Telegraph* (26 June 1930), 2.

Movie review.

D 93

Franey Delaney, "Big Business Boom," *Morning Telegraph* (26 June 1930), 3.

Radio feature.

D 94

Franey Delaney, "Jones Arrival on Air," *Morning Telegraph* (27 June 1930), 3.

Radio feature.

D 95

Franey Delaney, "Mike in Golf Gallery," *Morning Telegraph* (28 June 1930), 2.

Radio feature.

D 96

" 'Swing High' at George M. Cohan Theatre a Film for Whole Family," *Morning Telegraph* (28 June 1930), 3.

Movie review.

D 97

"Dandy Outdoor Film," *Morning Telegraph* (29 June 1930), 5.

Movie review.

D 98

" 'Czar of Broadway' Finds Death's Disgrace in Pack of Cards at Roxy," *Morning Telegraph* (30 June 1930), 2.

Movie review.

D 99

Franey Delaney, "Radio on Vacation," *Morning Telegraph* (30 June 1930), 2.

Radio feature.

D 100

" 'The Big Fight' Comparatively Good; Has Competent Cast, Happy End," *Morning Telegraph* (1 July 1930), 2.

Movie review.

D 101

Franey Delaney, "For A.M. Thinkers," *Morning Telegraph* (2 July 1930), 2.

Radio feature.

D 102

" 'Juno and the Paycock,' Fine Characterization, Comes to the Cameo," *Morning Telegraph* (2 July 1930), 3.

Movie review.

D 103

Franey Delaney, "Belle Baker on Air," *Morning Telegraph* (3 July 1930), 2.

Radio feature.

D 104

Franey Delaney, "Puff for Mr. Lopez," *Morning Telegraph* (4 July 1930), 2.

Radio feature.

D 105

" 'Holiday' Well Done Version of Barry Play, Comes to Rivoli," *Morning Telegraph* (4 July 1930), 3.

Movie review.

D 106

" 'On the Level' with McLaglen Found an Entertaining Picture at Roxy," *Morning Telegraph* (5 July 1930), 2.

Movie review.

D 107

Franey Delaney, "Radio Odds and Ends," *Morning Telegraph* (5 July 1930), 3.

Radio feature.

D 108

" 'The Unholy Three,' " *Morning Telegraph* (6 July 1930), 3.

Movie review.

D 109
Franey Delaney, "Royal Broadcast," *Morning Telegraph* (7 July 1930), 2.

Radio feature.

D 110
Richard Watts, Jr. "A Defense of the Film Star Who Has to Live His Parts," *New York Herald Tribune* (13 July 1930), VIII, 3.

Letter.

D 111
"Dancing School," *New York Herald Tribune* (3 August 1930), II, 7.

Column.

D 112
"The Decline of Jazz," *New York Herald Tribune* (14 September 1930), II, 7.

Column.

D 113
"Giants of a Vanished Race," *New York Herald Tribune* (28 September 1930), II, 7.

Column.

D 114
"Jazz Artists," *New York Herald Tribune* (14 December 1930), II, 9.

Column.

D 115
"A Jazz Leader," *New York Herald Tribune* (25 January 1931), II, 9.

Column.

D 116
"Jazz from the West," *New York Herald Tribune* (1 March 1931), II, 9.

Column.

D 117
Ads for *The Public Enemy, New York Times* (22 April 1931), 29; (23 April), 29; (24 April), 27.

Also in other newspapers.[3]

D 118
"The Little Boys Blue," "The Conning Tower," *New York Herald Tribune* (10 July 1931), 20.

Letter.

D 119
Letter to the Editor, *Vanity Fair,* XXXVI (August 1931), 17.

---

3. Attributed to O'Hara by Charles Einfeld, former head of the RKO publicity office in New York.

D 120
Ads for *The Star Witness, New York Times* (1 August 1931), 16; (2 August), VIII, 4; (3 August), 15.

Also in other newspapers.[4]

D 121
"Sing Us the Old Songs," *New York Herald Tribune* (9 August 1931), II, 9.

Column.

D 122
"When Dinner Coats Were Tucks and Young Men Toddled," *New York Herald Tribune* (30 August 1931), II, 9.

Column.

D 123
"Barrymore's *Real* Ambition," *Screenland,* XXIII (October 1931), 58–59, 116.

Possibly by another John O'Hara.

D 124
"Home in the Mud," "The Talk of the Town," *The New Yorker,* VII (5 December 1931), 16.

Unsigned, but credited to O'Hara and McConnell by *The New Yorker*'s records.

D 125
"Joe: Straight Man," *Pittsburgh Bulletin Index,* CII (18 May 1933), 4, 12.

Unsigned.[5]

D 126
"Adart Attention"—"Art," *Pittsburgh Bulletin Index,* CII (25 May 1933), 14.

Unsigned.

D 127
Items on Kenneth O'Brien, *Anthony Adverse,* and Yale-in-China, "The Rambler," *Pittsburgh Bulletin Index,* CII (1 June 1933), 7.

Unsigned.

D 128
"Erratum"—"Art," *Pittsburgh Bulletin Index,* CII (1 June 1933), 14.

Unsigned.

D 129
"Space-Grabber"—"Press," *Pittsburgh Bulletin Index,* CII (1 June 1933), 14.

Unsigned.

---

4. Attributed to O'Hara by Charles Einfeld.
5. None of O'Hara's work for the *Bulletin Index* was by-lined. The items listed here have been assigned to him by former staff members of the *Bulletin Index* or have been attributed to him on the basis of internal evidence. O'Hara also wrote some unidentified movie reviews.

D 130

"Apparel"—"Letters," *Pittsburgh Bulletin Index,* CII (8 June 1933), 15.

Unsigned reply to letter.

D 131

"Introducing Veritas"—"Politics," *Pittsburgh Bulletin Index,* CII (15 June 1933), 11–12.

Unsigned.

D 132

"Mazy Motion"—"Letters," *Pittsburgh Bulletin Index,* CII (15 June 1933), 15.

Unsigned reply to letter.

D 133

"Telephone Call"—"Letters," *Pittsburgh Bulletin Index,* CII (15 June 1933), 15.

Unsigned reply to call.

D 134

"Rhodes Scholar"—"Education," *Pittsburgh Bulletin Index,* CII (22 June 1933), 12–13.

Unsigned.

D 135

"Oars"—"Letters," *Pittsburgh Bulletin Index,* CII (29 June 1933), 15.

Unsigned reply to letter.

D 136

"Plush & Velvet"—"Crime," *Pittsburgh Bulletin Index,* CIII (6 July 1933), 12.

Unsigned.

D 137

"Tops"—"Press," *Pittsburgh Bulletin Index,* CIII (20 July 1933), 4.

Unsigned.

D 138

"Training"—"Letters," *Pittsburgh Bulletin Index,* CIII (20 July 1933), 15.

Unsigned reply to letter.

D 139

"Polo"—"Sport," *Pittsburgh Bulletin Index,* CIII (27 July 1933), 6–7.

Unsigned.

D 140

"Portland's Porter"—"Letters," *Pittsburgh Bulletin Index,* CIII (27 July 1933), 15.

Unsigned reply to letter.

D 141

Reply to request for Manhattan addresses—"Letters," *Pittsburgh Bulletin Index,* CIII (27 July 1933), 15.

Unsigned.

D 142

"Torch Singer"—"Music," *Pittsburgh Bulletin Index,* CIII (3 August 1933), 12.

Unsigned.

D 143

"Broun's Piece"—"Press," *Pittsburgh Bulletin Index,* CIII (17 August 1933), 10.

Unsigned.

D 144

"Underground"—"Letters," *Pittsburgh Bulletin Index,* CIII (17 August 1933), 15.

Unsigned reply to letter.

D 145

"Football: Up Boston Way," *The New Yorker,* IX (18 November 1933), 30–32.

D 146

"Football: Four Downs and a Fumble," *The New Yorker,* IX (25 November 1933), 61–62.

D 147

"Football: Requests and Demands," *The New Yorker,* IX (2 December 1933), 52, 54.

D 148

"Football: Princeton Visits the Bowl," *The New Yorker,* IX (9 December 1933), 85–87.

D 149

Contributions to *The Kungsholm Cruise News.*

See A 1.

D 150

John McClain, "On the Sun Deck," *New York Sun* (12 April 1934), 29.

Letter.

D 151

"John O'Hara says—," unlocated ad for *Appointment in Samarra* (1934).

Statement.

D 152

"Football: The Coming Boom in Stadiums," *The New Yorker,* X (29 September 1934), 30, 32.

D 153

"So They Say," *Golden Book Magazine,* XX (October 1934), 405.

Statement—possibly reprinted.

D 154

"Good Reading," *New York Herald Tribune Books* (22 November 1934), 17.

Reading list. See A 37.

D 155
"Essay on O'Hara Won First Prize for Bob Brown," *Pottsville Republican* (13 February 1935), 9.

Based on interview or letter.

D 156
"Why They'll Never Forget the Trial of the Century," *Hearst's International-Cosmopolitan,* XCVIII (May 1935), 180.

Article.

D 157
John McClain, "On the Sun Deck," *New York Sun* (21 August 1935), 22.

Interview.

D 158
"Unverbosity," "The Conning Tower," *New York Herald Tribune* (14 October 1935), 13.

Couplet.

D 159
Phil H. Storch, "Pottsville Native Now Famous as an Author Writes of Life Plainly as He Sees It," *Allentown Morning Call* (13 December 1935).

Possibly based on interview.

D 160
"Movie Fans Like Me Should Know All!" *New York Journal* (9 May 1936), "Saturday Home Magazine" section, 2.

King Features Syndicate. Article.

D 161
"Cesar Romero and the Three Dollar Bills," *New York Journal* (13 June 1936), "Saturday Home Magazine" section, 16.

King Features Syndicate. Article.

D 162
"Backstage with Esquire," *Esquire,* VI (August 1936), 24.

Statement.

D 163
Letter to the Editor, *Time,* XXX (6 September 1937), 8.

D 164
Stanley Woodward's column, *New York Herald Tribune* (16 January 1938), III, 3.

Letter.

D 165
Letter to the Editor, *New York Herald Tribune* (3 March 1938), 16.

D 166
"The English . . . They Are a Funny Race," *For Men,* II (September 1938), 47–50.

Article. See B 12.

D 167
"Are the English Human?" *For Men,* II (December 1938), 44–47.

Article.

D 168
"Stars in My Eyes," *The New Yorker,* XV (6 May 1939), 61.

Verse.

D 169
Letter to the Editor, *The New Republic,* C (25 October 1939), 343.

D 170
*Jazzmen,* Frederic Ramsey, Jr., and Charles Edward Smith, *The New Republic,* CI (27 December 1939), 287.

Book review.

D 171
Letter to the Editor, *The New Republic,* CII (15 January 1940), 88.

D 172
Letter to the Editor, *The New Republic,* CII (12 February 1940), 215.

D 173
Letter to the Editor, *The New Republic,* CII (29 April 1940), 579.

D 174
Robert Van Gelder, "John O'Hara, Who Talks Like His Stories," *New York Herald Tribune Books* (26 May 1940), 12.

Interview. See A 37 and B 11.

D 175
H. Allen Smith, "Pal Joey Gets Earful About O'Hara," *New York World-Telegram* (8 November 1940), 22.

Parody based on interview.

D 176
Harold Hadley, "Pal O'Hara's in Town to Keep Appointment Backstage," *Philadelphia Evening Bulletin* (11 December 1940), E 5.

Interview.

D 177
Thomas O'Hara, "John O'Hara Interviewed by Brother at Show Here," *Philadelphia Evening Public Ledger* (11 December 1940).

Interview.

D 178

Mary Morris and Robert Rice, "How a Musical Is Made," *PM* (22 December 1940), 51, 54.

Facsimiles letter to Richard Rodgers and portion of *Pal Joey* script. See B 18.

D 179

"Pal Joey Is Just a Boob to His Creator," *New York Post* (8 January 1941), 3.

Interview.

D 180

Lucius Beebe, "Stage Asides," *New York Herald Tribune* (12 January 1941), VI, 1–2.

Interview.

D 181

Benjamine Welles, "John O'Hara and His Pal Joey," *New York Times* (26 January 1941), IX, 2.

D 182

Nathaniel Benchley, "The Hard Luck Story of John O'Hara," *Stage,* I (February 1941), 42.

Interview.

D 183

"In Memory of Scott Fitzgerald: II—Certain Aspects," *New Republic,* CIV (3 March 1941), 311.

Article. See A 37 and B 28.

D 184A

"Who's Who Gives O'Hara Chance to Startle Strangers," *New York World-Telegram* (8 March 1941), 3.

Interview.

D 184B

"Touchiness and Mediocrity Prove Fatal to Movie Script Writers," *Chicago Sun* (28 February 1942), 14.

D 185

Stanley Woodward's column, *New York Herald Tribune* (8 January 1944), 13.

Letter.

D 186

"Some Fond Recollections of Larry Hart," *New York Times* (27 February 1944), II, 1.

Article.

D 187

"Dorothy Parker, Hip Pocket Size," *New York Times Book Review* (28 May 1944), 5, 29.

Review of *The Portable Dorothy Parker.* See A 37.

D 188
"Nothing from Joe?" *Liberty,* XXI (9 December 1944), 20–21.

Article.

D 189
Letter to the Editor, *New York Herald Tribune* (7 March 1945), 22.

D 190
"Scott Fitzgerald, Odds and Ends," *New York Times Book Review* (8 July 1945), 3.

Review of *The Crack-Up.* See A 37.

D 191
Lucius Beebe, "Stage Asides: Paul Douglas Talks of 'Born Yesterday,' " *New York Herald Tribune* (10 February 1946), VI, 1.

O'Hara quoted.

D 192
Earl Wilson's column, *New York Post* (28 March 1946), 41.

Interview ("The only good thing I ever got out of booze"). See A 37.

D 193
"That Benny Greenspan," *New York Times Book Review* (8 December 1946), 7, 59.

Review of Arthur Kober's *That Man Is Here Again.* See A 37.

D 194
"A High Priest of Jazz Sets Down His Life Story," *New York Times Book Review* (2 November 1947), 6.

Review of Eddie Condon's *We Called It Music.*

D 195
"The Stutz Bearcat," *Holiday,* IV (August 1948), 84–86, 89.

Article.

D 196
Charles Poore, "Books of the Times," *New York Times* (1 January 1949), 11.

Includes excerpt from letter by "A well-known author who will one day, we hope, write a novel called 'New York 21, N.Y.' "

D 197
"The Novels Novelists Read, or 'Taking in the Washing,' " *New York Times Book Review* (21 August 1949), 3.

Reading list. See A 37.

D 198
"On an Author," *New York Herald Tribune Book Review* (28 August 1949), VII, 2.

Interview.

D 199
Harvey Breit, "Talk with John O'Hara," *New York Times Book Review* (4 September 1949), 11.

Interview. See A 37 and B 21.

D 200
David Dempsey, "In and Out of Books," *New York Times Book Review* (6 November 1949), 8.

Interview.

D 201
"The Sander Case," *Boston Daily Record* (20 February 1950), 30.

Between 20 February and 10 March 1950, O'Hara wrote 14 articles on the mercy-killing trial of Dr. Hermann Sander for the INS syndicate. 13 of these articles have been located in the *Boston Daily Record* and 1 in the *Boston Sunday Advertiser.*

D 202
"Novelist O'Hara Tells Mercy Drama," *Boston Daily Record* (21 February 1950), 20.

D 203
"The Sander Case," *Boston Daily Record* (22 February 1950), 40.

D 204
"O'Hara Watches Sander, Unmoved at Death Room," *Boston Daily Record* (23 February 1950), 34.

D 205
"O'Hara Points out Sander Strategy," *Boston Daily Record* (24 February 1950), 16.

D 206
"Nurse Shows Anger, Says Writer O'Hara," *Boston Daily Record* (25 February 1950), 20.

D 207
" 'Trained Seals' at Sander Trial," *Boston Sunday Advertiser* (26 February 1950), 2.

D 208
"O'Hara Sees Sander Trial Tense," *Boston Daily Record* (27 February 1950), 33.

D 209
"O'Hara Likens Nurse to Actress in Drama," *Boston Daily Record* (28 February 1950).

D 210
"Opposing Witnesses Helped Dr. Sander," *Boston Daily Record* (1 March 1950), 25.

D 211
"Chicken Question Scores for Sander," *Boston Daily Record* (2 March 1950), 26.

D 212
"Defense Met Match in Helpern—O'Hara," *Boston Daily Record* (3 March 1950), 45.

D 213
"O'Hara's M.D. Dad Rushed, Like Sander," *Boston Daily Record* (8 March 1950), 21.

D 214
"The Sander Case," *Boston Daily Record* (9 March 1950), 30.

D 215
"M.D.'s Long 10 Minutes," *Boston Daily Record* (10 March 1950), 16.

D 216
"The New Expense-Account Society," *Flair,* I (May 1950), 22–23, 110–111.

Article.

D 217
"The Author's Name Is Hemingway," *New York Times Book Review* (10 September 1950), 1, 30–31.

Review of *Across the River and Into the Trees.* See A 37.

D 218
"Famous Author Writes of His Early Days on Journal; Is Now Big Literary Figure," *Pottsville Journal* (2 October 1950), 5.

Article. See B 40.

D 219
"Quogue," *Hampton Pictorial* (27 July 1951), 8.

Article.

D 220
"Some Authors of 1951 Speaking for Themselves: John O'Hara," *New York Herald Tribune Book Review* (7 October 1951), 6.

Statement ("How do I write?"). See A 37.

D 221
Ward Morehouse, "Broadway After Dark," *New York World-Telegram & Sun* (14 December 1951), 34.

Interview.

D 222
Leslie Midgley, "Hit Musical of the '40s Returns," *New York Herald Tribune* (20 December 1951), IV, 1.

Interview.

D 223
"O'Hara's Hotel," *Newsweek,* XXXIX (21 January 1952), 83.

Brief quote.

D 224
William M. Dwyer, "O'Hara Writes Play, Amateurs Stage It," *New York Herald Tribune* (18 May 1952), IV, 2.

Interview.

D 225

Red Smith's column, *New York Herald Tribune* (12 June 1952), 31.

Letter.

D 226

" 'Joey' Comes of Age," *New York Herald Tribune* (23 November 1952), IV, 1, 3.

Article.

D 227

Harry Evans, "Broadway Diary," *Family Circle,* XLI (December 1952), 108.

Brief quote.

D 228

"There Is Nothing Like a Norfolk," *Holiday,* XIV (September 1953), 14, 17.

Article.

D 229

"We Have with Us Today: Mr. John O'Hara," *The Fire Islander* (28 May 1954), 5, 7.

Article.

D 230

Lewis Nichols, "Talk with John O'Hara," *New York Times Book Review* (27 November 1955), 16.

Interview. See A 37.

D 231

John K. Hutchens, "John O'Hara from Pottsville, Pa.," *New York Herald Tribune Book Review* (4 December 1955), 2.

Interview. See A 37.

D 232

John K. Hutchens, "Authors, Critics, Speeches, Prizes," *New York Herald Tribune Book Review* (12 February 1956), 2, 4.

Interview.

D 233

John Cook Wyllie, "Book Editor Keeps Appointment with O'Hara," *Richmond News-Leader* (22 February 1956), 11.

Interview.

D 234

Robert L. Perkin, "John O'Hara: Rugged, Talented, Bitter," *Rocky Mountain News* (Denver) (23 February 1956), 40.

Interview.

D 235

Louis Cook, "O'Hara Book Naughty, Police Say; It's Banned," *Detroit Free Press* (18 January 1957), 3, 11.

Statement. O'Hara also quoted in 18 January 1957 syndicated INS article on Detroit action against *Ten North Frederick.*

D 236
Letter to the Editor, *New York Herald Tribune* (3 May 1957), 16.

D 237
Letter to the Editor, *Princeton Packet* (20 June 1957), 12.

D 238
"My Ten Favorite Plays," *Theatre Arts,* XLI (November 1957), 9.

List. See A 37.

D 239
"Novelist Likes the Film Translation," *New York Herald Tribune* (18 May 1958), IV, 3.

Article.

D 240
Red Smith's column, *New York Herald Tribune* (31 August 1958), III, 1.

Letter.

D 241
"As 'From the Terrace' Goes to Press: Appointment with O'Hara," *Publishers Weekly,* CLXXIV (3 November 1958), 22–23.

Interview. See A 37.

D 242
Lewis Nichols, "Mr. O'Hara," *New York Times Book Review* (16 November 1958), 8.

Interview. See A 37.

D 243
Rollene Waterman, "Appt. with O'Hara," *Saturday Review,* XLI (29 November 1958), 15.

Interview. See A 37.

D 244
"Talk with the Author," *Newsweek,* LII (1 December 1958), 93–94.

Interview. See A 37.

D 245
Letter to the Editor, *Princeton Packet* (4 December 1958), 11.

D 246
Robert Kirsch, "The Book Report," *Los Angeles Times* (28 December 1958), V, 7.

Letter.

D 247
Robert A. Burt and Charles E. Ruas, "Appointment with O'Hara," *Daily Princetonian* (7 January 1959), 2.

Includes O'Hara's written replies to questions. See A 37.

D 248

Susie Schildkraut, "Author O'Hara Interviewed," *The Inkling* (Miss Fine's School, Princeton), XIV (February 1959), 1.

Interview.

D 249

Maurice Dolbier, "What NBA Means to Some Past Winners," *New York Herald Tribune Book Review* (1 March 1959), 2, 11.

Statement ("Good writers get published."). See A 37.

D 250

Letter to the Editor, *New York Herald Tribune* (22 May 1959), 12.

D 251

A. H. Weiler, "Passing Picture Scene," *New York Times* (31 May 1959), II, 5.

Interview.

D 252

Letter to the Editor, *Holiday,* XXVI (December 1959), 4.

D 253

Letter to the Editor, *Princeton Packet* (17 March 1960), 10.

D 254

Hoke Norris, "O'Hara Attacks His Attackers," *Chicago Sun-Times* (3 April 1960), III, 1, 5.

Letter.

D 255

Letter to the Editor, *New York Herald Tribune* (5 April 1960), 18.

D 256

Hal Boyle, "John O'Hara at 55 Weaving Prose World," AP column (3 May 1960).

Syndicated interview.

D 257

Jack Keating, "John O'Hara's World of Yale, Society, and Sex," *Cosmopolitan,* CXLIX (September 1960), 59–63.

Interview.

D 258

Contribution to symposium on teaching creative writing, *four quarters,* X (January 1961), 17.

Letter ("If you're going to write, nothing will stop you"). See A 37.

D 259

Walter Farquhar, "Editorial Musings," *Pottsville Republican* (5 April 1961), 4.

Letter.

D 260

Statement on the death of Ernest Hemingway, *New York Times* (3 July 1961), 6.

D 261

Letter to the Editor, *New York Times* (5 July 1961), 32.

D 262

Letter to the Editor, *New York Herald Tribune* (20 August 1961), II, 3.

D 263

[Kenneth D. Munn], "A Writer's Look at His Town, Career, and Future," *Princeton Packet* (23 November 1961), 1, 4.

Interview. Revised as AP article and syndicated. See A 37.

D 264

Letter to the Editor, *New York Times* (30 December 1961), 18.

D 265

Letter to the Editor, *New York Herald Tribune* (26 January 1962), 16.

D 266

Letter to the Editor, *Princeton Packet* (1 February 1962), 8.

D 267

"Don't Say It Never Happened," *New York Herald Tribune Books* (8 April 1962), 3.

Article, See A 37.

D 268

Letter to the Editor, *New York Herald Tribune* (29 April 1962), II, 3.

See D 28.

D 269

Kate Lloyd, "On the American Scene: John O'Hara," *Glamour,* XLVII (May 1962), 125, 197.

Interview.

D 270

Letter to the Editor, *Princeton Packet* (10 May 1962), 6. Reprinted in *The Bermudian,* XXXIII (July 1962), 18.

D 271

Letter to the Editor, *New York Herald Tribune* (5 June 1962), 20.

D 272

Lewis Nichols, "In and Out of Books," *New York Times Book Review* (29 July 1962), 8.

Interview.

D 273

Letter to the Editor, *New York Herald Tribune* (19 September 1962), 24.

D 274
Letter to the Editor, *New York Herald Tribune* (28 September 1962), 24.

D 275
Letter to the Editor, *Yale Alumni Magazine,* XXVI (November 1962), 7.

D 276
"November March," Red Smith's column, *New York Herald Tribune* (6 November 1962), 25.

Verse.

D 277
Red Smith's column, *New York Herald Tribune,* Paris Edition (18 January 1963), 9.

Letter.

D 278
Letter to the Editor, *New York Herald Tribune* (17 April 1963), 24.

D 279
"Bleeck's: John O'Hara Recalls a Cave of Journalism Greats," *New York Herald Tribune* (24 April 1963), 28.

Article.

D 280
[Richard Boeth], "John O'Hara at 58: A Rage to Write," *Newsweek,* LXI (3 June 1963), 53–57.

Cover article based on interviews.

D 281
Sam Zolotow, "John O'Hara Finds Playwriting Fun," *New York Times* (29 July 1963), 16.

Interview.

D 282
Headnote for "The Lawbreaker," *The Saturday Evening Post,* CCXXXVI (16 November 1963), 53.

Letter ("I have recently been putting action back into my stories."). See A 37.

D 283
Red Smith's column, *New York Herald Tribune* (28 January 1964), 26.

Letter.

D 284
"John O'Hara Hears 'Influential People' Selling Bermuda Short," *Royal Gazette* (Bermuda), (20 March 1964), 6.

Interview.

D 285
Red Smith's column, *New York Herald Tribune* (10 June 1964), 25.

Letter.

D 286
"Dept. of Correction and Amplification," *The New Yorker,* XL (19 September 1964), 164–165.

Letter.

D 287
Note on "The Tackle," *Sports Illustrated,* XXI (21 September 1964), 6.

Possibly from letter.

D 288
"Appointment on Long Island," *Time,* LXXXIV (25 September 1964), 42.

Interview.

D 289
Ray Erwin, "John O'Hara Comes 'Home' to Newspapers," *Editor & Publisher,* XCVII (26 September 1964), 120.

Interview.

D 290
Lewis Nichols, "In and Out of Books," *New York Times Book Review* (29 November 1964), 8.

Interview.

D 291
"The Wayward Reader," *Holiday,* XXXVI (December 1964), 31–34.

Article.

D 292
"Memoirs of a Sentimental Duffer," *Holiday,* XXXVII (May 1965), 66–67, 118, 120, 122.

Article.

D 293
Douglas Watt's column, *New York Daily News* (6 August 1965), 60.

Letter.

D 294
Arthur Pottersman, "The World, I Think, Is Better Off That I'm a Writer," *London Sun* (21 September 1965), 3.

Interview.

D 295
Arthur Pottersman, "John O'Hara," *Books and Bookmen,* XI, 20–22.

Interview. See A 37.

D 296
Dorothy Manners' column, *New York Journal-American* (8 April 1966), 12.

Letter.

D 297

James Kerney, Jr., "The Simple Life . . . But in Style," *Trenton Evening Times* (23 May 1966), 13.

Interview.

D 298

"On Cars and Snobbism," *Holiday,* XL (August 1966), 52–53.

Article.

D 299

Homer Bigart, "Staff of Tribune Sad, Not Shocked," *New York Times* (16 August 1966), 26.

Statement.

D 300

"Bored by Fame," *London Evening Standard* (3 May 1967), 6.

Interview.

D 301

Peter Grosvenor, "John O'Hara . . . Two Blows He Had to Beat," *London Daily Express* (4 May 1967), 6.

Interview. See A 37.

D 302

P.H.S., "Much-Mauled O'Hara," *London Times* (4 May 1967), 10.

Interview.

D 303

"Mr. John O'Hara," *Foylibra* (June 1967), iii–iv.

Report of Foyles luncheon speech.

D 304

"Celibacy, Sacred and Profane," *Holiday,* XLII (August 1967), 28–29.

Article.

D 305

Alden Whitman, "O'Hara, in Rare Interview, Calls Literary Landscape Fairly Bleak," *New York Times* (13 November 1967), 45.

Interview. See A 37.

D 306

Alden Whitman, untitled interview, *New York Times Book Review* (26 November 1967), 5.

D 307

"Hello Hollywood Good-bye," *Holiday,* XLIII (May 1968), 54–55, 125–126, 128–129.

Article.

D 308
Don A. Schanche, "John O'Hara Is Alive and Well in the First Half of the Twentieth Century—He Owns It," *Esquire,* CXXII (August 1969), 84–86, 142, 144–149.

Based on interviews.

D 309
Shirley Stewart, "Evening School Eulogizes Literary Giant," *The Night Rider* (4 May 1970), 4.

Letters.

D 310
Joel Sayre, "John O'Hara A Reminiscence," *Washington Post Book World* (18 March 1973), 2.

Letter.

D 311
Robert Moses' column, *Park East* (10 January 1974), 5.

Letter.

D 312
Robert Moses' column, *Park East* (17 January 1974), 5.

Letter.

D 313
Geoffrey T. Hellman, "Profiles: Some Splendid and Admirable People," *The New Yorker,* LII (23 February 1976), 43–81.

Includes letters, pp. 69–70.

D 314
"After 45 Years In Medicine, Jacob Lichstein '32 Reminisces," *Jefferson Medical College Alumni Bulletin,* XXVII (Summer 1977), 36–37.

Includes letter.

# E. Columns

Newspaper and magazine columns by O'Hara, arranged chronologically.

E 1

"After Four O'Clock," *Pottsville Journal,* 2 April 1925–1926.

No surviving example.

E 2

"Entertainment Week," *Newsweek,* 15 July 1940–16 February 1942.

"An American in Memoriam," XVI (15 July 1940), 34.
"Into the Silences," XVI (22 July 1940), 36.
"The Theater's Annual Hay-Day," XVI (29 July 1940), 37.
"Hart Time," XVI (5 August 1940), 36.
"Pastor Hall—Not by Beethoven," XVI (12 August 1940), 41.
"Things to Come," XVI (19 August 1940), 44.
"Taking the Sleeper," XVI (26 August 1940), 50.
"Personal History," XVI (2 September 1940), 48.
"Heigh-ho, Wanger!" XVI (9 September 1940), 61.
"The Groaner," XVI (16 September 1940), 62.
"The Sun Shines East," XVI (23 September 1940), 50.
"You'll Have to Speak a Little Louder," XVI (30 September 1940), 58.
"With the Greatest of Ease," XVI (7 October 1940), 58.
"Yes, and No," XVI (14 October 1940), 74.
"Watch the O'Fearnas Go By," XVI (21 October 1940), 61.
"Charlie, Charley," XVI (28 October 1940), 60.
"100,000 Bucks Country, Pa.," XVI (4 November 1940), 62.
"De Sylva Standard," XVI (11 November 1940), 60.
"Once Is a Lifetime," XVI (18 November 1940), 60.
"New York Is Calling," XVI (25 November 1940), 52.
"The Hayes Department," XVI (2 December 1940), 46.
" 'That's All There Is . . . ,' " XVI (9 December 1940), 64.
" 'Delicatessen Story,' " XVI (16 December 1940), 66.
"The Pace that Kills," XVI (23 December 1940), 50.
"Pshaw!" XVI (30 December 1940), 38.
"Christmas Presents," XVII (6 January 1941), 52.
"Rice to the West," XVII (13 January 1941), 52.
"Brewster Bodies," XVII (20 January 1941), 63.
"Whoopee and Stuff," XVII (27 January 1941), 46.
"Critic in the Dark," XVII (3 February 1941), 59.
"Valentine's Day Massacre," XVII (10 February 1941), 63.
"Have You Met Miss Jones?" XVII (17 February 1941), 67.
"All Wack and Some Play," XVII (24 February 1941), 60.
"What's on Your Mind?" XVII (3 March 1941), 60.
"A Claire," XVII (10 March 1941), 66.
" 'Citizen Kane,' " XVII (17 March 1941), 60. See B 31.
"George Rx," XVII (24 March 1941), 70.

297

"The Coast Is Clear," XVII (31 March 1941), 67.
"The Tables down at Ciro's," XVII (7 April 1941), 62.
"Stumping the Expert," XVII (14 April 1941), 70.
"Bang, Bang, Bong," XVII (21 April 1941), 62.
"Prize Collection," XVII (28 April 1941), 64.
"Notes on Notes," XVII (5 May 1941), 66.
"All Packed?" XVII (12 May 1941), 62.
"Mutiny on a Bounty," XVII (19 May 1941), 76.
"Hallelujah," XVII (26 May 1941), 70.
"No Passports Required," XVII (2 June 1941), 52.
"What's Wrong?" XVII (9 June 1941), 60.
"Harvard: Fair," XVII (16 June 1941), 60.
"Chatter Column," XVII (23 June 1941), 54.
"Good Man in a Room," XVII (30 June 1941), 58.
"My Year," XVIII (7 July 1941), 52.
"Urgent!" XVIII (14 July 1941), 63.
"Thisa and Thata," XVIII (21 July 1941), 54.
"Conscientious Objector," XVIII (28 July 1941), 54.
"Hepburn or Snakes," XVIII (4 August 1941), 48.
"The Lady of 'The Lake,' " XVIII (11 August 1941), 62.
"America, I Love You," XVIII (18 August 1941), 58.
"Vox, Possibly, Humana," XVIII (25 August 1941), 52.
"One Season Coming Up," XVIII (1 September 1941), 48.
"Tramp, Tramp, Tramp," XVIII (8 September 1941), 70.
"Ahm a Poller," XVIII (15 September 1941), 54.
"Win with Wookey," XVIII (22 September 1941), 52.
"Boo!" XVIII (29 September 1941), 54.
"Senators vs. Dodgers," XVIII (6 October 1941), 58.
"The Children's Hour," XVIII (13 October 1941), 68.
"Complaint Department," XVIII (20 October 1941), 74.
"Grab-Bag," XVIII (27 October 1941), 60.
"Cool for 'Candle,' " XVIII (3 November 1941), 58.
"Show Enough," XVIII (10 November 1941), 70.
"Out of This World," XVIII (17 November 1941), 57.
"Hold, Enough!" XVIII (24 November 1941), 74.
"Hit and Misses," XVIII (1 December 1941), 71.
"Stage Wait," XVIII (8 December 1941), 68.
"What's New," XVIII (15 December 1941), 72.
"Broadway, Too," XVIII (22 December 1941), 61.
"Introduction to Tosca," XVIII (29 December 1941), 42.
"The Mantle of Mantle," XIX (5 January 1942), 55.
"Desire Under the Rose," XIX (12 January 1942), 46.
"N.Y. to L.A.," XIX (19 January 1942), 58.
"You're Like a Sweetheart of Mine," XIX (26 January 1942), 64.
"Report to the Nation," XIX (2 February 1942), 60.
"Harvard List," XIX (9 February 1942), 63.
"Is Evvabody Happy?" XIX (16 February 1942), 74.

E 3
"Sweet and Sour," *Trenton Sunday Times-Advertiser*, 27 December 1953–27 June 1954.

See A 13.

27 December 1953, part 4, p. 10

3 January 1954, part 4, p. 12

10 January 1954, part 4, p. 12

17 January 1954, part 4, p. 12

24 January 1954, part 4, p. 10

31 January 1954, part 4, p. 12

7 February 1954, part 4, p. 12

14 February 1954, part 4, p. 12

21 February 1954, part 4, p. 12

28 February 1954, part 4, p. 12

7 March 1954, part 4, p. 12

14 March 1954, part 4, p. 12

21 March 1954, part 4, p. 12

28 March 1954, part 4, p. 12

4 April 1954, part 4, p. 12

11 April 1954, part 4, p. 12

18 April 1954, part 4, p. 12

25 April 1954, part 4, p. 14

2 May 1954, part 4, p. 12

9 May 1954, part 4, p. 12

16 May 1954, part 4, p. 12

23 May 1954, part 4, p. 12

30 May 1954, part 4, p. 10

6 June 1954, part 4, p. 12

13 June 1954, part 4, p. 12

20 June 1954, part 4, p. 16

27 June 1954, part 4, p. 10

E 4

"Appointment with O'Hara," *Collier's,* 5 February 1954–28 September 1956.

*CXXXIII:*

5 February 1954, 6, 8

19 February 1954, 6, 8

5 March 1954, 16

19 March 1954, 6, 8

2 April 1954, 6

16 April 1954, 6, 8

30 April 1954, 6, 8

14 May 1954, 6, 8

28 May 1954, 6, 8

11 June 1954, 6

25 June 1954, 6, 8

*CXXXIV:*

9 July 1954, 6, 8

23 July 1954, 6

6 August 1954, 6

20 August 1954, 6

3 September 1954, 6

17 September 1954, 6, 8

1 October 1954, 6, 8

15 October 1954, 6, 8

29 October 1954, 6, 8

12 November 1954, 6, 8

26 November 1954, 6, 8

10 December 1954, 6, 8

24 December 1954, 6, 8

*CXXXV:*

7 January 1955, 12–13

21 January 1955, 6, 8

4 February 1955, 6, 8

18 February 1955, 6

4 March 1955, 6

18 March 1955, 6, 8

1 April 1955, 6, 8

15 April 1955, 6, 8

29 April 1955, 6, 8

13 May 1955, 6, 8

27 May 1955, 6, 8

10 June 1955, 6, 8

24 June 1955, 6, 8

*CXXXVI:*

8 July 1955, 6, 8

22 July 1955, 6, 8

5 August 1955, 6–7

19 August 1955, 6, 8

2 September 1955, 6

16 September 1955, 6, 8

30 September 1955, 6, 8

14 October 1955, 6, 8

28 October 1955, 6, 8

9 December 1955, 6, 8

23 December 1955, 6, 8

*CXXXVII:*

6 January 1956, 6

20 January 1956, 8

3 February 1956, 6, 8

17 February 1956, 6

2 March 1956, 6

16 March 1956, 6, 8

30 March 1956, 6, 8
13 April 1956, 6, 8
27 April 1956, 6
11 May 1956, 6

25 May 1956, 6, 8
8 June 1956, 8
22 June 1956, 6, 8

*CXXXVIII:*
6 July 1956, 6, 8
20 July 1956, 6
3 August 1956, 6
17 August 1956, 6

31 August 1956, 6
14 September 1956, 6
28 September 1956, 6

E 5

'My Turn," *Newsday* (Long Island), 3 October 1964–2 October 1965.

Syndicated. See A 27.

3 October 1964, 4W
10 October 1964, 4W
17 October 1964, 4W
24 October 1964, 4W
31 October 1964, 4W
7 November 1964, 4W
14 November 1964, 4W
21 November 1964, 4W
28 November 1964, 4W
5 December 1964, 4W
12 December 1964, 4W
19 December 1964, 4W
26 December 1964, 4W
2 January 1965, 4W
9 January 1965, 4W
16 January 1965, 4W
23 January 1965, 4W
30 January 1965, 4W
6 February 1965, 4W
13 February 1965, 4W
29 February 1965, 4W
27 February 1965, 4W
6 March 1965, 4W
13 March 1965, 4W
20 March 1965, 4W
27 March 1965, 4W
3 April 1965, 4W

10 April 1965, 4W
17 April 1965, 4W
24 April 1965, 4W
1 May 1965, 4W
8 May 1965, 4W
15 May 1965, 4W
22 May 1965, 4W
29 May 1965, 4W
5 June 1965, 4W
12 June 1965, 4W
19 June 1965, 4W
26 June 1965, 4W
3 July 1965, 4W
10 July 1965, 4W
17 July 1965, 4W
24 July 1965, 4W
31 July 1965, 6W
7 August 1965, 4W
14 August 1965, 4W
21 August 1965, 4W
28 August 1965, 4W
4 September 1965, 4W
11 September 1965, 4W
18 September 1965, 4W
25 September 1965, 4W
2 October 1965, 4W

E 6

"The Whistle Stop," *Holiday*, September 1966–May 1967.

"Eunuchs in the Harem," XL (September 1966), 16, 20–21.
"Egos and Actors," XL (October 1966), 34, 37–38.
"Put up Your Dukes," XL (November 1966), 20, 24–25.
"The Error of Our Ways," XL (December 1966), 22, 24, 27.
"Reflections of a Non-Travel Writer," XLI (January 1967), 24, 26, 28–29.
"The Follies of Broadway," XLI (February 1967), 23, 25.
"A Harvest of Sour Grapes," XLI (March 1967), 20, 24, 26.
"When Big Bands Were Big," XLI (April 1967), 20, 23, 26.
"If the Name Fits," XLI (May 1967), 28, 30–31.

# F. Blurbs

Statements specially written by O'Hara on dust jackets of books by other authors, arranged chronologically. Quotes from his reviews are not included.

F 1

Budd Schulberg, *What Makes Sammy Run?* New York: Random House, [1941].

Letter from O'Hara to Bennett Cerf (28 January 1941) printed on back of dust jacket.

F 2

Ernest Hemingway, *Green Hills of Africa*. New York: Permabooks, [1954].

#P 296. O'Hara quoted on p. [1]: "As good as anything I have read in English." Previous publication—if any—not located.

F 3

Charles Mercer, *The Reckoning*. [New York]: Dell, [1963].

#7270. O'Hara quoted on front cover: "If you want to see a good writer at work, read *The Reckoning*."

F 4.

John K. Hutchens, *One Man's Montana*. Philadelphia & New York: Lippincott, [1964].

O'Hara quoted on front dust jacket: "John Hutchens' ONE MAN'S MONTANA could only have been written by one man, and that's the man who wrote it. The State is lucky to have as its portraitist a word-painter who produces an affectionate picture without hiding the pock marks. The old realist, Charlie Russell, would have been pleased."

# Appendices / Index

# Appendix 1

## Newspaper and Magazine Employment

O'Hara's journalism jobs, listed chronologically.

1.1
Reporter and columnist, *Pottsville Journal,* July 1924–late 1926.

There is no surviving file of the *Journal* for this period. See A 35 and D 1.

1.2
Reporter, *Tamaqua Courier,* January–March 1927.

No by-lines.

1.3
Reporter and rewrite man, *New York Herald Tribune,* March–August 1928.

No by-lines.

1.4
Reporter and checker, *Time,* August 1928–March 1929.

No by-lines.

1.5
Reporter, *Editor and Publisher,* spring 1929.

No by-lines.

1.6
Rewrite man, *New York Daily Mirror,* July 1929.

See D 28.

1.7
Critic and radio columnist (as John O'Hara and Franey Delaney), *New York Morning Telegraph,* May–July 1930.

See Section D.

1.8
Managing editor (without title), *Pittsburgh Bulletin Index,* May–August 1933.

No by-lines. See Section D.

1.9
Editor, *The Kungsholm Cruise News,* March 1934.

See A 1.

# Appendix 2

## Movie Employment

O'Hara's work for the movies, listed chronologically—including movies made from O'Hara's writings.

| | |
|---|---|
| 1934 | 12 June–20 August. Paramount. O'Hara worked on scripts for "Dad's Day" and "Soldier Woman" (neither film released with these titles). |
| 1936–1937 | Acted in *The General Died at Dawn.* O'Hara worked on treatments for Goldwyn and MGM. |
| 1939 | 17 March–13 April. RKO. O'Hara worked on *In Name Only.* |
| 1939 | 18 September–6 December. Twentieth Century–Fox. O'Hara worked on *I Was an Adventuress* (screen credit to Karl Tunberg, Don Ettlinger, and O'Hara); also worked on *He Married His Wife* (screen credit to Sam Hellman, Darrell Ware, Lynn Starling, Erna Lazarus, Scott Darling, and O'Hara). Possibly worked on *These Glamour Girls* at MGM. |
| 1940 | 2 January–5 April. Twentieth Century–Fox. O'Hara worked on *Down Argentine Way.* |
| 1941 | 24 March–26 July. Twentieth Century–Fox. O'Hara received sole screen credit for *Moontide* screenplay. |
| 1945 | August–January 1946. MGM. O'Hara worked on *Cass Timberlane.* |
| 1946 | June. United Artists. O'Hara worked on *A Miracle Can Happen (On Our Merry Way)* from own original story. Received screen credit for James Stewart–Henry Fonda material. |
| 1946 | O'Hara possibly worked on *Strange Journey* and *Sentimental Journey* for Twentieth Century–Fox. |
| 1955 | Spring–Summer. Twentieth Century–Fox. O'Hara received screen credit for original story of *Best Things in Life Are Free.* Script by William Bowers and Phoebe Ephron. |
| 1956 | Fall. Twentieth Century–Fox. O'Hara wrote screenplay for "Bravados"; not produced. |
| 1957 | Twentieth Century–Fox. O'Hara wrote original story, "The Man Who Could Not Lose"; not produced. |
| 1957 | *Pal Joey* (Columbia). O'Hara not involved in screenplay. |
| 1958 | *10 North Frederick* (Twentieth Century–Fox). O'Hara not involved in screenplay. |
| 1960 | *Butterfield 8* (MGM). O'Hara not involved in screenplay. |
| 1960 | *From the Terrace* (Twentieth Century–Fox). O'Hara not involved in screenplay. |
| 1965 | *A Rage to Live* (Mirisch–United Artists). O'Hara not involved in screenplay. |

# Appendix 3

## Compiler's Notes

See "A Cub Tells His Story" (A 37 and D 1) for O'Hara's account of his work on the *Pottsville Journal*.

"Famous Author Writes of His Early Days on Journal; Is Now Big Literary Figure," *Pottsville Journal* (D 218): "I have found employment—however brief—on . . . The Morning Telegraph (twice, yet!) . . . The New York Journal-American . . . I have seen the color of the money of . . . The London Express. . . ." Only one of O'Hara's stints on the *Morning Telegraph* has been identified (see Section D). Nothing by him has been located in the *London Express*. The *Journal-American* appearances may be D 160 and D 161.

*Sweet and Sour*, p. 136: " . . . I got stuck for two stories in a magazine called *Carnival*." No copies located.

*Sweet and Sour*, p. 137: "In an extremely active career I once wrote for an if-money publication that was being brought along by two men named Fred Palmer and Malcolm Ross. My recollection is that it was called *Today—In New York*, but I won't swear to it." *Today—In New York* was distributed in hotels in 1929–1930. No copies located.

*Sweet and Sour*, p. 138: "You can find an article on the martini cocktail in a magazine called *For Men*, but you have to find *For Men*." The Library of Congress has an incomplete run of *For Men*, lacking an issue with this article.

*Sweet and Sour*, p. 138: "I sold a short story to *The Strand*." No story by-lined by O'Hara has been found in *The Strand*.

There may be unlocated contributions by O'Hara in *The Hampton Chronicle* and other Quogue area newspapers *(Hampton Bays News, Southampton Press)*.

Only two of O'Hara's contributions to *The New Yorker*'s "Talk of the Town" have been identified (D 30 and D 124). There were probably more.

None of O'Hara's prep-school writings has been located. He was an "athletic correspondent" at Niagara University Preparatory School in 1923–1924.

"A Trip to Sea," *Blackwood's Magazine*, CCLXXXII (October 1962), is by-lined John O'Hara, but is not by this John O'Hara.

# Appendix 4

## Works About John O'Hara

All books about O'Hara and selected articles.

Bassett, Charles W. "O'Hara's Roots," *Pottsville Republican* (20 March 1971–8 January 1972).

Bruccoli, Matthew J. *The O'Hara Concern.* New York: Random House, 1975.

Carson, Edward Russell. *The Fiction of John O'Hara.* Pittsburgh: University of Pittsburgh Press, 1961.

Farr, Finis. *O'Hara.* Boston: Little, Brown, 1973.

Gary, Beverly. "A Post Portrait: John O'Hara," *New York Post* (18–22, 24 May 1959).

Grebstein, Sheldon Norman. *John O'Hara.* New York: Twayne, 1966.

McCormick, Bernard. "A John O'Hara Geography," *Journal of Modern Literature,* I (second issue, 1970–71), 151–158.

Schanche, Don A. "John O'Hara Is Alive and Well in the First Half of the Twentieth Century," *Esquire,* CXXII (August 1969), 84–86, 142, 144–149.

Walcutt, Charles C. *John O'Hara.* Minneapolis: University of Minnesota Press, 1969.

# Index

# Pittsburgh Series in Bibliography

HART CRANE: A DESCRIPTIVE BIBLIOGRAPHY
Joseph Schwartz and Robert C. Schweik

F. SCOTT FITZGERALD: A DESCRIPTIVE BIBLIOGRAPHY
Matthew J. Bruccoli

WALLACE STEVENS: A DESCRIPTIVE BIBLIOGRAPHY
J. M. Edelstein

EUGENE O'NEILL: A DESCRIPTIVE BIBLIOGRAPHY
Jennifer McCabe Atkinson

JOHN BERRYMAN: A DESCRIPTIVE BIBLIOGRAPHY
Ernest C. Stefanik, Jr.

RING W. LARDNER: A DESCRIPTIVE BIBLIOGRAPHY
Matthew J. Bruccoli and Richard Layman

MARIANNE MOORE: A DESCRIPTIVE BIBLIOGRAPHY
Craig S. Abbott

NATHANIEL HAWTHORNE: A DESCRIPTIVE BIBLIOGRAPHY
C. E. Frazer Clark, Jr.

JOHN O'HARA: A DESCRIPTIVE BIBLIOGRAPHY
Matthew J. Bruccoli

*Forthcoming*

MARGARET FULLER: A DESCRIPTIVE BIBLIOGRAPHY
Joel Myerson

RAYMOND CHANDLER: A DESCRIPTIVE BIBLIOGRAPHY
Matthew J. Bruccoli

DASHIELL HAMMETT: A DESCRIPTIVE BIBLIOGRAPHY
Richard Layman

SUPPLEMENT TO F. SCOTT FITZGERALD: A DESCRIPTIVE BIBLIOGRAPHY
Matthew J. Bruccoli